The
Columbian
Exchange

THE COLUMBIAN EXCHANGE

Biological and Cultural Consequences of 1492

30th Anniversary Edition

ALFRED W. CROSBY, JR.

Forewords by J. R. McNeill and Otto von Mering

Westport, Connecticut
London

Library of Congress Cataloging in Publication Data

Crosby, Alfred W.
  The Columbian exchange.

  (Contributions in American studies, no. 2)
  Bibliography: p.
  1. Indians—Diseases. 2. Indians—Agriculture. 3. Medical geography—
History. 4. Geographical distribution of animals and plants. I. Title.
E98. D6C7   574.5   73-140916
ISBN 0-8371-5821-4

Chapter 2, originally entitled "Conquistador y Pestilencia: The First New World
Pandemic and the Fall of the Great Indian Empires," first published in *Hispanic
American Historical Review*, XLVII (August 1967), 321–327.
© Duke University Press.

A large part of chapter 4 first published in *American Anthropologist*, LXXI
(April 1969), 218–27.

Library of Congress Catalog Card Number: 73-140916

ISBN: 0-275-98073-1
       0-275-98092-8(pbk)

First published in 2003

Praeger Publishers, 88 Post Road West, Westport, CT 06881
An imprint of Greenwood Publishing Group, Inc.
www.praeger.com

Printed in the United States of America

The paper used in this book complies with the
Permanent Paper Standard issued by the National
Information Standards Organization (Z39.48-1984).

10 9 8 7 6 5 4 3 2

TO ALL THE RULEY GIRLS

Contents

List of Illustrations

Foreword

In *A Sand County Almanac,* published in 1949, Aldo Leopold, the American naturalist, essayist, and godfather of modern environmentalism, called for a rewriting of history from an ecological perspective. A generation of historians ignored him. In the social ferment and intellectual tumult of the 1960s, Alfred W. Crosby came, by his own path, to the same conclusion as Leopold. But he then took the further step of actually writing a book that took seriously the importance of ecological shifts in human affairs. You hold that book in your hands.

Leopold would have been pleased; Crosby's professional colleagues were less than pleased. *The Columbian Exchange* had difficulty finding a publisher until Greenwood published it in 1972. The reviews in scholarly journals ranged from ungenerous to polite, and many journals did not bother to review it. Crosby's colleagues at his own university expressed some skepticism as to whether this was really history or not, but the book refused to go away. It dealt in a clear, compact manner with subjects that seemed ever more important, which helped it to find its way onto reading lists at many colleges across the United States. It was also translated into Spanish and Italian.

My first encounter with the book came on a rainy afternoon in 1982 when I picked it off of a shoulder-high shelf in an office I temporarily occupied. I read it in one gulp, neglecting the possibility of supper. Only rarely can I recall precisely the circumstances in which I read a book long ago, but *The Columbian Exchange,* and the sense of excitement it provoked in me, etched itself into my memory. History has never seemed quite the same for me since. Perhaps I was unusually receptive, having been steeped for many, many months in works concerning the constitutional histories of the British Commonwealth.

Many others found new vistas on American, Latin American, European, African, and world history in Crosby's book. It became one of the foundational texts for the field of environmental history, which emerged in the U.S. in the 1970s. Mainstream historians gradually took notice too, and by the 1990s the notion of the Columbian Exchange had worked its way into several textbooks on American and world history.

The phrase "The Columbian Exchange" did as well. It is not often that a historian coins a new phrase that becomes standard shorthand for some complex phenomenon, but today almost every practicing historian in the U.S., and many overseas, recognize the words "The Columbian Exchange." Most could give a fair rendition of what Crosby meant by the phrase, even those who had not read the book. Whereas thirty years ago Crosby's ideas met with indifference from most historians, neglect from many publishers, and hostility from at least some reviewers, they now figure prominently in conventional presentations of modern history.

Crosby, of course, built on the work of previous scholars. He did not poke around in archives looking for documents dealing with measles, sheep, and bluegrass. But geographers were interested in crop dispersals. Anthropologists and a few historians tried to make sense of the epidemics and the demographic catastrophe that befell the Americas after 1492. Readers will find their works in Crosby's footnotes. No one had put these pieces together before, and no one had written on these subjects with such wit and verve.[1]

So for historians Crosby framed a new subject. He pursued the issue of ecological factors in his 1986 book *Ecological Imperialism*, which looked at some other parts of the world, including Australia and New Zealand, and argued for a systematic, asymmetrical impact of biological exchange which helped Europeans dominate much of the world in recent centuries. Others have enriched his account by drawing attention to some of the West African components of the Columbian Exchange, such as the rice that underpinned the plantation economy of the Carolina lowlands after 1690.[2]

Crosby did not discuss Africa very much in *The Columbian Exchange*, but he had a very good reason. In the 1960s, the historiography of Africa was just taking shape, and information of the sort he needed was not as easily available as it became. He explored the importance of American crops for modern Africa, but African crops, diseases, and people formed a crucial part— in some places the dominant part—of the Old World's biotic donations to the Americas. It is well to remember that before 1880 most of the people who crossed the Atlantic to the Americas were Africans, and before 1820 four out of every five transatlantic migrants hailed from Africa. Although they came in chains, parts of their flora and fauna came with them, including African rice, okra, yams, black-eyed peas, millets, sorghum, sesame, and the pathogens that cause yellow fever and malaria. Coffee came from Africa, although not in slave ships. Africans also brought their highly effective techniques of growing rice and their not so effective means of healing yellow fever and malaria sufferers.

Crosby's legacy lies not in the comprehensiveness of chronicling the Columbian Exchange, but in the establishment of a perspective, a model for understanding ecological and social events. Indeed, with a little imagination one can find exchanges of the sort Crosby illuminated almost everywhere. Most of these are shrouded in the mists of time and will never be understood in the detail that Crosby was able to provide for the Columbian Exchange. Long before Columbus, mariners on the Indian Ocean learned to navigate the monsoon winds and sail between the coasts of East Africa and India. They carried crops, pests, weeds, and diseases back and forth, bringing sorghum, pearl millet, and finger millet to India. Similar exchanges on the monsoon winds took place between the archipelagoes of southeast Asia and China. Champa rice, an early-ripening variety, made southern China much more productive from the thirteenth century onwards and helped underwrite the prosperity and power of Song and Ming China. More recently, as Crosby explored in his later book, a large-scale, if rather one-sided, biological exchange took place between Pacific Islands and Australia on the one hand, and Eurasia on the other. This took place after the navigations of Captain James Cook in the late eighteenth century, uniting previously separate ecosystems with dramatic results that paralleled the Columbian Exchange. The antipodes had no equivalent of the potato or maize to give to the world (eucalyptus trees are perhaps their most successful biological export), but for the peoples and ecosystems of Australia, New Zealand, or Tahiti, the Cook Exchange, as it might be called, proved jarring in the extreme.

Parallels to the Columbian Exchange occurred on land as well. When caravan traffic first sustained commercial exchanges between China and the Mediterranean world at around 100 B.C.E., seeds, spores, and germs went along for the bumpy ride. Cherries, and perhaps smallpox and measles, came to the Roman world; China acquired grapes, alfalfa, donkeys, camels, and also perhaps smallpox and measles, among other items.

Something similar must have happened when caravans crossed the Sahara Desert between the Maghreb and the West African sahel. An African Columbus, whose name we will never know, inaugurated regular traffic sometime before 500 C.E. Horses came to West Africa, with revolutionary political consequences that roughly paralleled the impact of horses upon the Plains Indian of North America, although the difficulty of raising horses in West

Africa altered the situation somewhat. Nonetheless, the military use of horses, especially against peoples who did not have them, helped reorganize West Africa, giving rise to large empires such as Ghana, Mali, and Songhai.

Trans-Saharan caravans probably also exchanged pathogens between West Africa and the Mediterranean world. The syphilis outbreak of the 1490s, which may have resulted from an import from the Americas, could also represent a mutation of West African yaws. In the reverse direction, some of the crowd and herd diseases of Eurasia may have entered West Africa in the tissues of camel drivers. Rats and fleas may have crossed the Sahara this way too, bringing bubonic plague to the sahel in the great pandemic of the fourteenth century.

These biological exchanges, if indeed they occurred as I suggest, helped shape the history of Eurasia and Africa as surely as the Columbian Exchange. Their impacts were perhaps smaller in scale and, at least at the moment, less well documented than the impacts that Crosby put in the spotlight. But perhaps one day they too will find their Crosby, who will write books that would both please Aldo Leopold's ghost and change someone's vision of history on a damp afternoon.

J. R. McNEILL

NOTES

1. A predecessor of sorts was Hans Zinsser's delightful *Rats, Lice, and History* (1934), a medical doctor's irreverent biography of typhus.

2. E.g. Judith Carney, *Black Rice* (Cambridge, MA: Harvard University Press, 2001).

Preface to the 2003 Edition

I don't read my books after they come out because publication is a hard freeze that makes imprecisions, lapses in taste, and mistakes permanent and painful to the touch. However, in preparation for writing this preface I pulled *The Columbian Exchange* down from the shelf and did go through it. Flaws? Oh, yes; I'll talk over a few of them with you. But it is a good book; I'll talk some about that, too.

First, my apologies. Thirty years ago I used "man" to mean all members of the *Homo sapiens* species. So did most people, but it was stupid then and it is now. I used the word "race" as if I actually knew what it meant. I referred to the Maya as the most "sensitive" of all the indigenous peoples of the Americas without realizing how patronizing that is. Was I implying that Cortés might have invited the Maya for cocktails, but certainly not the Aztecs?

And so on. I invite you to make your own selection of yesterday's plastic blossoms pressed between the pages of my book.

I made some flat-out mistakes, some of them pretty good. All smallpox epidemics in previously uninfected populations did *not* produce thirty percent mortality rates. Only the worst epidemics did that. The indigenous inhabitants of the Antilles were not almost all extinct by the mid-sixteenth century, only those of the Greater Antilles. The Caribs hung on in the Lesser Antilles. Ancestral wheat was not, like the ancestors of maize, markedly inferior in yield to its cultivated descendents. Wild wheat was awkward to harvest but very productive, which may be one of the reasons why the peoples of southwest Asia got the jump on the rest of humanity in farming, urbanization, etc.

My biggest mistake was a matter of general ignorance at the time and I like it a lot. On page 218 I announced, *ex cathedra,* that there has been no extreme and permanent physical change affecting the entire globe in half a billion years. Since the publication of *The Columbian Exchange,* geologists and paleontologists have amassed evidence that an asteroid or some such object hit the Earth about sixty-five million years ago, killing off the dinosaurs, clearing the way for mammals, and making a fool out of me.

The chapter which has weathered the last thirty years the least successfully, though it has not been completely superseded, is number four, "The Early History of Syphilis: A Reappraisal." The geographical homeland of the disease was a mystery when I wrote of it and still is, whatever the newspapers proclaim, as they do at least once every five years. Did syphilis exist in the New World before 1492? There are a good many skeletons with distorted and scarred bones that seem to indicate that it did. But by "it" do we mean venereal syphilis or one of the nonvenereal "syphilises," or are they all just manifestations of the same thing?

Did "it" exist in the Old World before 1492? There are pre-Columbian skeletons in the Old World similar to those termed syphilitic in the New World, but only a very few. Their tiny number doesn't, of course, prove that their wretched owners did *not* have syphilis, but if they did the disease must have been of a different character, certainly less communicable, than sixteenth-century Europe's venereal pox. Either that, or before 1492 Old World people must have been close to one hundred percent celibate or monogamous, an admirable, and therefore unlikely, state of affairs.

To my knowledge the oldest cadaver thus far proved syphilitic by actual evidence of the presence of *Treponema pallidum* in its tissues is that of Maria d'Aragona of Naples. This noblewoman died in 1568, long after Columbus sailed, so her tissues tell us no more than that the disease was circulating in Europe in her lifetime, which we knew for sure anyway.[1] Unfortunately, treponemal traces fade with time and any in pre-Columbian bones would probably be so faint as to defy investigators using present technology.

We don't know where venereal syphilis started. It could have come from here or there or here *and* there and have leaped in deadlines when mild strains of treponemas met and crossed the Atlantic in 1492, or its increase in virulence circa 1500 may have had nothing whatsoever to do with Columbus and simply have been a coincidence.

Anyway, I should not have ennobled syphilis with a whole chapter as if it were Montezuma's Revenge. Its Old World debut was spectacular and, like all things venereal, fascinating, but it was not a history-maker like the plague in the fourteenth century or smallpox in the sixteenth century. I cast it in a major role because I was uneasy about so many diseases crossing west over the Atlantic and none crossing east. I was like the geographers who believed for generations, before Captain Cook proved otherwise, that there must be a continent, a *Terra Australis,* in the far, far south vast enough to balance all off of Eurasia, the bulk of Africa, and North America. Chapter four was my try for a sort of epidemiological-geographical symmetry. The aforesaid geographers were wrong, and so was I. There was little symmetry in the exchange of diseases between the Old and New Worlds, and there are few factors as influential in the history of the last half millennium as that.

I should have no more than nodded to the French Pox and included not pages but a whole chapter on the crops of the post-

Columbian slave plantations, particularly southeast Asia's sugar and America's tobacco. European desire (addiction might be a better word) for the sweetener served as a motivation to transport millions of Africans across the Atlantic. Tobacco, which has killed many more than syphilis, is the true Montezuma's Revenge.

But enough of my self-abasement, however noble. Let's proceed to what is worthwhile about my book. It is about something so huge that we often overlook it, much as we tend to be unconscious of the air we breathe, and that is the full story of our species since the melting back of the continental glaciers. That is to say, it is the story of the divergent evolution of the ecosystems and associated societies, isolated by rising sea levels, and when they did meet, the catastrophic and bountiful effects they had on each other. Those effects are so great as to defy containment in our usual intellectual divisions: archaeology, history, botany, medicine, demography, etc.

Thirty years ago I was so naïve that I thought I could function usefully in all these disciplines. Naivité, if insisted upon, can guide you through the trees to some very interesting forests, which it did in my case.

I doubt that I would have gone hiking there but for the tumble and tumult of the 1960s (which in defiance of the decimal system lasted to the Watergate crisis of the early seventies.) I had studied for a doctorate in United States history in the starchy 1950s. I had been trained by men (always) who, most of them, were veterans of the Second World War, men who rarely entertained doubts about the basic goodness of the society for which they had fought. For these men American history was political before all else and came in four-year presidential compartments occasionally illuminated by wars, which the good guys always won. The good guys consisted of people who looked quite a lot like me. History was the story of people like me (Americans or, if not so blessed, at least European) and was, all and all, a record of progress, and would continue to be.

Then, just as I started teaching, along came the Civil Rights struggle and the Black Power movement, which taught me that people who didn't look like me had been appallingly mistreated by people who did look like me. Then came the Vietnam War, which taught me that the world was much more than North America and Europe, that people who looked like me did not necessarily win all the wars, and that there were big pieces missing from the kind of history I was teaching.

The sixties "globalized" my mind a quarter century before that word entered journalistic jargon. For instance, if the Viet Cong were successful against the American armed forces, despite all the latter's technological advantages, and if Africa had somehow repelled European imperialists for centuries before succumbing, then why were American Indians, all and all, so easily conquered? Did Cortés just huff and puff and blow Monctezuma's house down or were there other factors at work?

The sixties, which made ideologues of some, drove me to biology. I had always had an interest in biological matters, though nothing that leafing through *Natural History* or watching *Nova* on TV could not satisfy. That mild interest now came to my rescue. I recommend such professionally irrelevant inclinations to young historians—linguistics, architecture, jazz, etc. They may provide you with new questions to ask when you are weary of the old questions. Good questions are harder to come by than good answers.

I fled from ideological interpretations of history and went in search of the basics, life and death. Alive is alive and dead is dead, whatever Adam Smith or Karl Marx, Richard Nixon or Leonid Brezhnev had to say. What kept people alive long enough to reproduce, and what killed them? Perhaps food and disease?

Asking big questions like that is like replacing the standard film in your camera with infrared or ultraviolet film. You see things you have never seen before. The indigenous peoples of the Greater Antilles appear and then disappear. Chinese peasants eating corn on the cob, not rice, loom up.

Big questions can, of course, lead to over-simplified answers. I probably did that with my telling of the arrival and first spread of smallpox in America, which, I indicated, led *ipso facto* to European triumph. Epidemics among immunologically unprepared populations (often called virgin soil epidemics) often do produce high mortality rates, but if left alone the population will recover in numbers.

Europe, for instance, lost one-third of its population to the Black Death in the fourteenth century and recovered in time. If the Black Death had been accompanied by the arrival of Genghis Khan's hordes, miraculously plague-proof, the story would have been very different. It might have been similar to what happened when European settlers followed on the heels of smallpox and other infections previously unknown to American Indians.

If, by the way, the plague and the Mongols had arrived in tandem, I think it is unlikely that I would be writing this preface in an Indo-European language.

If Columbus had sailed directly from the western extreme to the eastern extreme of Eurasia—if there had been no Americas—Spain and Europe would have probably been the richer for his success and perhaps the Ottoman Empire a bit poorer. There would have been major shifts of power, technologies, and possibly of religions. But even so, post-Columbian developments would have been only more of what had gone before. Columbus, however, couldn't get to Asia—there were two continents full of biological and cultural improbabilities in his way—and life on our planet changes drastically and forever as the eastern and western hemispheres began to exchange life forms, both macro and micro.

NOTES

1. Gino Fornaciari et al, "Syphilis in a Renaissance Italian Mummy," *Lancet* 2 (1989): 614.

Foreword

Alfred W. Crosby, Jr., belongs to a select company of social historians. He has devoted his special scholarly talents to re-examine the record of the perduring interaction between man's ways and changes in his condition since Columbus found the New World. As an exponent of what I should like to call "anthropomedical" historiography, he informs us succinctly about this many-faceted chain of altered conditions of life and well-being. His retelling of it is an eloquent testimony to man's unquenchable drive to explore his habitat and himself, not always wisely, sometimes too well.

The reader is taken on an engrossing intellectual voyage through the facts and interpretations of the salient cultural and bio-social consequences of 1492. He will gain a balanced view of the worldwide exchange and sociopolitical sequelae of the protean disease, syphilis, and the major communicable diseases of influenza, smallpox, measles, and pneumonia. He can also learn important historical answers to the complex connection between the international movement of disease and man, the cumulative transformation of world food suplies, and some of the noteworthy changes in world population growth.

Professor Crosby is commendably precise in delineating the global dispersal and exchange of the leading New World cultigens (e.g., maize, potato, sweet potato, bean, and manioc) and the characteristic Old World plant and animal food staples (e.g., rice, wheat, barley, oat, and fruit crops; cattle, pig, sheep, goat, chicken, and horse). We are also persuaded by his argument linking the progressive restructuring of national, regional, and local agricultural economies to notable historical declines in food supply and to the continuous rise in the quality, availability, and level of basic world food sources.

The author's thoughtful consideration of the historically significant human and ecological effects of the world exchange of cultigens and micro-organisms should appeal to all serious students of the present human condition. He concludes his well-paced history of the Columbian exchange with an evocative reexamination of the most recent, and, in the long run perhaps, most significant human "resultant" of 1492: the post-1800 phenomenon of vast intercontinental migration.

Is it not ironic that, although worldwide population movements profoundly influence our daily lives, we know far more about the cause, meaning, and consequences of migratory behavior among animals? Should we remain as grossly uninformed about it as at present, we will soon become foolishly uncertain about its probable role in the future course of man's way with fellow man. As a provisional antidote to our lack of knowledge in this area, the reader may wish to join me in pondering over Professor Crosby's observation that today "there are two Europes and two Africas: one on either side of the Atlantic."

OTTO VON MERING
October 1971

Preface

Nothing can be understood apart from its context, and man is no exception. He is a living entity, dependent on a number of other living entities for food, clothing, and often shelter. Many living things are dependent upon him for the same. Man is a biological entity before he is a Roman Catholic or a capitalist or anything else. Moreover, man's history did not start when he first began to keep records, nor is it limited to only the aspects of his existence of interest to the literati. The first step to understanding man is to consider him as a biological entity which has existed on this globe, affecting, and in turn affected by, his fellow organisms, for many thousands of years.

Once we have placed man in this proper spatial and temporal context, we can begin to examine single aspects or events of his history with the assurance—or at least the hope—that the results will have a meaningful relationship to that context and will not merely send us off down the weedy little paths that lead from one antiquarian's gazebo to another.

Before the historian can judge wisely the politcal skills of human groups or the strength of their economies or the meaning of their literatures, he must first know how successful their member human beings were at staying alive and reproducing themselves. He must have some idea of how their efforts in accomplishing these tasks affected their environments. It is to the ecologist and not to the philatelist that the historian should look for his model of scholarly virtue.

You may have been taught as children to recite:

> Columbus sailed the ocean blue
> In fourteen hundred and ninety-two . . .

and few of us really get beyond that kind of description of what happened in that year. We acquire more and more facts, which enable us to paint more and more elaborate pictures of that event and the sensational accomplishments of the conquistadors which followed quickly thereafter. These pictures are so hypnotically interesting that most of us never shake loose from their surface fascination to seek the real significance of the events they depict.

Tradition has limited historians in their search for the true significance of the renewed contact between the Old and New Worlds. Even the economic historian may occasionally miss what any ecologist or geographer would find glaringly obvious after a cursory reading of the basic original sources of the sixteenth century: the most important changes brought on by the Columbian voyages were biological in nature.

To illuminate just that point is the raison d'être of this book. It is a brief book and, I hope, an unpretentious one, but I am the first to appreciate that historians, geologists, anthropologists, zoologists, botanists, and demographers will see me as an amateur in their particular fields. I anticipate their criticism by agreeing with them in part and replying that, although the Renaissance is long past, there is great need for Renaissance-style attempts at pulling together the discoveries of the specialists to learn what we know, in general, about life on this planet.

I apologize to Native Americans for my constant use of the ambiguous and innacurate term *Indian*. I realize that Columbus's use of that word was an egregious error and that there is no reason except inertia to repeat it; however, the word *Amerindian* offends me as jerrybuilt, and few of my prospective readers are yet using *Native American*. For their sake I have continued with the time-hallowed and confusing *Indian*.

I would like to thank Washington State University for providing a grant to support the researching and writing of this book. I must also thank the editors of *The Hispanic American Historical Review* and *The American Anthropologist* for permisssion to republish those parts of Chapters 2 and 4 that first appeared in those journals. I owe a great debt to Barbara S. Crosby, for her perceptive stylistic criticisms. Last of all but most of all, I thank my whole family—Barbara, Kevin, and Carolyn—who endured so many twinkling little anecdotes about maize and smallpox.

The
Columbian
Exchange

King Ferdinand looks out across the Atlantic Ocean as Columbus lands in the West Indies.
COURTESY HOUGHTON MIFFLIN

The
Contrasts

1

On the evening of October 11, 1492, Christopher Columbus, on board the *Santa Maria* in the Atlantic Ocean, thought he saw a tiny light far in the distance. A few hours later, Rodrigo de Triana, lookout on the *Pinta*'s forecastle, sighted land. In the morning a party went ashore. Columbus had reached the Bahamas. The connection between the Old and New Worlds, which for more than ten millennia had been no more than a tenuous thing of Viking voyages, drifting fishermen, and shadowy contacts via Polynesia, became on the twelfth day of October 1492 a bond as significant as the Bering land bridge had once been.[1]

The two worlds, which God had cast asunder, were re-united, and the two worlds, which were so very different, began on that day to become alike. That trend toward biological homogeneity is one of the most important aspects of the history of life on this planet since the retreat of the continental glaciers.

The Europeans thought they were just off the coast of Asia—back to Eurasia again—but they were struck by the strangeness of the flora and fauna of the islands they had

3

discovered. The record kept by Columbus is full of remarks like:

> I saw neither sheep nor goats nor any other beast, but I have been here but a short time, half a day; yet if there were any I couldn't have failed to see them . . . .

> There were dogs that never barked . . . .

> All the trees were as different from ours as day from night, and so the fruits, the herbage, the rocks, and all things.[2]

The distinctiveness of the human inhabitants of these islands struck Columbus, as well. He found the Indians unlike even black Africans, the most exotic people he had ever met with before. The Indians' hair was "not kinky, but straight and course like horsehair; the whole forehead and head is very broad, more so than any other race that I have ever seen." These Arawak Indians were so impressed with the Europeans—their vessels, clothing, weapons, shapes, and colors—that they thought them demigods and gathered around to kiss the Spaniards' "hands and feet, marvelling and believing that they came from the sky . . . [and] feeling them to ascertain if they were flesh and bones like themselves."[3]

The differences between the life forms of the two worlds have amazed men ever since 1492. Most nonbotanists are inclined to pay more attention to animals than plants, so the contrast between the flora of the eastern and western hemispheres has never excited as much interest as that between the fauna, but the contrast is a marked one. It is not absolute—some 456 species of plants, for instance, are indigenous to both North America and Japan—but the uniqueness of American flora must be acknowledged. Cacti, for instance, are exclusively American in origin. Despite hundreds of years of contact via shipping between the northeastern part of the United States and adjacent Canada and the rest of the world, only about 18 percent of the total number of plant species growing in this part of America are of non-American origin.[4]

The pre-Columbian agriculturalists developed the American food plants from an assemblage of wild plants which was very different from that which the inventors of agriculture in the Old World had. Even the most optimistic of the early colonists of Virginia had to admit that the flora was alien more often than it was familiar. This difference becomes more and more pronounced as one moves south into Mexico and beyond. Jean de Léry, who was a member of the abortive French colony at Río de Janeiro in the 1550s, found only three plants with which he was familiar: purslane, basil, and a kind of fern. All the others were strange, leading to all sorts of difficulties. With no grapes, how were the Europeans to make the wine needed to celebrate the Lord's Supper? Was it better to forego the ceremony until wine could be obtained from Europe or to operate on the theory that Jesus used wine only because it was common in Palestine, and that, therefore, His sacrifice of Himself on the Cross could be commemorated with one of the local Indian beverages?[5]

The contrast between the Old and New World fauna has impressed everyone who has ever crossed the Atlantic or Pacific. Some species are common to both worlds, especially in the northern latitudes, but sometimes this only serves to point up other contrasts. In South and Central America the biggest native quadruped is the tapir, an animal also present in southeast Asia, but by no means the most impressive animal there.[6] The Old World elephant has a much more useful nose and is many times larger. Tropical America's four-legged carnivores are more impressive than the herbivorous tapir, but here, too, the strange disparity between New and Old World mammals appears. The jaguar is not an animal to treat with contempt, but compared to a lion or tiger, he is one of the middle-sized cats.

The early explorers wondered at the smallness of the American mammals they came upon in their early expeditions, most of which were limited to the torrid zone. It was the reptiles, snakes, birds, and insects that really impressed them. Europe has no reptile as big as the iguana; there is probably no animal quite as ugly. The iguana reminded Amerigo Vespucci of the flying serpent of legend, except for the lack of wings. Vespucci and his comrades reacted to the iguanas exactly as nature intended that the enemies of these harmless beasts should: "Their whole appearance," he wrote of the reptiles, "was so strange that we, supposing them to be poisonous, did not dare approach them." Many of the fellow jungle-dwellers of the iguanas were at least as strange, often as terrifying, and frequently a good deal more dangerous. In the rivers there were eels that defended themselves with electricity, and rays and piranhas. There were monkeys—no oddity in itself, but these swung by their tails! Who had ever seen a bird as strange as the toucan, who seemed more beak than body, and who had ever seen a land bird as large as the Andean condor actually fly? And who, outside of a nightmare, had ever seen bats that drank blood or a snake quite as long as the anaconda?[7]

Europeans found the animals of temperate North America less alien than those of the lands to the south, but still very unlike the animals of Europe. The rivers contained more kinds of fish than had ever swum in the Ebro or Guadalquivir. One of the biggest kind swam in the Mississippi and had whiskers like a cat, "the third part of which was head, with gills from end to end and along the sides were great spines, like very sharp awls." There was a snake with a castanet on his tail (rattlesnake, no doubt) whose bite left the victim with enough time for his last confession, but for little more. Strangest of all, when Coronado rode onto the plains, he found no gold but a kind of huge cattle as numerous as fish in the sea (buffalo or bison). They were as large or larger than oxen and had short, thick horns and humps like camels and when they ran, they carried their tails erect like scorpions. The Spanish horses were frightened of them "for they have a narrow short face, the brow two palms across from eye to eye, the eyes sticking out at the side, so that, when they are running, they can see who is following them. They have very long beards, like goats, and when they are running they throw their heads back with the beard dragging on the ground."[8]

Men returned from America with stories of mythical beasts—like that of the Mexican bird which never lands as long as it lives and even lays and hatches its eggs in the air[9]—but there was no need to resort to fiction. American fauna is richer in species of unique animals than any imagination could devise. In the 1850s Philip L. Sclater, on the basis of what he knew about the geographic distribution of bird genera, decided that our planet is divided into six regions, each one with a characteristic bird population: two of these regions make up the New World. Twenty years later, Alfred Russel Wallace, co-originator with Darwin of the modern concept of evolution, saw that Sclater's six-part division of the planet is as valid for animals in general as for birds in particular. The animals of the six sections are prevented or at least inhibited from intermingling by oceans, mountain ranges, deserts, differences in temperature. The fauna of these regions are not absolutely distinctive—the tapir is native to both tropical America and tropical Asia; the cougar, rattlesnake, and hummingbird are native to both North and South America—but, to quote a modern zoogeographer, "the animals in different parts of one faunal realm are on the whole more related to those of other parts of the same region than to those of other regions." To illustrate, although there are many similarities among the fauna of the Irrawaddy, lower Niger, and Amazon valleys, a zoologist can differentiate between them at a glance.[10]

South and Central America plus the West Indies and part of Mexico make up one of the Sclater–Wallace regions. The rest of Mexico, plus the United States, Canada, and Greenland make up another. Of the two, the southernmost is the richest zoologically, with forty-five families of backboned animals peculiar to it alone, according to Wallace. (Research since his time has shown that neither this southern region of the New World nor any of the other five regions is quite so clearly distinctive as he thought—accumulation of data always points up exceptions to any rule—but the general validity of the Sclater–Wallace system is still accepted.) It seems clear to the layman that southern America, with its unique anteaters, sloths, monkeys with prehensile tails, vampire bats, rodents as big as dogs, and wild profusion of insects and birds must rank as a separate region. Only Australia equals it in being truly exceptional.

Northern America is not nearly as distinctive. At most, Wallace grants only thirteen families of vertebrates as native to it exclusively, but it does have claim to uniqueness. A number of mammalian genera are peculiar to it, including several kinds of moles and species like the Rocky Mountain goat and the prong-buck. It shares with the region to the south the distinction of being home to the only marsupials outside of Australia and the only hummingbirds in the world. It is very rich in kinds of reptiles and amphibia, despite the fact that temperate and cold climates usually limit the numbers of such animals. And its peerless system of lakes and rivers give it a wealth of fresh water mollusca and fish unequalled anywhere else on this planet.[11]

Alfred Russel Wallace's careful accumulation of evidence and guarded generalities confirmed what Jean de Léry had guessed on the basis of one trip to Brazil more than three hundred years before: that America is so truly "different from Europe, Asia and Africa in the living habits of its people, the forms of its animals, and, in general, in that which the earth produces, that it can well be called the new world. . . ."[12]

The contrasts between the two worlds piqued European curiosity. Not everything was different. American palms were quite like those of Africa, and the jaguar was very much like the leopard. But why even slight differences, and why the great ones? Why were there no horses or cattle anywhere in the Americas? Why were there no four-legged beasts bigger than a fox in the West Indies? Even those who had voyaged to Africa for slaves and to the Far East for spices found little in America that was familiar, and many things that were utterly strange.

The Europeans had emerged from the Middle Ages with intellectual systems, Christian and Aristotelian, claimed by the orthodox (and so few even guessed there was anything beyond orthodoxy) to explain everything from the first and last ticks of history to what happens in the egg prior to the hatching of the chick. These systems proved too cramped to accommodate the New World. Aristotle had quite logically supposed the equatorial zone of the earth so hot that life could not exist there. Joseph de Acosta crossed directly under the sun on his way to America in 1570 and "felt so great cold, as I was forced to go into the sunne to warme me: what could I else do then but laugh at Aristotle's Meteors and his philosophie. . . ." Pliny's *Natural History* contains thirty-seven books, and yet he did not mention the llama in any of them. The works of Hippocrates, Galen, and Avicenna occupied whole shelves of every good fifteenth-century library from Baghdad to Oxford to Timbuktu, but these three giants of medicine had not a word to say about syphilis. Ancient and medieval geographers had made fine maps of all the world, but the men of the Columbian generation discovered that "Ptolomeus, and others knewe not the halfe."[13]

The ancient and medieval pronouncements on humans and human behavior seemed to leave Europeans little choice but to condemn the Indians as allies of the Devil. For instance, Christians agreed that heterosexual monogamy was the way to handle the sex relationship. The Indians, with a kind of abandon unmentioned in even the candid pages of the Old Testament, practiced promiscuity, polygamy, incest, and sodomy. The Europeans had either to conceive of the naturalness of cultural diversity and invent cultural toleration to go along with it, or to assume that Indians were in league with Hell. Most made the latter choice. The exception, of course, was Montaigne, who found nothing barbarous in what he heard of America, except insofar as "everyone gives the title barbarism to everything that is not according to his usage. . . ."[14]

The Bible was the source of most wisdom, and the book of Genesis told all that one needed to know about the beginning of the heavens, earth, angels, plants, animals, and men. There was one God and there had been one Creation; when mankind had offended God, God caused a great flood in which all land creatures, including men, had perished, except those preserved in Noah's ark. This explanation seemed sufficiently broad to include within its bounds all the diversity of life—plant, animal, and human—which the European was obliged to acknowledge up to the end of the fifteenth century. Then da Gama and Columbus brought whole new worlds crashing into the area of European perception.

The problems of explaining Africa and Asia were difficult but surmountable. After all, it had always been known that they were there and, if Europeans had not seen elephants, they had at least always known about them. But America, who had ever dreamed of America? The uniqueness of the New World called into question the whole Christian cosmogony. If God had created all of the life forms in one week in one place and they had then spread out from there over the whole world, then why are the life forms in the eastern and western hemispheres so different? And if all land animals and men had drowned except for those in the ark, and all that now exist are descended from those chosen few, then why the different kinds of animals and men on either side of the Atlantic? Why are there no tree sloths in the African and Asian tropics, and why do the Peruvian heathens worship Viracocha instead of Baal or some other demon familiar to the ancient Jews? The effort to maintain the Hebraic version of the origin of life and man was to "put many learned Christians upon the rack to make it out."[15]

The problem tempted a few Europeans to toy with the concept of multiple creations, but the mass of people clung to monogeneticism. They had to; it was basic to Christianity. For example, what would happen to the validity of the Pope's 1493 grant to Spain of "all islands and mainlands found and to be found, discovered, and to be discovered," in the western Atlantic unless their inhabitants were truly men and women and thus under papal jurisdiction? The famous Requirement of 1512, which the Spanish monarchs ordered the conquistadors to read to the Indians so that they would realize that their subsequent slaughter and subjugation were justified, opened with a statement that "the Lord our God, Living and Eternal, created Heaven and Earth, and one man and one woman, of whom you and I, and all the men of the world, were and are descendants. . . ." Being descendants of Adam and Eve, the American aborigines were subject to the Pope and, by his donation of America to Spain, to Ferdinand and Isabella.

If monogeneticism in this instance worked against the Indians, in 1537 it worked for them. The Pope denounced as satellites of the Devil those who claimed the Indians "should be treated as dumb brutes created for our service," a view common among the conquistadors. The Pope proclaimed "that the Indians are truly men, and that they are not only capable of understanding the Catholic faith but, according to our information, they desire exceedingly to receive it."[16]

Thus it was decided by Rome that the aborigines of America were worthy of conquest and too worthy to be treated as domesticated animals. Again and again during the centuries of European imperalism, the Christian view that all men are brothers was to lead to persecution of non-Europeans—he who is my brother sins to the extent that he is unlike me—and to the tempering of imperialism with mercy—he who is my brother deserves brotherly love.

The papacy remained undisturbed in its confidence that the book of Genesis provided all the paleontology that a Christian needed. But America was such a very square peg to fit into the round hole of Genesis. In 1520 Philippus Paracelsus, whose mind was ballasted with little dogma of any variety, is supposed to have said that no one would easily believe that "those who have been found in the out-of-the-way islands . . . are the posterity of Adam and Eve. . . . It is most probable that they are descended from another Adam."[17] Joseph de Acosta was a churchman, but the contrast between the creatures of the Old and New Worlds, which he had seen with his own eyes, also led him to the brink of heresy. There are in America, he wrote,

> a thousand different kindes of birdes and beasts of the forrest, which have never beene knowne, neither in shape nor name; and whereof there is no mention made, neither among the Latins nor Greeks, nor any other nations of the world.

He offered the explanation that "it may be God hath made a new creation of beasts."[18]

The problem of America troubled the seventeenth century, too, helping to lead some few men into unorthodoxy and at least one right into jail. If Eden and Mount Ararat were both in Asia, then how could man and animals be in America? The most influential of the men opposed to orthodox views on the subject was Isaac de La Peyrère. He was more inspired to heresy by biblical ambiguities and references in an-

cient documents to seemingly pre-Adamite events in Egypt
and Phoenicia than by the enigma of a biologically unique
America, but his theory provided explanations for all three
sources of confusion. Adam was the product of a second creation and father only to the Jews. The first Creation, which
preceded that of Adam by a very long time, had included
the creation of the ancestors of all the non-Jews—the pre-
Adamites—and the Flood had been only Palestinian in extent and had not affected them. Among the descendants of
the pre-Adamites were "the Mexicans whom Columbus discovered not so long ago." La Peyrère's book was burned and
he was arrested, but polygeneticism lived on.[19]

In 1857 Philip L. Sclater, one of Britain's leading zoologists and originator of the six faunal zone scheme referred
to previously, read before the Linnean Society a paper in
which he showed himself to be one who still entertained the
idea of multiple creations. This idea would explain how his
birds and all other land animals, including man, were distributed as they were. Like all polygeneticists, he started with
the false premise that

> every species of animal must have been created within or over
> the geographical area which it now occupies. Such being the
> case, if it can be shown that the areas now occupied by the
> primary varieties of mankind correspond with the primary zoologi-
> cal provinces of the globe. it would be an inevitable deduction,
> that these varieties of Man had their origin in the different parts
> of the world where they are now found, and the awkward necessity
> of supposing the introduction of the red man into America by
> Behring's Straits, and of colonizing Polynesia by stray pairs of
> Malays floating over the water like cocoa-nuts, and all similar
> hypotheses would be avoided.

It was in this paper that Sclater put forth his hypothesis that
the birds of the world are distributed in six distinctive regions. These regions he divided into two groups, one for the
Old World and one for the New. The titles he chose for the

two prove him a brother of Acosta: *Creatio Palaeogeana* and *Creatio Neogeana,*[20] or Old World and New World Creation.

Sclater was among the last of the respectable polygeneticists. In 1858 Charles Darwin and Alfred Russel Wallace presented essays to the Linnean Society in which they put forth the modern theory of evolution. One year later, Darwin published *On the Origin of Species,* shattering the concept of multiple creations (while also knocking loose a large part of the foundation of traditional Judaism and Christianity). Once the new theory of evolution was accepted, polygeneticism lived on only as a rationale for racism, in which capacity it still serves.[21]

The real source of conflict between orthodox Christians and the tiny but stubborn number of polygeneticists was that Christians had no adequate concept of change on which to base an explanation of how the earth and the life on earth had reached their present condition. The concept of evolution had existed from at least the time of Aristotle, but it was neither popular nor orthodox: the task of the Christian philosopher and biologist was to provide man with the intellectual means to freeze reality into a stable system, and not to send it slipping and tumbling down the slope of time toward no destination in particular. The accepted belief was that all the kinds of plants and animals, plus the first two people, had been created during the first week of time and that all species were complete as of that first Sunday and were without possibility of developing into new species.

Even if the European had had the concept of evolution to help him explain how the differences between the Old and New Worlds had come to be, he had no concept whatsoever of the amount of time the forces of evolution had been working on the life forms of this planet. A theory of biological evolution is useful only when thought of in terms of millions of years. The Requirement of 1512 set the date of creation at five thousand years prior to the writing of that document.

By the next century the date had been calculated with more exactness. Bernabé Cobo, the great expert on America, stated in 1651 that God had created the world "5,199 years before the birth of his Only Begotten Son and Redeemer our Jesus Christ." James Ussher, bishop of Ireland and a contemporary of Cobo, reckoned the date to be 4004 B.C. Disagreements on the exact age of the universe became more and more common, but everyone did agree that Adam had been dead for only a few thousand years. There had barely been enough time for mankind to move from pictography to the alphabet, and not nearly enough for the differentiation of the llama from the dromedary or the jaguar from the leopard.[22] Not until the geologist Sir Charles Lyell published his work in the 1830s did man really begin to know how old the world is, and how long natural forces have had to mold life into different forms.

It was approximately 60 million years ago that the world began to resemble the one we now know. The grasses, deciduous trees and shrubs, and all the plants that flower were already pushing in beside the ferns and conifers and were already beginning to differentiate into the quarter million species that now exist.[23] The dinosaurs died off and the mammals became prevalent, differentiating into bats and whales, sloths and antelopes, and, after most of the 60 million years had passed, men.

If one has some slight familiarity with this 60 million year period, the Cenozoic Era, and the course of evolution during it, then the difference between the Old and New World flora and fauna can be explained without resorting to extra creations. The course of that evolution was profoundly influenced by the emerging and submerging of the various great land bridges of the world, joining or separating the continents where various experiments in new types of life were going on. The most obvious example of the importance of a land bridge or, in this case, the lack of one, is Australia, which has been separated from Asia since the very beginning of the Cenozoic, and where the rule of the marsupials was nearly uncontested until the arrival of the Europeans and their placental mammals: horses, sheep, rabbits, and so on.[24]

The existing intercontinental land bridge, which was probably under water for the longest time in the Cenozoic, is the isthmus of Central America. For tens of millions of years, beginning early in the Cenozoic, South America was another Australia, where mammals that could not have survived the competition of their cousins in the Old World and North America proliferated. Then the land connection with the north reappeared, and many of the species native to South America disappeared beneath the wave of more efficient mammals rolling down from North America. The few who survived were those which missed by the widest margins fitting sixteenth-century European preconceptions of what mammals should be: the armadillo, tree sloth, and American anteater.[25]

Far to the northwest of the Central American isthmus is the most notoriously retractable land bridge of them all and one which had the greatest influence on evolution during the Cenozoic. It now lies beneath the Bering Sea, but it was once 1,500 kilometers of dry land from north to south, and thousands of species of plants and animals, super- and submicroscopic, moved across it from world to world. If the water level today fell forty meters, the Bering Strait would again be dry land.[26]

The existence or nonexistence of an isthmus between the Old and New Worlds began to fascinate Europeans almost as soon as they realized that Columbus had found not Asia but a new continent. The possibility of a land bridge from Tierra del Fuego to Asia never stirred as much interest as the possibility of an Arctic equivalent. The English, finding the southern sea passages to Cathay and the Spice Islands an Iberian monopoly, permitted their desire for a waterway to the Orient to persuade them that such a bridge *did not* exist between America and Siberia, and therefore that northwest and northeast passages between England and the Orient *did* exist. Sir Humphrey Gilbert cited Plato, Aristotle, Pliny, Strabo, and a number of contemporary geographers, none of whom had ever been within half a world of the Bering Strait, to prove "that America was an Iland; and that there lyeth a great Sea betweene it, Cathay and Greenland. . . ." He had not only authorities for this view but also reason: if America were connected with Asia then certainly the people of northwestern America, "hoping to have found some like commodities to their owne . . . ," or the Tartars, fleeing the cold and poverty of their country, would each have found their way to the other's continent. Furthermore, "there hath not at ani time been found any of ye beasts proper to Cathay, or Tartarie, etc., in America: nor of those proper to America, in Tartarie, Cathay, etc., or ani part of Asia." Off the English sailed to freeze their toes and lose their lives from Nova Zembla to Hudson Bay.[27]

Sir Francis Drake was among the first to disagree with Gilbert on the basis of practical experience. Drake coasted along California and northward in the 1570s, probably looking for an easy way home with his Spanish loot, but found no indication of a strait. The search was given up because of "the large spreading of the Asian and American continent which (somewhat northward of these parts), if they be not fully joined, yet seem they to come very neer one to the other."[28]

Joseph de Acosta reasoned along a different line than in his statement quoted on page 12 and re-created the isthmus that Gilbert had erased. If God had created life only once and if all land animals had passed through only one ark, then how could there be animals in both the eastern and western hemispheres if the two worlds were and always had been separate? "I have long beleeved that the one and the other world are joyned and continued with another in some part, or at least very neere."[29]

The participants in this argument, which lasted until the eighteenth-century voyages of Bering and others, were each both right and wrong. Their disagreements not only reflected their ignorance about the northern Pacific but also the simple fact that evidence existed for both the union and disunion of Asia and America. The history of the land bridge area has been one of successive submergences and emergences. During the former periods the Old and New Worlds developed independently and divergently. During the latter, biological revolutions swept both worlds, as life forms native to one, foreign to the other, crossed over into virgin territory.[30]

It is probable that these cross-migrations usually affected the New World more profoundly than the Old, because the latter, being larger, usually had produced a greater variety of life forms during the period of separation and isolation. But America, too, developed unique and long-lived life forms. The modern camel and horse, for instance, are North American in origin. The camels migrated west to become the dromedaries and Bactrian camels of Asia and Africa, and south to become the llamas of Peru. The horses trotted along with them into Asia and thence to Africa and Europe. Both animals disappeared in their homeland, the last of them dying during the latter millennia of the last epoch of the Cenozoic, the Pleistocene.[31]

The demise of the horse and camel in North America is part of one of the most mysterious chapters of the last million years. In a period of about 40,000 to 10,000 years ago at least two hundred kinds of animals disappeared, leaving us to inherit, in the words of Alfred Russel Wallace, "a zoologically impoverished world, from which all the hugest, and fiercest, and strongest forms have recently disappeared. . . ." Mammoths, mastodons, giant sloths, saber-toothed tigers, woolly rinoceroses, giant bisons, and others, all disappeared completely. The extinct animals were usually of the largest kinds, although the huge whales in the oceans were not affected. There was no dramatic decrease in the ranks of the plants. These large land mammals were not replaced by similarly sized rivals. This is extinction without replacement, which makes it something of an oddity.[32]

The explanation that climatic changes at the end of the Pleistocene caused these extinctions is not satisfactory. Climatic changes were gradual, which would have permitted the animals to adjust by means of the survival and reproduction of the fittest. Or the animals could simply have moved over a period of generations to regions where the climate was comfortable for them. Disease, cosmic rays, "racial senility," and other such deus ex machina explanations have been offered, but why would these forces have affected only the largest animals?[33]

The last of the large mammals to attain its present form and to arrive in America was man, and a currently popular explanation for the Pleistocene extinctions points to him as the extinguisher. He, seeking food in quantity, would choose the large rather than the small herbivores to prey upon. As these herbivores decreased in numbers, so would the large carnivores and scavengers that depended on them for food. The chief weakness of this theory is that it obliges one to believe that a scattered population of Stone Age hunters could have eliminated millions of gigantic and presumably very dangerous animals. The Indians of recorded history never wiped out the herds of American bison, even with the help of musket and rifle. Could prehistoric hunters have eliminated similarly large herds of scores of different animals, even if they had thousands of years to try?[34]

It is much easier to deprecate the prehistoric hunters as *the* great murderers of the Pleistocene than to suggest a better explanation for the Pleistocene extinctions. The theory seems more satisfactory for America than for the Old World. In Australia, Madagascar, New Zealand, and America—the areas most difficult to reach from the lands of man's origin—the extinctions took place most recently, within the last 15,000 years. The most inaccessible of all these areas, except possibly for New Zealand, was America.[35]

During the late Pleistocene the Bering land bridge was high and dry for long periods, and a corridor free from ice led down from Alaska between the glaciers through Canada. It is generally thought that during one or more of these periods men crossed from Siberia into America. The first came possibly as long ago as 28,000 years, and there is no proof that there were not even earlier migrations. These people, who for many thousands of years had been perfecting their hunting skills against animals who had had an equal amount of time to adjust to these two-legged predators, moved into a world teeming with animals which had never seen a single man. The hunting was superb.[36]

Whether it was some proto-Indian who drove his spear into the heart of the last mammoth in the Americas is, of course, a matter for debate. It is true that man's arrival and the disappearance of the larger animals in America do roughly coincide. And the advantage of "the element of surprise" which the abruptness of man's appearance in the Americas gave him would help account for the strange fact that the extinction of the larger fauna in the New World was more thorough than in the Old.

The presence of so many fewer large animals in the western than in the eastern hemisphere struck the sixteenth-, seventeenth-, and eighteenth-century Europeans as very odd, indeed. The eighteenth-century naturalist, the Comte de Buffon, leaped to the conclusion that if the quadrupeds of the New World were inferior to those of the Old in size, then so was most everything else American inferior to its counterpart in Europe, Africa, and Asia. One of the most glaring examples of American inferiority, according to Buffon and those of his school, was the American Indian. He was inferior in technology, political organization, military prowess, resistance to disease, intelligence, and—most important of all—in "ardour for women."[37] In the twentieth century, we are perhaps sophisticated enough to grant that the Indians have as rich a sex life as any people and also that their "stupidity" was simply evidence of the cultural gap between Europeans and Indians, but we must admit that the Old World snob was roughly correct in much of the rest of his estimation. When Columbus arrived, even the most advanced Indians were barely out of the Stone Age, and their armies were swept aside by tiny bands of conquistadors. Their agriculture was impressive, but they had few domesticated animals, and those were not very impressive. What European could but smile when comparing the Indian's dog, turkey, duck, llama, and guinea pig to his own horse, ass, cattle, sheep, pigs, chickens, geese? The Indians died in droves of diseases the Europeans, Africans, and Asians had accommodated themselves to long, long ago. As one indignant Spaniard put it, Indians "died like fish in a bucket."[38]

It was clear and still is clear that American Indians are different from the rest of mankind in a number of important ways, none of which worked to their advantage in their confrontation with Columbus and those who followed him. It may be accurate to say that the Indians were *more* different from the rest of mankind in 1492 than any other major group of humanity. A probable exception to this rule are the Australian aborigines, who were also isolated from the rest of humanity for a period of thousands of years.

The uniqueness of the American Indian is measurable. It lies not so much in his color, height, weight, bone formation, and other physical attributes—he is obviously some sort of cousin to the Mongoloid people, as Amerigo Vespucci noted—as in the physical uniformity of Indians from Hudson

Bay to Tierra del Fuego. Three hundred years ago Bernabé
Cobo remarked on this uniformity, and many anthropologists
of the twentieth century agree with him.[39] There are no contrasts among the Indians to equal those between the Watutsi
and pygmies, or the blond Prussians and swarthy Sicilians.
It is not true that "if you have seen one Indian, you have
seen them all"—no one would mistake a San Blas Indian
for an Iroquois—but, to quote the physical anthropologist
Frederick S. Hulse, "Compared to the diversity in bodily
form and genetical constitution found among the peoples on
the eastern side of the Atlantic, the American Indians show
a surprising degree of uniformity."[40] Some anthropologists
have gone so far as to rate the Indians not as a subgroup
of the Mongoloid people, but as an entirely separate race.[41]

This unique uniformity is especially apparent in the distribution of blood types among American aborigines. Unlike
superficial racial and cultural characteristics, blood type distribution provides a scientific way of differentiating between
groups of human beings. A human's blood type is irrevocably
dictated by heredity. No change in training, food, climate
or anything else can alter an individual's blood type; and
there is no way in which a people of blood type O, for instance, can suddenly start having great numbers of children
of blood type B unless there has been an infusion of genetic
material from outside the original group. It is also true that
a people whose blood type distribution is, let us say, 60 percent O, 30 percent B, and 10 percent A is very unlikely to
produce children or grandchildren or even great grandchildren whose blood type distribution is markedly different, unless they breed with outsiders.

The accompanying maps show dramatically how uniform
and unique is the blood type distribution of the Indians.[42]
The maps do not prove that the American aborigines are
an utterly homogeneous people. No one claims the Eskimos
to be Indian. There are other ways of measuring the

physical properties of the Indian population which do not produce as homogeneous a picture as do these maps.[43] Even the maps for type A and type O seem to indicate that the Indians of Canada and the northernmost part of the United States and their—quite literally—blood brothers, the Athapascans of southwestern United States, have not exactly the same ancestors as the aborigines elsewhere in America. But it is still safe to say, after proper acknowledgment of the law that all generalities are false, that either something happened to kill off most of the Indians with A and B type blood, which is most unlikely, or that almost all Indians are closely related to each other.

Their uniformity of blood types becomes even more impressive when contrasted with the disuniformity of distribution in the Old World. Blood type maps of the eastern hemisphere aborigines are of great complexity, with one variety of distribution here and a different one a hundred or a thousand miles beyond. There has obviously been a great mixing of peoples in the Old World. In contrast, the American Indians are so "purebred" that T. D. Stewart states "that no population of comparable size has remained so uniform after expanding, in whatever time has been involved, over such a large area."[44]

This uniformity of the Indians and the extent to which they are like and yet unlike the Mongoloid people, taken together with what we know about the Bering land bridge, suggest the following interpretation of the prehistoric history of the Indians. Some tens of thousands of years ago, when the Bering Straits were dry land, Asians began to cross into America. They were not Mongoloids, but probably of the people who were the common ancestors both of the present-day Chinese and Japanese, and of the American Indians. These immigrants and those who followed them were few in number. The climate of Siberia was such that few people lived near the Bering land bridge; hence relatively few people

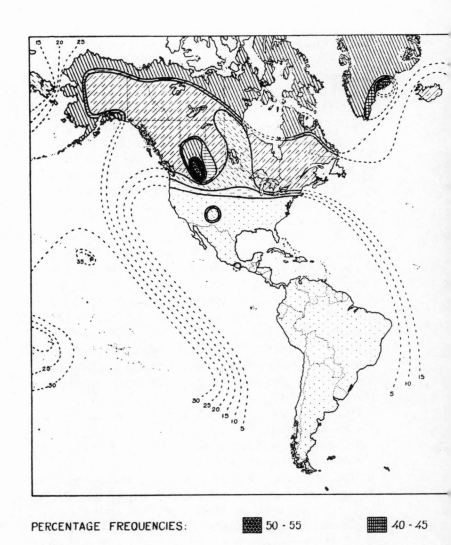

PERCENTAGE FREQUENCIES: ▓ 50 - 55   ▤ 40 - 45

▨ 15 - 20   ▧ 10 - 15

Distribution of blood group gene A in the aboriginal populations of the world.
COURTESY BLACKWELL SCIENTIFIC PUBLICATIONS LTD.

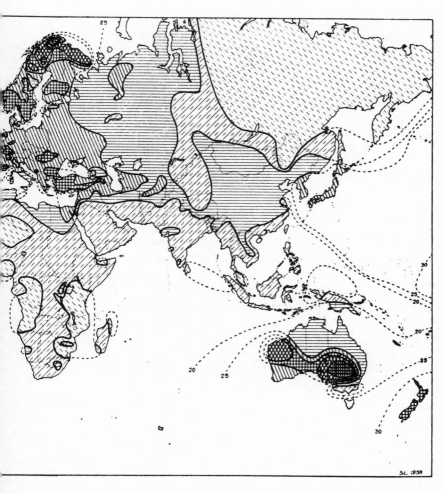

▨ 35 - 40	▦ 30 - 35	▨ 25 - 30	▤ 20 - 25
▤ 5 - 10	▢ 0 - 5		

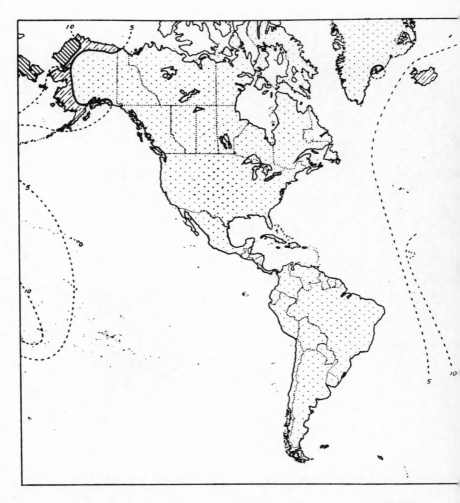

PERCENTAGE FREQUENCIES: ▓ 25 - 30   ▒ 20 - 25

Distribution of blood group gene B in the aboriginal populations of the world.
COURTESY BLACKWELL SCIENTIFIC PUBLICATIONS LTD.

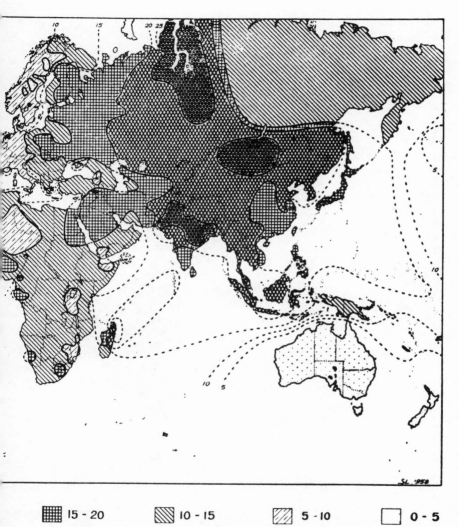

| ▦ 15 - 20 | ▨ 10 - 15 | ▧ 5 -10 | ☐ 0 - 5 |

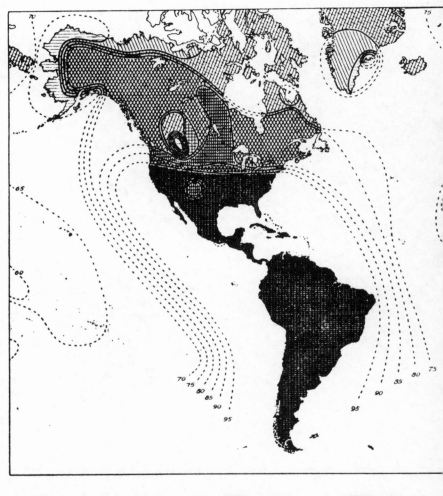

PERCENTAGE FREQUENCIES:

■ 95 - 100 ▓ 90 - 95

▨ 65 - 70 ▤ 60 - 65

Distribution of blood group gene O in the aboriginal populations of the world.

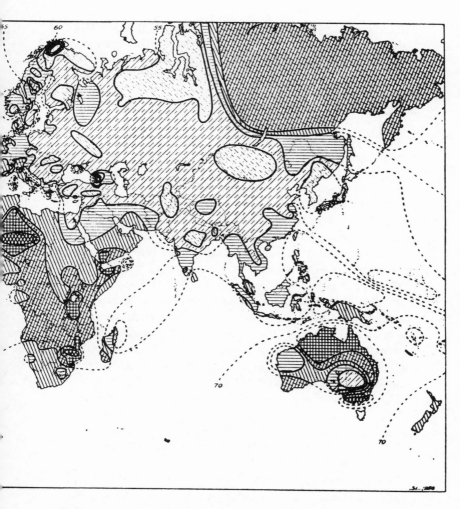

85 - 90	80 - 85	75 - 80	70 - 75
55 - 60	50 - 55	45 - 50	35 - 40

made the journey to America. The question of how the large
Indian population of 1492 could have descended from only
a few ancestors is easily answered. To give an extreme example, only four hundred males and females, reproducing once
every twenty years at an increase per generation of only 1.4
percent would have 10 million sons and daughters in 15,000
years.[45]

Then 10,000 years or so ago, the Bering land bridge sub-
merged again. Thereafter very few types of terrestrial life
found their way from the one world to the other. *Homo
sapiens* and moose and elm trees and all the life forms of
the two worlds were left in isolation, and the differences between the geographically separated life forms began to become greater. A few scattered groups of men continued to
find their way from Siberia to Alaska, just as a tiny number
of Asians, Polynesians, and Americans undoubtedly managed to drift across the Pacific, perhaps carrying ideas and
a handful or two of seeds. It has been demonstrated to be
possible: in 1815 a Japanese junk set out from Osaka to
Yedo, lost its masts and rudder, and drifted seventeen
months before the three men left alive out of a crew of at
least seventeen were taken aboard an American brig off
Santa Barbara, California.[46] But quantitatively the basis constitution of the human population of the New World as it
existed from circa 8,000 B.C. to 1492 A.D. was completed
by the former date. This is also true of the plants and animals that man in the New World was to live with and learn
to adapt to his own purposes.

The ancestors of the Indians crossed into the isolation of
America probably before agriculture had been invented, and
certainly before the people of Siberia had taken it up. The
first Americans entered the cul-de-sac of the New World before the major domestications of wild animals had been accomplished, or they came at a time when only the first domestications had taken place, such as that of the dog.[47] They

crossed over long before the foundation of the first Sumerian city had been laid, long before the Chinese began to write. The American Indians developed their ways of life in very nearly complete isolation.

That isolation not only hampered the growth of their civilizations, but also weakened their defenses against the major diseases of mankind. In the first place, the climate of Siberia, the land bridge, and Alaska screened out many diseases: the cold killed the germs and, more important, the cold and the rigor of the life in those latitudes eliminated all humans suffering from debilitating diseases. In the crudest sense, the life of the earliest Americans was a matter of the survival of the fittest.[48]

These first emigrants carried few diseases with them and found no humans in America, diseased or healthy. They lived, died, and bred alone for generation after generation, developing unique cultures and working out tolerances for a limited, native American selection of pathological micro-life. When the isolation of the New World was broken, when Columbus brought the two halves of this planet together, the American Indian met for the first time his most hideous enemy: not the white man nor his black servant, but the invisible killers which those men brought in their blood and breath.

NOTES

1. The theoretical basis of this chapter and this book in general is neatly summed up in George Gaylord Simpson, *The Geography of Evolution,* 69–132.

2. Christopher Columbus, *Journals and Other Documents on the Life and Voyages of Christopher Columbus,* trans. Samuel Eliot Morison, 72–73, 84.

3. Ibid., 66, 90.

4. Hui-Lin Li, "Floristic Relationships Between Eastern Asia and Eastern North America," 403; Henry A. Gleason and Arthur Cronquist, *The Natural Geography of Plants*, 34; Ronald Good, *The Geography of the Flowering Plants*, 64.

5. Jean de Léry, *Journal de Bord de Jean de Léry*, ed. M. R. Mayeux, 129, 293; William Strachey, *The Historie of Travell into Virginia Britania*, 117–133; Stefan Lorant, ed., *The New World*, 230–262.

6. Carl H. Lindroth, *The Faunal Connections Between Europe and North America*, 15–134; Léry, *Journal*, 239. The tapir is an odd sort of animal with a stubby semi-prehensile nose; at the most, it is only three feet high and six feet long. The best that Léry could say of the Brazilian tapir was that it was something like an ass, something like a cow, and entirely unlike either.

7. Martin Waldseemüller, *Cosmographiae Introductio by Martin Waldseemüller . . . To Which Are Added the Four Voyages of Amerigo Vespucci*, trans. Joseph Fischer and Franz von Wiesser, 106; Simpson, *Geography of Evolution*, 167–208.

8. Pedro Castañeda, *The Journey of Coronado*, trans. George Parker Winship, 140–141; Frederick W. Hodge and Theodore H. Lewis, eds., *Spanish Explorers in the Southern United States, 1528–1543*, 210.

9. Samuel Champlain, *Narrative of a Voyage to the West Indies and Mexico in the Years 1599–1602*, trans. Alice Wilmere, 36.

10. Philip J. Darlington, *Zoogeography, The Geographical Distribution of Animals*, 423; Philip L. Sclater, "On the General Geographical Distribution of the Members of the Class Aves," 137–145; Alfred Russel Wallace, *The Geographical Distribution of Animals*, 1:58ff.

11. Wallace, *Distribution of Animals*, 2:5–19, 115–125. For a corrective for Wallace's oversimplification, see Darlington, *Zoogeography*, 442–449.

12. Léry, *Journal*, 406.

13. Joseph de Acosta, *The Natural and Moral History of the Indies*, trans. Edward Grimston, 1:90; André Thevet, *The New Found Worlde, or Antartike*, trans. Thomas Hacket, 138.

14. Michel Eyquem de Montaigne, *Montaigne, Selected Essays*, ed. Blanchard Bates, 77.

15. Quoted in T. Bendyshe, "The History of Anthropology," 365.

16. Henry Steele Commager, ed., *Documents of American History*, 3; Lewis Hanke, ed., *History of Latin American Civilization*,

Sources and Interpretations, 1:123–124; Lewis Hanke, *The Spanish Struggle for Justice in the Conquest of America*, 33, 72–73.

17. Bendyshe, "History of Anthropology," 353.

18. Acosta, *Natural and Moral History*, 1:277–278.

19. Bendyshe, "History of Anthropology," 355–366, Matthew Hale, *The Primitive Origination of Mankind*, 182ff; Lee Eldridge Huddleston, *Origins of the American Indians, European Concepts, 1492–1729*, 139–140; David Rice McKee, "Issac de La Peyrère, A Precursor of Eighteenth Century Critical Deists," 456–485; Margaret T. Hodgen, *Early Anthropology in the Sixteenth and Seventeenth Century*, 207–253; Isaac de La Peyrère, *Prae-Adamitae*, 23.

20. Sclater, "Geographical Distribution of the Class Aves," 131, 145.

21. For an example of polygenetic racism, see Alexander Winchell, *Preadamites, or a Demonstration of the Existence of Men Before Adam*.

22. Bernabé Cobo, *Obras*, 1:13–14; Hanke, *Latin American Civilization*, 1:124; Paul Hazard, *The European Mind (1680–1715)*, 47.

23. Raymond C. Moore, *Introduction to Historical Geology*, 578–579.

24. Edwin H. Gilbert, *Evolution of the Vertebrates*, 424.

25. Ibid., 262–267, 338, 348.

26. David M. Hopkins, "The Cenozoic History of Beringia–A Synthesis," 410; Hansjurgen Müller-Beck, "On Migrations Across the Bering Land Bridge in the Upper Pleistocene," 380.

27. David Beers Quinn, ed., *The Voyage and Colonizing Enterprises of Sir Humphrey Gilbert*, 1:137–142.

28. Quoted in A. L. Rowse, *The Elizabethans and America*, 29.

29. Acosta, *Natural and Moral History*, 1:60.

30. Hopkins, "Cenozoic History," 451ff.

31. Ibid., 475; Colbert, *Evolution of Vertebrates*, 360, 364, 386.

32. Wallace, *Distribution of Animals*, 1:150; P. S. Martin, "Prehistoric Overkill," 78.

33. William E. Edwards, "The Late-Pleistocene Extinction and Diminution in Size of Many Mammalian Species," 143–145.

34. Martin, "Prehistoric Overkill," 75–120.

35. Ibid., 77.

36. Müller-Beck, "Migration," 373, 381; Edwards, "Late-Pleistocene Extinction," 145–148.

37. Henry Steele Commager and Elmo Giordanetti, eds., *Was America a Mistake? An Eighteenth Century Controversy*, 53ff.

38. Quoted in D. P. Mannix and Malcolm Cowley, *Black Cargoes*, 5–6.

39. Cobo, *Obras*, 2:13; Waldseemüller, *Cosmographiae Introductio*, 92.

40. Frederick S. Hulse, *The Human Species, An Introduction to Physical Anthropology*, 346.

41. J. V. Neel and F. M. Salzano, "A Prospectus for Genetic Studies on the American Indians," 249.

42. A. E. Mourant, Ada Kópec, and Kazimiera Domaniewska-Sobczak, *The ABO Groups, Comprehensive Tables and Maps of World Distribution*, 268–270.

43. Neel and Salvano, "Genetic Studies," 253.

44. T. D. Stewart, "A Physical Anthropologist's View of the Peopling of the New World," 262.

45. W. S. Laughlin, "Human Migration and Permanent Occupation in the Bering Sea Area," 416.

46. Charles W. Brooks, *Japanese Wrecks Stranded and Picked up Adrift in the North Pacific Ocean*, 10.

47. Fredeick E. Zeuner, *A History of Domesticated Animals*, 436–439.

48. Stewart, "Peopling of the New World," 265.

Conquistador y Pestilencia 2

Why were the Europeans able to conquer America so easily? In our formal histories and in our legends, we always emphasize the ferocity and stubbornness of the resistance of the Aztec, Sioux, Apache, Tupinamba, Araucanian, and so on, but the really amazing thing about their resistance was its ineffectiveness. The Orientals held out against the Europeans much more successfully; they, of course, had the advantage of vast numbers and a technology much more advanced than that of the Indians. The Africans, however, were not "thousands of years ahead" of the Indians, except in possessing iron weapons, and yet the great mass of black Africans did not succumb to European conquest until the nineteenth century.

There are many explanations for the Europeans' success in America: the advantage of steel over stone, of cannon and firearms over bows and arrows and slings; the terrorizing effect of horses on foot soldiers who have never seen such beasts before; the lack of unity among the Indians, even within their empires; the prophecies in Indian mythology about the arrival of white gods. All these factors combined

35

to deal to the Indian a shock such as only H. G. Wells's *War of the Worlds* can suggest to us. Each factor was undoubtedly worth many hundreds of soldiers to Cortés and Pizarro and other great Indian-killers.

For all of that, one might have at least expected the highly organized, militaristic societies of Mexico and the Andean highlands to survive the initial contact with the European societies. Thousands of Indian warriors, even if confused and frightened and wielding only obsidian-studded war clubs, should have been able to repel the first few hundred Spaniards to arrive. And what is the explanation for the fact that Indians were really only a little more successful in defending themselves and their lands after they learned that the invaders were not gods, after they obtained their own horses and guns and developed tactics to deal with the Europeans?

After the Spanish conquest an Indian of Yucatan wrote of his people in the happier days before the advent of the European:

> There was then no sickness; they had no aching bones; they had then no high fever; they had then no smallpox; they had then no burning chest; they had then no abdominal pain; they had then no consumption; they had then no headache. At that time the course of humanity was orderly. The foreigners made it otherwise when they arrived here.[1]

It would be easy to attribute this statement to the nostalgia that the conquered always feel for the time before the conqueror appeared, but the statement is probably in part true. During the millennia before the European brought together the compass and the three-masted vessel to revolutionize world history, men moved slowly, seldom over long distances and rarely across the great oceans. Men lived in the same continents where their great-grandfathers had lived and seldom caused violent and rapid changes in the delicate balance between themselves and their environments. Diseases tended to be endemic rather than epidemic. It is true that man did not achieve perfect accommodation with his microscopic parasites. Mutation, ecological changes, and migration brought the Black Death to Europe, and few men lived to the proverbial age of three-score years and ten without knowing epidemic disease. Yet ecological stability did tend to create a crude kind of mutual toleration between human host and parasite. Most Europeans, for instance, survived measles and tuberculosis, and most West Africans survived yellow fever and malaria.

Migration of man and his maladies is the chief cause of epidemics. And when migration takes place, those creatures who have been longest in isolation suffer most, for their genetic material has been least tempered by the variety of world diseases. Among the major divisions of the species homo sapiens, with the possible exception of the Australian aborigine, the American Indian probably had the dangerous privilege of longest isolation from the rest of mankind. Medical historians guess that few of the first rank killers among the diseases are native to the Americas.[2]

These killers came to the New World with the explorers and the conquistadors. The fatal diseases of the Old World killed more effectively in the New, and the comparatively benign diseases of the Old World turned killer in the New. There is little exaggeration in the statement of a German missionary in 1699 that "the Indians die so easily that the bare look and smell of a Spaniard causes them to give up the ghost."[3]

The most spectacular period of mortality among the American Indians occurred during the first hundred years of contact with the Europeans and Africans. Almost all the contemporary historians of the early settlements, from Bartolomé de las Casas to William Bradford of Plymouth Plantation, were awed by the ravages of epidemic disease among the native populations of America. In Mexico and Peru, where there were more Europeans and Africans—and, therefore, more contact with the Old World—and a more careful chronicle of events kept than in most other areas of America, the record shows something like fourteen epidemics in the former and perhaps as many as seventeen in the latter between 1520 and 1600.[4]

The annals of the early Spanish empire are filled with complaints about the catastrophic decline in the number of native American subjects. When Antonio de Herrera wrote his multivolume history of that empire at the beginning of the seventeenth century, he noted as one of the main differences between the Old and New Worlds the extreme susceptibility of the natives of the latter to diseases, especially smallpox. Indian women, he wrote, were especially quick to succumb to it, but it rarely infected anyone of European birth. The Indians became so enraged by the invulnerability of the Spaniards to epidemic disease that they kneaded infected blood into their masters' bread and secreted corpses in their wells—to little effect.[5]

The victims of disease were probably greatest in number in the heavily populated highlands of New Spain (Mexico) and Peru, but, as a percentage of the resident population, were probably greatest in the hot, wet lowlands. By the 1580s disease, ably assisted by Spanish brutality, had killed off or driven away most of the peoples of the Antilles and the lowlands of New Spain, Peru, and the Caribbean littoral, "the habitation of which coasts is . . . so wasted and condemned, that of thirty parts of the people that inhabit it, there wants twenty-nine; and it is likely the rest of the Indians will in short time decay."[6]

It has often been suggested that the high mortality rates of these post-Columbian epidemics were due more to the brutal treatment of the Indians by the Europeans than to the Indians' lack of resistance to imported maladies. But the early chroniclers reported that the first epidemics following the arrival of Old World peoples in a given area of the New World were the worst, or at least among the worst. European exploitation had not yet had time to destroy the Indians' health.

The record shows that several generations of Indian contact with Europeans and Africans seemed to lead not to the total destruction of the Indians, but only to a sharp diminution of numbers, which was then followed by renewed population growth among the aborigines.[7] The relationships between these phenomena are too complex to be explained by any one theory. However, their sequence is perfectly compatible with the theory that the Indians had little or no resistance to many diseases brought from the Old World, and so first died in great numbers upon first contact with immigrants from Europe and Africa; and when those Indians with the weakest resistance to those maladies had died, interbreeding among the hardy survivors and, to some unmeasured extent, with the immigrants, led to the beginning of population recovery.

The record of early post-Columbian medical history of America was never kept carefully and much of it has been erased since, but it does seem to show a greater number of epidemics, characterized by a higher mortality rate, than was typical even in insalubrious Europe of that time. The very first was a pandemic which began in 1519 in the Greater Antilles and swept through Mexico, Central America, and—probably—Peru. It caused "in all likelihood the most severe single loss of aboriginal population that ever occurred," to quote one expert who has examined its history carefully.[8] It is the best documented of all of the first epidemics. We have no more than snatches of information on the others. Hans Staden, captive to the Tupinamba of Brazil in the early 1550s, was—ironically—saved from death by what may have been an epidemic. He convinced the local chief that the malady carrying off many of the Indians had been sent by the Christian God to punish them for their intention to eat Staden. In 1552 a respiratory disease killed many natives around Pernambucò. In the same decade epidemic broke out among the· famished Frenchmen at Río de Janeiro, spread to the mission Indians there and killed eight hundred of them. In 1558 pleurisy and bloody flux spread along the coast from Río to Espírito Santo. In 1558 and 1560 smallpox arrived in Río de la Plata and swept off thousands of Indians, without touching a single Spaniard. Smallpox came to Brazil in 1562 and 1563 and carried off tens of thousands of Indians, but left the Portuguese unscathed. In some villages no one was left who was healthy enough to tend the sick, "not even someone who could go to the fountain for a gourdfull of water."[9]

The English were as efficient disease carriers as the Latins. In 1585 Sir Francis Drake led a large expedition against Spain's overseas possessions. His men picked up some highly contagious fever—probably typhus—in the Cape Verde Islands and brought it along with them to the Caribbean and Florida. The malady spread to the Indians in the environs of St. Augustine and, "The wilde people . . . died verie fast and said amongest themselves, it was the Inglisshe God that made them die so faste."[10]

In 1587 the English founded a colony at Roanoke Island, a few hundred miles north of St. Augustine. The colonists' diagnoses of their immediate and fatal effect on many of the Indians was similar in medical philosophy to that expressed by the Florida Indians. Thomas Hariot wrote that there was no Indian village where hostility, open or hidden, had been shown,

> but that within a few dayes after our departure from everies such townes, that people began to die very fast, and many in short space; in some townes about twentie, in some fourtie, in some sixtie, & in one six score, which in trueth was very manie

in respect to their numbers. . . . The disease also was so strange that they neither knew what it was, nor how to cure it; the like by report of the oldest men in the countrey never happened before, time out of mind.[11]

The natives of what is now the Atlantic coast of Canada had contact with Europeans—fishermen and fur traders—from very early in the sixteenth century, long before the English attempted colonization at Roanoke or any other place in America. Depopulation was already apparent among their tribes by the time of French settlement. The Jesuit *Relations* contain a report dated 1616 from which the following paragraph is extracted. The Indians, it states,

> are astonished and often complain that, since the French mingle with and carry on trade with them, they are dying fast and the population is thinning out. For they assert that, before this association and intercourse, all their countries were very populous and they tell how one by one the different coasts, according as they have begun to traffic with us, have been more reduced by disease.[12]

These Indians looked south enviously to New England, where tribes were not diminishing. The turn of these Armouchiquois, as the Canadian Indians called them, came in the same year that the above report was written. In 1616 and 1617 a pestilence swept through New England, clearing the woods, in the words of Cotton Mather, "of those pernicious creatures, to make room for better growth." Whatever the sickness was, Europeans were immune to it. The handful of whites who passed the winter of 1616–1617 with the Indians of coastal Maine "lay in the cabins with those people that died, [but] not one of them ever felt their heads to ache, while they stayed there." The Massachusetts tribe was nearly completely exterminated, depopulating the area of Plymouth Bay at just about the same time that the Pilgrims were deciding to come to America. The same epidemic also swept the environs of Boston Bay. A European who lived in that area in 1622 wrote that the Indians had

> died on heapes, as they lay in their houses; and the living, that were able to shift for themselves, would runne away and let them dy, and let there Carkases ly above the ground without burial. . . . And the bones and skulls upon the severall places of their habitations made such a spectacle after my coming into those partes, that, as I travailed in the Forrest nere the Massachusetts, it seemed to me a new found Golgotha.[13]

There is no need to continue this lugubrious catalog. The records of every European people who have had prolonged contact with the native peoples of America are full of references to the devastating impact of Old World diseases. The Russians, the last to come, had the same experience as the Spanish, Portuguese, English, and French; and thousands of Aleuts, Eskimos, and Tlingits were thrust into their graves by the maladies which the promyshlenniki—as innocent of intent as the conquistadores—brought to the New World with them.[14]

It would take a work of many volumes to give the full history of Old World diseases and New World peoples. We will limit ourselves to a detailed study of the first recorded American epidemic, an epidemic whose influence on the history of America is as unquestionable and as spectacular as that of the Black Death on the history of the Old World.

We know that the most deadly of the early epidemics in America were those of the eruptive fevers—smallpox, measles, typhus, and so on. The first to arrive and the deadliest, said contemporaries, was smallpox. Even today, however, smallpox is occasionally misdiagnosed as influenza, pneumonia, measles, scarlet fever, syphilis, or chicken pox.[15] Four hundred years ago such mistakes were even more common, and writers of the accounts upon which we must base our examination of the early history of smallpox in America did not have any special interest in accurate diagnosis. The early historians were much more likely to cast their eyes skyward and comment on the sinfulness that had called down such epidemics as obvious evidence of God's wrath than to describe in any detail the diseases involved. It should also be noted that conditions which facilitate the spread of one disease will usually encourage the spread of others, and that "very rarely is there a pure epidemic of a single malady." Pneumonia and pleurisy, for instance, often follow after smallpox, smothering those whom it has weakened.[16]

Furthermore, although the Spanish word *viruelas,* which appears again and again in the chronicles of the sixteenth century, is almost invariably translated as "smallpox," it specifically means not the disease but the pimpled, pustuled appearance which is the most obvious symptom of the disease. Thus the generation of the conquistadores may have used "viruelas" to refer to measles, chicken pox, or typhus. One must remember that people of the sixteenth century were not statistically minded, so their estimates of the numbers killed by epidemic disease may be a more accurate measurement of their emotions than of the numbers who really died.

When the sixteenth-century Spaniard pointed and said "viruelas," what he meant and what he saw was usually smallpox. On occasion he was perfectly capable of distinguishing among diseases: for instance, he called the epidemic of 1531 in Central America *sarampión*—measles—and not viruelas.[17] We may proceed on the assumption that smallpox was the most important disease of the first pandemic in the recorded history of the Americas.

Smallpox has been so successfully controlled by vaccination and quarantine in the industrialized nations of the twentieth century that few North Americans or Europeans have ever seen it. But it is an old companion of humanity, and for most of the last millennium it was one of the commonest diseases in Europe. It was long thought, with reason, to be one of the most infectious maladies. Smallpox is usually communicated through the air by means of droplets or dust particles; its virus enters the new host through the respiratory tract. There are many cases of hospital visitors who have contracted the disease simply by breathing the air of a room in which someone lies ill with the disease.[18]

Because it is extremely communicable, before the eighteenth century it was usually thought of as a necessary evil of childhood, such as measles is today. Sometimes the only large group untouched by it was also that which had been relatively unexposed to it—the young. Yet even among Spanish children of the sixteenth century, smallpox was so common that Ruy Díaz de Isla, a medical writer, recorded that he had once seen a man of twenty years sick with the disease, "and he had never had it before."[19]

Where smallpox has been endemic, it has been a steady, dependable killer, taking every year from 3 to 10 percent of those who die. Where it has struck isolated groups, the death rate has been awesome. Analysis of figures for some twenty outbreaks shows that the case mortality among an unvaccinated population is about 30 percent. Presumably, in people who have had no contact whatever with smallpox, the disease will infect nearly every single individual it touches. When in 1707 smallpox first appeared in Iceland, in two years 18,000 out of the island's 50,000 inhabitants died of it.[20]

The first people of the New World to meet the white and black races and their diseases were Arawaks of the Greater Antilles and the Bahamas. On the very first day of landfall in 1492 Columbus noted that they "are very unskilled with arms . . . [and] could all be subjected and made to do all that one wished."[21] These Arawaks lived long enough to provide the Spaniards with their first generation of slaves in America and Old World diseases with their first beachhead in the New World.

Oviedo, one of the earliest historians of the Americas, estimated that a million Indians lived on Santo Domingo when the Europeans arrived to plant their first permanent colony in the New World. "Of all those," Oviedo wrote, "and of all those born afterwards, there are not now believed to be at the present time in this year of 1548 five hundred persons, children and adults, who are natives and are the progeny or lineage of those first."[22]

The destruction of the Arawaks has been largely blamed on the Spanish cruelty, not only by the later Protestant historians of the "Black Legend" school but also by such contemporary Spanish writers as Oviedo and Bartolomé de Las Casas. Without doubt the early Spaniards brutally exploited the Indians. But it was obviously not in order to kill them off, for the early colonists had to deal with a chronic labor shortage and needed the Indians. Disease would seem to be a more logical explanation for the disappearance of the Arawaks, because they, like other Indians, had little immunity to Old World diseases. At the same time, one may concede that the effects of Spanish exploitation undoubtedly weakened their resistance to disease.

Yet it is interesting to note that there is no record of any massive smallpox epidemic among the Indians of the Antilles for a quarter of a century after the first voyage of Columbus. Indians apparently suffered a steady decline in numbers, which was probably due to extreme overwork, other diseases, and a general lack of will to live after their whole culture had been shattered by alien invasion.[23] How can the absence of smallpox be explained, if the American Indian was so susceptible and if ships carrying Europeans and Africans from the pestilential Old World were constantly arriving in Santo Domingo? The answer lies in the nature of the disease. It is a deadly malady, but it lasts only a brief time in each patient. After an incubation period of twelve days or so, the patient suffers from high fever and vomiting followed three or four days later by the characteristic skin eruptions. For those who do not die, these pustules dry up in a week or ten days and form scabs which soon fall off, leaving the disfiguring pocks that give the disease its name. The whole process takes a month or less, and after that time the patient is either dead or immune, at least for a period of years. Also there is no nonhuman carrier of smallpox, such as the flea of typhus or the mosquito of malaria; it must pass from man to man. Nor are there any long-term human carriers of smallpox, as, for instance, with typhoid and syphilis. It is not an over-simplification to say that one either has smallpox and can transmit it, or one has not and cannot transmit it.

Except for children, most Europeans and their slaves had had smallpox and were at least partially immune, and few but adults sailed from Europe to America in the first decades after discovery. The voyage was one of several weeks, so that, even if an immigrant or sailor contracted smallpox on the day of embarkation, he would most likely be dead or rid of its virus before he arrived in Santo Domingo. Moist heat and strong sunlight, characteristic of a tropical sea voyage, are particularly deadly to the smallpox virus. The lack of any rapid means of crossing the Atlantic in the sixteenth century delayed the delivery of the Old World's worst gift to the New.

It was delayed; that was all. An especially fast passage from Spain to the New World; the presence on a vessel of several nonimmune persons who could transmit the disease from one to the other until arrival in the Indies; the presence of smallpox scabs, in which the virus can live for weeks, accidentally packed into a bale of textiles—by any of these means smallpox could have been brought to Spanish America.[24]

In December 1518 or January 1519 a disease identified as smallpox appeared among the Indians of Santo Domingo, brought, said Las Casas, from Castile. It touched few Spaniards, and none of them died, but it devastated the Indians. The Spaniards reported that it killed one-third to one-half of the Indians. Las Casas, never one to understate the appalling, said that it left no more than one thousand alive "of that immensity of people that was on this island and which we have seen with our own eyes."[25]

Undoubtedly one must question these statistics, but they are not too far out of line with mortality rates in other smallpox epidemics, and with C. W. Dixon's judgment that populations untouched by smallpox for generations tend to resist the disease less successfully than those populations in at least occasional contact with it. Furthermore, Santo Domingo's epidemic was not an atypically pure epidemic. Smallpox seems to have been accompanied by respiratory ailments (*romadizo*), possibly measles, and other Indian-killers. Starvation probably also took a toll, because of the lack of hands to work the fields. Although no twentieth-century epidemiologist or demographer would find these sixteenth-century statistics completely satisfactory, they probably are crudely accurate.[26]

In a matter of days after smallpox appeared in Santo Domingo, it appeared in Puerto Rico. Before long, the Arawaks were dying a hideous and unfamiliar death throughout the islands of the Greater Antilles.[27] Crushed by a quarter-century of exploitation, they now performed their last function on earth: to act as a reserve of pestilence in the New World from which the conquistador drew invisible biological allies for his assault on the mainland.

Smallpox seems to have traveled quickly from the Antilles to Yucatán. Bishop Diego de Landa, the chief sixteenth-century Spanish informant on the people of Yucatán, recorded that sometime late in the second decade of that century "a pestilence seized them, characterized by great pustules, which rotted their bodies with a great stench, so that the limbs fell to pieces in four or five days." The *Book of Chilam Balam of Chumayel,* written in the Mayan language with European script after the Spanish settlement of Yucatán, also records that some time in the second decade "was when the eruption of pustules occurred. It was smallpox." It has been speculated that the malady came with Spaniards shipwrecked on the Yucatán coast in 1511 or with the soldiers and sailors of Hernández de Cordoba's expedition which coasted along Yucatán in 1517. Both these explanations seem unlikely, because smallpox had not appeared in the Greater Antilles, the likeliest source of any smallpox epidemic on the continent, until the end of 1518 or the beginning of 1519. Be that as it may, there is evidence that the Santo Domingan epidemic could have spread to the continent before Cortés's invasion of Mexico. Therefore, the epidemic raging there at that time may have come in two ways—north and west from Yucatán and directly from Cuba to central Mexico, brought by Cortés's troops.[28]

The melodrama of Cortés and the conquest of Mexico needs no retelling. After occupying Tenochtitlán and defeating the army of his rival, Narváez, he and his troops had to fight their way out of the city to sanctuary in Tlaxcala. Even as the Spanish withdrew, an ally more formidable than Tlaxcala appeared. Years later Francisco de Aguilar, a former follower of Cortés who had become a Dominician friar, recalled the terrible retreat of the *Noche Triste.* "When the Christians were exhausted from war, God saw fit to send the Indians smallpox, and there was a great pestilence in the city. . . ."[29]

With the men of Narváez had come a black man suffering from smallpox, "and he infected the household in Cempoala where he was quartered; and it spread from one Indian to another, and they, being so numerous and eating and sleeping together, quickly infected the whole country." The Mexicans had never seen smallpox before and did not have even the European's meager knowledge of how to deal with it. The old soldier-chronicler, Bernal Díaz del Castillo, called the Negro "a very black dose [for Mexico] for it was because of him that the whole country was stricken, with a great many deaths."[30]

Probably, several diseases were at work. Shortly after the retreat from Tenochtitlán Bernal Díaz, immune to smallpox like most of the Spaniards, "was very sick with fever and was vomiting blood." The Aztec sources mention the racking cough of those who had smallpox, which suggests a respiratory complication such as pneumonia or a streptococcal infection, both common among smallpox victims. Great numbers of the Cakchiquel people of Guatemala were felled by a devastating epidemic in 1520 and 1521, having as its most prominent symptom fearsome nosebleeds. Whatever this disease was, it may have been present in central Mexico along with smallpox.[31]

The triumphant Aztecs had not expected the Spaniards to return after their expulsion from Tenochtitlán. The sixty days during which the epidemic lasted in the city, however, gave Cortés and his troops a desperately needed respite to reorganize and prepare a counterattack. When the epidemic subsided, the siege of the Aztec capital began. Had there been no epidemic, the Aztecs, their war-making potential unimpaired and their warriors fired with victory, could have pursued the Spaniards, and Cortés might have ended his life spread-eagled beneath the obsidian blade of a priest of Huitzilopochtli. Clearly the epidemic sapped the endurance of Tenochtitlán. As it was, the siege went on for seventy-five days, until the deaths within the city from combat, starvation, and disease—probably not smallpox now—numbered many thousands. When the city fell "the streets, squares, houses, and courts were filled with bodies, so that it was almost impossible to pass. Even Cortés was sick from the stench in his nostrils."[32]

Peru and the Andean highlands were also hit by an early epidemic, and if it was smallpox it most probably had to pass through the Isthmus of Panama, as did Francisco Pizarro himself. The documentation of the history of Panama in the first years after the conquest is not as extensive as that of Mexico or the Incan areas, because the Isthmus had fewer riches and no civilized indigenous population to learn European script from the friars and write its own history. We do know that in the first decades of the sixteenth century the same appalling mortality took place among the Indians in Central America as in the Antilles and Mexico. The recorded medical history of the Isthmus began in 1514 with the death, in one month, of seven hundred Darien settlers, victims of hunger and an unidentified disease. Oviedo, who was in Panama at the time of greatest mortality, judged that upwards of two million Indians died there between 1514 and 1530, and Antonio de Herrera tells us that forty thousand died of disease in Panama City and Nombre de Dios alone in a twenty-eight year period during the century. Others wrote of the depopulation of "four hundred leagues" of land that had "swarmed" with people when the Spanish first arrived.[33]

What killed the Indians? Contemporaries and many historians blame the carnage on Pedrarias Dávila, who executed Balboa and ruled Spain's first Central American settlements with such an iron hand that he was hated by all the chief chroniclers of the age. It can be effectively argued, however, that he was no more a berserk butcher of Indians than Pizarro, for the mortality among Indians of the Isthmus during his years of power is parallel to the high death rates among the Indians wherever the Spaniards went.[34] When charges against Pedrarias were investigated in 1527, his defenders maintained that the greatest Indian-killer had been an epidemic of smallpox. This testimony is hard to reject, for another document of 1527 mentions the necessity of importing aboriginal slaves into Panama City, Nata, and the port of Honduras, because smallpox had carried off all the Indians in those areas.[35]

The Spaniards could never do much to improve the state of public health in Panama. In 1660 those who governed Panama City listed as resident killers and discomforters smallpox, measles, pneumonia, suppurating abscesses, typhus, fevers, diarrhea, catarrh, boils, and hives—and blamed them all on the importation of Peruvian wine![36] Of all the killers operating in early Panama, however, smallpox was undoubtedly the most deadly to the Indians.

If we attempt to describe the first coming of Old World disease to the areas south of Panama, we shall have to deal with ambiguity, equivocation, and simple guesswork, for eruptive fever, now operating from continental bases, apparently outstripped the Spaniards and sped south from the Isthmus into the Incan Empire before Pizarro's invasion. Long before the invasion, the Inca Huayna Capac was aware that the Spaniards—"monstrous marine animals, bearded men who moved upon the sea in large houses"—were pushing down the coast from Panama. Such is the communicability of smallpox and the other eruptive fevers that any Indian who received news of the Spaniards could also have easily received the infection of the European diseases. The biologically defenseless Indians made vastly more efficient carriers of such pestilence than the Spaniards.[37]

Our evidence for the first post-Columbian epidemic in Incan lands is entirely hearsay, because the Incan people had no system of writing. Therefore, we must depend on secondary accounts by Spaniards and by Indians born after the conquest, accounts based on Indian memory and written down years and even decades after the epidemic of the 1520s. The few accounts we have of the great epidemic are associated with the death of Huayna Capac. He spent the last years of his life campaigning against the people of what is today northern Peru and Ecuador. There, in the province of Quito, he first received news of an epidemic raging in his empire, and there he himself was stricken. Huayna Capac and his captains died with shocking rapidity, "their faces being covered with scabs."

Of what did the Inca and his captains die? One of the most generally reliable of our sources, Garcilaso de la Vega, describes Huayna Capac's death as the result of "a trembling chill . . . , which the Indians call *chucchu,* and a fever, called by the Indians *rupu.* . . ." We dare not, four hundred years later, state unequivocally that the disease was not one native to the Americas. Most accounts call it smallpox, or suggest that it was either smallpox or measles. Smallpox seems the best guess because the epidemic struck in that period when the Spaniards, operating from bases where smallpox was killing multitudes, were first coasting along the shores of Incan lands.[38]

The impact of the smallpox pandemic on the Aztec and Incan Empires is easy for the twentieth-century reader to underestimate. We have so long been hypnotized by the daring of the conquistador that we have overlooked the importance of his biological allies. Because of the achievements of modern medical science we find it hard to accept statements from the conquest period that the pandemic killed one-third to one-half of the populations struck by it. Toribio Motolinía claimed that in most provinces of Mexico "more than one half of the population died; in others the proportion was little less. . . . They died in heaps, like bedbugs."

The proportion may be exaggerated, but perhaps not as much as we might think. The Mexicans had no natural resistance to the disease at all. Other diseases were probably operating quietly and efficiently behind the screen of smallpox. Add the factors of food shortage and the lack of even minimal care for the sick. Motolinía wrote, "Many others died of starvation, because as they were all taken sick at once, they could not care for each other, nor was there anyone to give them bread or anything else." We shall never be certain what the death rate was, but from all evidence, it must have been immense. Sherburne F. Cook and Woodrow Borah estimate that, for one cause and another, the population of central Mexico dropped from about 25 million on the eve of conquest to 16.8 million a decade later. This estimate strengthens confidence in Motolinía's general veracity.[39]

South of Panama, in the empire of the Incas, our only means of estimating the mortality of the epidemic of the 1520s is by an educated guess. The population there was thick, and it provided a rich medium for the transmission and cultivation of communicable diseases. If the malady which struck in the 1520s was smallpox, as it seems to have been, then it must have taken many victims, for these Indians probably had no more knowledge of or immunity to smallpox than the Mexicans. Most of our sources tell us only that many died. Cieza de León gives a figure of 200,000, and Martín de Murúa, throwing up his hands, says, "infinite thousands."[40]

We are reduced to guesswork. Jehan Vellard, student of the effect of disease on the American Indian, states that the epidemics in Peru and Bolivia after the Spanish conquest killed fewer than those in Mexico and suggests the climatic conditions of the Andean highlands as the reason. But smallpox generally thrives under dry, cool conditions. Possibly historians have omitted an account of the first and, therefore, probably the worst post-Columbian epidemic in the Incan areas because it preceded the Spanish conquest.[41] A half century or so after the conquest, Indians in the vicinity of Lima maintained that the Spanish could not have conquered them if, a few years before Pizarro's invasion, respiratory disease had not "consumed the greater part of them."[42] Was this the great killer of the 1520s in the Incan Empire? Perhaps future archaeological discoveries will give us more definite information.

The pandemic not only killed great numbers in the Indian empires, but it also affected their power structures, striking down the leaders and disrupting the processes by which they were normally replaced. When Montezuma died, his nephew, Cuitláhuac, was elected lord of Mexico. It was he who directed the attacks on the Spaniards during the disastrous retreat from Tenochtitlán, attacks which nearly ended the story of Cortés and his soldiers. Then Cuitláhuac died of smallpox. Probably many others wielding decisive power in the ranks of the Aztecs and their allies died in the same period, breaking dozens of links in the chain of command. Bernal Díaz tells of an occasion not long after Tenochtitlán when the Indians did not attack "because between the Mexicans and the Texcocans there were differences and factions"[43] and, of equal importance, because they had been weakened by smallpox.

Outside Tenochtitlán the deaths due to smallpox among the Indian ruling classes permitted Cortés to cultivate the loyalty of several men in important positions and to promote his own supporters. Cortés wrote to Charles V about the city of Cholula: "The natives had asked me to go there, since many of their chief men had died of the smallpox, which rages in these lands as it does in the islands, and they wished me with their approval and consent to appoint other rulers in their place." Similar requests, quickly complied with, came from Tlaxcala, Chalco, and other cities. "Cortés had gained so much authority," the old soldier Bernal Díaz remembered, "that Indians came before him from distant lands, especially over matters of who would be chief or lord, as at the time smallpox had come to New Spain and many chiefs died."[44]

Similarly in Peru the epidemic of the 1520s was a stunning

blow to the very nerve center of Incan society, throwing that society into a self-destructive convulsion. The government of the Incan Empire was an absolute autocracy with a demi-god, the Child of the Sun, as its emperor. The loss of the emperor could do enormous damage to the whole society, as Pizarro proved by his capture of Atahualpa. Presumably the damage was greater if the Inca were much esteemed, as was Huayna Capac. When he died, said Cieza de León, the mourning "was such that the lamentation and shrieks rose to the skies, causing the birds to fall to the ground. The news traveled far and wide, and nowhere did it not evoke great sorrow." Pedro Pizarro, one of the first to record what the Indians told of the last days before the conquest, judged that had "this Huayna Capac been alive when we Spaniards entered this land, it would have been impossible for us to win it, for he was much beloved by all his vassals."[45]

Not only the Inca but many others in key positions in Incan society died in the epidemic. The general Mihcnaca Mayta and many other military leaders, the governors Apu Hilaquito and Auqui Tupac (uncle and brother to the Inca), the Inca's sister, Mama Coca, and many others of the royal family all perished of the disease. The deaths of these important persons must have robbed the empire of much resiliency. The most ominous loss of all was the Inca's son and heir Ninan Cuyoche.[46]

In an autocracy no problem is more dangerous or more chronic than that of succession. One crude but workable solution is to have the autocrat himself choose his successor. The Inca named one of his sons, Ninan Cuyoche, as next wearer of "the fringe" or crown, on the condition that the *calpa*, a ceremony of divination, show this to be an auspicious choice. The first *calpa* indicated that the gods did not favor Ninan Cuyoche, the second that Huascar was no better a candidate. The high nobles returned to the Inca for another choice, and found him dead. Suddenly a terrible gap had opened in Incan society: the autocrat had died, and there was no one to take his place. One of the nobles moved to close the gap. "Take care of the body," he said, "for I go to Tumipampa to give the fringe to Ninan Cuyoche." But it was too late. When he arrived at Tumipampa, he found that Ninan Cuyoche had also succumbed to the smallpox pestilence.[47]

Among the several varying accounts of the Inca's death the one just related best fits the thesis of this chapter. And while these accounts may differ on many points, they all agree that confusion over the succession followed the unexpected death of Huayna Capac. War broke out between Huascar and Atahualpa, a war which devastated the empire and prepared the way for a quick Spanish conquest. "Had the land not been divided between Huascar and Atahualpa," Pedro Pizarro wrote, "we would not have been able to enter or win the land unless we could gather a thousand Spaniards for the task, and at that time it was impossible to get together even five hundred Spaniards."[48]

The psychological effect of epidemic disease is enormous, especially of an unknown disfiguring disease which strikes swiftly. Within a few days smallpox can transform a healthy man into a pustuled, oozing horror, whom his closest relatives can barely recognize. The impact can be sensed in the following terse, stoic account, drawn from Indian testimony, of Tenochtitlán during the epidemic.

> It was [the month of] Tepeilhuitl when it began, and it spread over the people as great destruction. Some it quite covered [with pustules] on all parts—their faces, their heads, their breasts, etc. There was a great havoc. Very many died of it. They could not walk; they only lay in their resting places and beds. They could not move; they could not stir; they could not change position, nor lie on one side; nor face down, nor on their backs. And if they stirred, much did they cry out. Great was its [smallpox] destruction. Covered, mantled with pustules, very many people died of them.[49]

In some places in Mexico the mortality was so great that, as Motolinía recorded, the Indians found it impossible to bury the great number of dead. "They pulled down the houses over them in order to check the stench that rose from the dead bodies," he wrote, "so that their homes became their tombs." In Tenochtitlán the dead were cast into the water, "and there was a great, foul odor; the smell issued forth from the dead."[50]

For those who survived, the horror was only diminished, for smallpox is a disease which marks its victims for the rest of their lives. The Spanish recalled that the Indians who survived, having scratched themselves, "were left in such a condition that they frightened the others with the many deep pits on their faces, hand, and bodies." "And on some," an Indian said, "the pustules were widely separated; they suffered not greatly, neither did many [of them] die. Yet many people were marred by them on their faces; one's face or nose was pitted." Some lost their sight—a fairly common aftereffect of smallpox.[51]

The contrast between the Indians' extreme susceptibility to the new disease and the Spaniards' almost universal immunity, acquired in Spain and reinforced in pestilential Cuba, must have deeply impressed the native Americans. The Indians, of course, soon realized that there was little relationship between Cortés and Quetzalcoatl, and that the Spaniards had all the vices and weaknesses of ordinary men, but they must have kept a lingering suspicion that the Spaniards were some kind of supermen. Their steel swords and arquebuses, their marvelously agile galleys, and, above all, their horses could only be the tools and servants of supermen. And their invulnerability to smallpox—surely this was a shield of the gods themselves!

One can only imagine the psychological impact of smallpox on the Incans. It must have been less than in Mexico, because the disease and the Spaniards did not arrive simul-

taneously, but epidemic disease is terrifying under any circumstances and must have shaken the confidence of the Incans that they still enjoyed the esteem of their gods. Then
came the long, ferocious civil war, confusing a people accustomed to the autocracy of the true Child of the Sun. And
then the final disaster, the coming of the Spaniards.

The Mayan peoples, probably the most sensitive and bril-
liant of all American aborigines, expressed more poignantly
than any other Indians the overwhelming effect of epidemic.
Some disease struck into Guatemala in 1520 and 1521,
clearing the way for the invasion shortly thereafter by Pedro
de Alvarado, one of Cortés's captains. It was apparently not
smallpox, for the accounts do not mention pustules but emphasize nosebleeds, coughs, and illness of the bladder as the
prominent symptoms. It may have been influenza;[52] whatever
it was, the Cakchiquel Mayas, who kept a chronicle of the
tragedy for their posterity, were helpless to deal with it. Their
words speak for all the Indians touched by Old World disease in the sixteenth century:

> Great was the stench of the dead. After our fathers and grand-
> fathers succumbed, half of the people fled to the fields. The
> dogs and vultures devoured the bodies. The mortality was terrible.
> Your grandfathers died, and with them died the son of the king
> and his brothers and kinsmen. So it was that we became orphans,
> oh, my sons! So we became when we were young. All of us
> were thus. We were born to die![53]

NOTES

1. *The Book of Chilam Balam of Chumayel*, trans. Ralph L.
Roy, 83.

2. P. M. Ashburn, *The Ranks of Death. A Medical History
of the Conquest of America*, passim; Henry H. Scott, *A History
of Tropical Medicine*, 1:128, 283; Sherburne F. Cook, "The Incidence
and Significance of Disease Among the Aztecs and Related Tribes,"

321, 335; Jehan Vellard, "Causas Biológicas de la Desparición de los Indios Americanos," 77–93; Woodrow Borah, "America as Model: The Demographic Impact of European Expansion upon the Non-European World," 379–387.
3. Quoted in E. Wagner Stern and Allen E. Stearn, *The Effect of Smallpox on the Destiny of the Amerindian*, 17.
4. Charles Gibson, *The Aztecs Under Spanish Rule*, 448–451; Henry F. Dobyns, "An Outline of Andean Epidemic History to 1720," 494.
5. Antonio de Herrera y Tordesillas, *Historia General*, 2:35; Charles Gibson, *Spain in America*, 141–142.
6. Joseph de Acosta, *The Natural and Moral History of the Indies*, 1:160. For specific references on depopulation see Antonio Vazquez de Espinosa, *Compendium and Description of the West Indies*, paragraphs 98, 102, 115, 271, 279, 334, 339, 695, 699, 934, 945, 1025, 1075, 1079, 1081, 1102, 1147, 1189, 1217, 1332, 1342, 1384, 1480, 1643, 1652, 1685, 1852, 1864, 1894, 1945, 1992, and 2050. An interesting comparison can be made between Spanish America and the Spanish Philippines. The aborigines of each suffered exploitation, but there were fewer epidemics and much less depopulation in the Philippines. Contact between these islands and the mainland of Asia had existed for many generations, and the Filipinos had acquired mainland immunities. See John L. Phelan, *The Hispanization of the Philippines*, 105–107; Emma H. Blair and James A. Robertson, eds., *Philippine Islands*, 12:311; 13:71; 30:309; 32:93–94; 34:292.
7. Sherburne F. Cook and Woodrow Borah, *The Indian Population of Central Mexico, 1531–1610;* Sherburne F. Cook and Woodrow Borah, *The Aboriginal Population of Central Mexico on the Eve of the Spanish Conquest.*
8. Dobyns, "Andean Epidemic History," 514.
9. *Hans Staden, The True History of His Captivity*, trans. Malcolm Letts, 85–89; Alexander Marchant, *From Barter to Slavery: The Economic Relations of the Portuguese and Indians in the Settlement of Brazil, 1500–1580*, 116–117; Claude Lévi-Strauss, *A World on the Wane*, 87; Juan López de Velasco, *Geografía y Descripción Universidad de las Indias*, 552.
10. David B. Quinn, ed., *The Roanoke Voyages*, 1:378.
11. Ibid.
12. Quoted in Alfred G. Bailey, *The Conflict of European and Eastern Algonkian Cultures, 1504–1700: A Study in Canadian Civilization*, 13.

13. Charles Francis Adams, *Three Episodes of Massachusetts History*, 1:1–12.

14. Hubert Howe Bancroft, *History of Alaska, 1730–1885*, 350, 560–563.

15. C. W. Dixon, *Smallpox*, 68.

16. Franklin H. Top et al., *Communicable and Infectious Diseases*, 515; Hans Zinsser, *Rats, Lice and History*, 87–88.

17. Donald B. Cooper, *Epidemic Disease in Mexico City, 1761–1813*, 87–88; Raúl Porras Barrenechea, ed., *Cartas del Perú, 1524–1543*, 22, 24, 33, 46.

18. Dixon, *Smallpox*, 171, 299–301.

19. Ashburn, *Ranks of Death*, 86.

20. Dixon, *Smallpox*, 325; John Duffy, *Epidemics in Colonial America*, 20, 22; Stearn and Stearn, *Effect of Smallpox*, 14.

21. Samuel Eliot Morison, *Admiral of the Ocean Sea, A Life of Christopher Columbus*, 1:304–305.

22. Gonzalo Fernández Oviedo y Valdés, *Historia General y Natural de las Indias*, 2d ed., 1:66–67.

23. Ibid.; *Colección de Documentos Inéditos Relativos al Descubrimiento, Conquista y Colonización de las Posesiones Españolas en América y Oceanía*, 1:428.

24. S. P. Bedson et al., *Virus and Rickettsial Diseases*, 151–152, 157; Dixon, *Smallpox*, 174, 189, 296–297, 304, 359; Jacques M. May, ed., *Studies in Disease Ecology*, 1, 8.

25. *Colección de Documentos Inéditos*, 1:367, 369–370, 429; *Colección de Varios Documentos para la Historia de la Florida y Tierras Adyzacentes*, 1:44; Fray Bartoloméde Las Casas, *Obras Escogidas de Bartolomé de Las Casas*, 2:484.

26. *Colección de Documentos Inéditos*, 1:368, 397–398, 428–429; Dixon, *Smallpox*, 317–318, 325.

27. Pablo Alvarez Rubiano, *Pedrarias Dávila*, 608; *Colección de Varios Documentos para la Historia de la Florida*, 1:45.

28. Diego de Landa, *Landa's Relación de las Cosas de Yucatán*, trans. Alfred M. Tozzer, 42; *Book of Chilam Balam*, 138.

29. Patricia de Fuentes, ed. and trans., *The Conquistadors. First-Person Accounts of the Conquest of Mexico*, 159. For the argument that this was measles, not smallpox, see Horacio Figueroa Marroquin, *Enfermedades de los Conquistadores*, 49–67.

30. Bernal Díaz del Castillo, *The Bernal Díaz Chronicles: The True Story of the Conquest of Mexico*, trans. Albert Idell, 250; Diego Durán, *The Aztecs: The History of the Indies in New Spain*, trans. Doris Heyden and Fernando Horcasitas, 323; Francisco López

de Gómara, *Cortés, the Life of the Conqueror by His Secretary,* trans. Lesley Byrd Simpson, 204–205; Toribio Motolinía, *Motolinía's History of the Indians of New Spain,* trans. Elizabeth A. Foster, 38; Bernardino de Sahagún, *Florentine Codex: General History of the Things of New Spain,* trans. Arthur J. O. Anderson and Charles E. Dibble, 9:4.

31. *Anales de Tlatelolco, Unos Anales Históricos de la Nación Mexicana y Códice de Tlatelolco,* 64. *The Annals of the Cakchiquels and Title of the Lords of Totonicapan,* trans. Adrian Recinos, Dioniscio José Chonay and Delia Goetz, 115–116; Bedson, *Virus,* 155; Díaz del Castillo, *Chronicles,* 289; Miguel Léon-Portilla, ed., *The Broken Spears: The Aztec Account of the Conquest of Mexico,* 132; Top, *Diseases,* 515.

32. Hernando Cortés, *Five Letters,* trans. J. Bayard Morris, 226; Díaz del Castillo, *Chronicles,* 405–406; López de Gómara, *Cortés,* 285, 293; León-Portilla, *Broken Spears,* 92; Sahagún, *Florentine Codex,* 13:81.

33. *Colección de Documentos Inéditos,* 37:200; Oviedo, *Historia General,* 2d ed., 3:353. For corroboration see M. M. Alba C., *Etnología y Población Historica,* passim; Porras Barrenechea, *Cartas del Perú,* 24; López de Velasco, *Geografía,* 341; *Relaciones Históricas y Geográficas de America Central,* 216–218.

34. Herrera, *Historia General,* 5:350; *Relaciones Históricas y Geográficas,* 200.

35. Alvarez, *Pedrarias Dávila,* 608, 619, 621, 623; *Colección de Documentos para la Historia de Costa Rica,* 4:8.

36. Pascual de Andagoya, *Narrative of the Proceedings of Pedrarias Dávila,* trans. Clements R. Markham, 6; *Colección de Documentos Inéditos,* 17:219–222; Herrera, *Historia General,* 4:217; Scott, *Tropical Medicine,* 1:192, 288.

37. Garcilaso de la Vega, *First Part of the Royal Commentaries of the Yncas,* trans. Clements R. Markham, 2:456–457. Fernando Montesinos, *Memorias Antiguas Historiales del Perú,* trans. Philip A. Means, 126. Pedro Sarmiento de Gamboa, *History of the Incas,* trans. Clements R. Markham, 187. It has been suggested that the source of the great epidemic in question was two men, Alonso de Molina and Ginés, left behind by Pizarro at Tumbez on the reconnaissance voyage of 1527. Pedro de Cieza de León, *The Incas of Pedro Cieza de León,* ed. Victor W. von Hagen, trans. Harriet de Onis, n. 51. If the epidemic was smallpox or measles, this explanation is unlikely, because these diseases are of short duration and have no carrier state. The expedition of which these men were

members had had no contact with pestilential Panama for some time before it returned there from Tumbez. If these two men caught smallpox or measles, it must have been already present among the Indians.

38. Felipe Guamán Poma Ayala, *Nueva Corónica y Buen Govierno*, 85–86. Cieza de León, *Incas*, 52, 253; Bernabé Cobo, *Obras*, 2:93. Garcilaso de la Vega, *Royal Commentaries*, 2:461; Martín de Murúa, *Historia General del Perú, Origen y Descendencia de los Incas*, 1:103–104; Clements R. Markham, ed. and trans., *Narratives of the Rites and Laws of the Incas*, 110; Pedro Pizarro, *Relation of the Discovery and Conquest of the Kingdoms of Peru,* trans. Philip A. Means, 1:196–198; Sarmiento de Gamboa, *History of the Incas*, 167–168; Miguel Cabello Valboa, *Miscelánea Antártica, una Historia del Perú Antiguo*, 393–394; Marcos Jiménez de la Espada, ed., *Relaciones Geograficas de Indias-Perú*, 2:267.

Did smallpox exist in the Incan lands before the 1520s? Fernando Montesinos, writing in the seventeenth century, claimed that Capac Titu Yupanqui, a pre-Columbian Peruvian, died of smallpox in a general epidemic of that disease. Also, some examples of the famous naturalistic Mochica pottery show Indians with pustules and pocks which bear a very close resemblance to those of smallpox. But Montesinos is regarded as one of the least reliable historians of Incan times, and there are several other diseases native to the northwestern section of South America, such as the dreadful verrugas, which have a superficial dermatological similarity to smallpox. Furthermore, the aborigines of the Incan Empire told Pedro Pizarro that they had had no acquaintance with smallpox in pre-Columbian times. Montesinos, *Memorias Antiguas*, 54; Pizarro, *Relation*, 1:196; Victor W. von Hagen, *Realm of the Incas*, 106; Myron G. Schultz, "A History of Bartonellosis (Carrion's Disease)," 503–515; see also Raoul and Marie D'Harcourt, *La Médicine dans l'Ancien Pérou*. passim.

39. Cook and Borah, *Aboriginal Population*, 4, 89; Motolinía, *History*, 38; Sahagún, *Florentine Codex*, 13:81.

40. Ashburn, *Ranks of Death*, 20; Cieza de León, *Incas*, 52; Murúa, *Historia General*, 1:104; Pizarro, *Relation*, 1:196.

41. Vellard, "Causas Biológicas," 85; Bedson, *Virus*, 157, 167; Dixon, *Smallpox*, 313.

42. Reginaldo de Lizárrago, *Descripción Colonial por Fr. Reginaldo de Lizárrago*, 1:136.

43. Díaz del Castillo, *Chronicles*, 282, 301; López de Gómara, *Cortés*, 238–239.

44. Cortés, *Five Letters*, 136; Díaz del Castillo, *Chronicles*, 289, 311.

45. Cieza de León, *Incas*, 53; Pizarro, *Relation*, 1:198–199.

46. Ayala, *Nueva Corónica*, 86; Cobo, *Obras*, 2:93; Sarmiento de Gamboa, *History of the Incas*, 167–168; Valboa, *Miscelánea Antártica*, 393.

47. Sarmiento de Gamboa, *History of the Incas*, 167–168, 197–199; for corroboration see Cieza de León, *Incas*, 253; Valboa, *Miscelánea Antártica*, 394.

48. Pizarro, *Relation*, 1:199.

49. Sahagún, *Florentine Codex*, 13:81.

50. Motolinía, *History*, 38; Sahagún, *Florentine Codex*, 9:4.

51. Sahagún, *Florentine Codex*, vol. 13:81; López de Gómara, *Cortés*, 204–205; Dixon, *Smallpox*, 94; A. J. Rhodes and C. E. van Rooyen, *Textbook of Virology*, 2d. ed., 319.

52. F. Webster McBryde, "Influenza in America During the Sixteenth Century," 296–297.

53. *Annals of the Cakchiquels*, trans. Recinos, Chonay, Goetz, 116.

Old World Plants and Animals in the New World

3

If pathogens could pass freely from the Old World to the New, so, fortunately, could other life forms. So could the life forms that provide man with food, fiber, hides, and labor, that is, cultivated plants and domesticated animals. To a notable extent, the whole migration of Spaniards, Portuguese, and the others who followed them across the Atlantic, and the successful exploitation of the New World by these people depended on their ability to "Europeanize" the flora and fauna of the New World. That transformation was well under way by 1500, and it was irrevocable in both North and South America by 1550.

In this matter, as in that of diseases, the impact of the Old World on the New was so great that we of the twentieth century can only imagine what pre-Columbian America must have been like. Bernabé Cobo, the seventeenth-century naturalist and historian, took an optimistic view of the effect of the eastern hemisphere on the western:

> All the regions of the globe have contributed their fruits and abundance to adorn and enrich this quarter part of the world, which we Spaniards found so poor and destitute of the plants

and animals most necessary to nourish and give service to mankind, howsoever prosperous and abundant the mineral resources of gold and silver.[1]

But before we examine the truth of his statement in detail, we must acknowledge that the Americas were not conquered by armies and bands of settlers marching on stomachs filled exclusively with wheat and pork and other items of European cuisine. Old World plants and animals obviously did not always precede the explorers and conquistadors (although sometimes this was the case), and there are wide stretches of the Americas where European flora and fauna did not and do not prosper. The colonists, particularly the early ones and those in the hot, wet areas, had to accept many items of the Indian diet. To Europeans wheat bread was probably the most indispensable item of diet, but the grains of Europe would not grow in climates where even the wafers used in the mass "did bend like to wet paper, by reason of the extreme humidity and heat." Nicolas Durand de Villegagnon wrote of Río de Janeiro that it was necessary to eat "foods entirely different from those of our Europe."[2]

In the West Indies and the hot, wet lowlands the Spaniard either had to import his wheat or eat bread made from manioc flour—"a thinne and broade cake, almost like unto a Moores target or buckler."[3] The littoral of Brazil is also inhospitable to wheat; and manioc or cassava, as it is often called, quickly became the staple of the diet there. The Brazilian historian, Caio Prado, calls it "the necessary accompaniment to man" in Brazil.[4]

Maize, also, had importance in the wet lowlands, but not nearly so much as in the higher, drier, cooler parts of the mainland. The Spanish always preferred wheat to maize bread, but could not always obtain or afford it and the lower classes among the Spanish colonists often ate the latter.[5]

The Iberians ate all kinds of other American foods— pumpkins, beans, potatoes, and so on—but none were as important in their diets as manioc and maize. The Europeans in America, like those at home, were very slow to accept potatoes as a staple food. Even in the Andean highlands, the homeland of the white potato, the Europeans at best considered it a semifood, although some were willing to make fortunes by raising potatoes to feed the Indian miners at Potosí.[6]

Europeans vastly enhanced their own ability to live in ever increasing numbers in the Americas by distributing Indian plants and seeds to areas where they had been unknown in pre-Columbian times. The white potato, to cite an example, was unknown in North America before the seventeenth century. It was first brought to New England by the Scotch-Irish, via Europe, in 1718.[7] It is also obvious that the European made large profits and shaped the land and histories of whole areas of the New World by raising American plants on extensive plantations—tobacco, cocoa, paprika, American cotton—and that he cut and gathered guaiacum, sassafras, and other native products for export across the Atlantic. But the fact that the European utilized native American plants is not so important as his importation of plant and animal sources of food from the eastern hemisphere. The European immediately set about to transform as much of the New World as possible into the Old World. So successful was he that he accomplished what was probably the greatest biological revolution in the Americas since the end of the Pleistocene era.

The European pathfinders are remembered for their courage and endurance, and hardly at all for their green thumbs. But agriculturalists they were (albeit, in the case of the Spanish, with limited enthusiasm), strewing seed from snowy north to snowy south. Who brought which plant to where is a question that rarely can be answered accurately. In the latter part of the sixteenth century José de Acosta asked who had planted the "whole woods and forests of orange trees" through which he walked and rode, and was told "that oranges being fallen to the ground, and rotten, their seeds did spring, and of those which the water carried away into diverse parts, these woods grew so thicke . . ."[8]

The first arrival dates of which we can be sure are those having to do with Española, that vestibule to the Americas where everything seems to have happened first. Let us start there with the initial attempts to raise European plants, trace the spread of those plants to the mainland, then return to Española to do the same for European livestock.

Columbus left seeds with the citizens of the abortive colony of Navidad in 1493, but, if they were ever planted, it is doubtful that they were ever harvested, because those citizens were massacred by the Arawaks. The history of European horticulture in the Americas really begins with the second voyage of Columbus, when he returned to Española with seventeen ships, 1,200 men, and seeds and cuttings for the planting of wheat, chickpeas, melons, onions, radishes, salad greens, grape vines, sugar cane, and fruit stones for the founding of orchards. The early results were marvelously encouraging, or so the enthusiastic colonists insisted. "All the seeds they had sown sprouted in three days and were ready to eat by the twenty-fifth day. Fruit stones planted in the ground sprouted in seven days; vine shoots sent out leaves at the end of the same period, and by the twenty-fifth day green grapes were ready to be picked." The Spanish wish was affecting the Spanish eyesight. The tradition of a "starving time" in the early history of a given American colony was initiated on Española in 1494; an unlikely event if European seeds were really bouncing out of the soil as fully mature plants in record times.[9]

The Antilles were less than a perfect base camp in the Americas for the European horticulturalists. Wheat and the other European grains failed, and so did grape vines and olive trees: no bread, wine, or oil. A Castilian could starve here! But many of the garden crops—cauliflowers, cabbages, radishes, lettuce, and European melons—prospered, and if the colonist could tolerate American Indian staples, he could always dessert on such familiar fruits as oranges, lemons, pomegranates, citrons, and figs that did well in the West Indies.[10]

Another important addition to the flora of the Antilles in the early years was the banana, brought in from the Canaries in 1516. Oviedo described this immigrant fruit as having an easily removed skin, and "inside it is all flesh which is very much like the marrow of the legbone of a cow." These banana trees, he wrote in the 1520s, "have multiplied so greatly that it is marvelous to see the great abundance of them on the islands and in Tierra Firme [southern coast of the Caribbean], where the Christians have settled."[11]

The economic underpinnings of most of the important European settlements in the tropical and semitropical zones of America historically have been the raising of a certain few crops on large plantations for export to Europe. These plantation areas, with their fields of sugar, cotton, rice, indigo, have, at one time and another, stretched all the way from Virginia's tobacco fields to Brazil's coffee fields. Mining produced the most spectacular profits in the colonial New World, but the plantations employed more people and, in the end, produced greater wealth.

It all began in Española with sugar, which was already a profitable plantation crop in the Canaries and Portugal's Atlantic islands in the fifteenth century. Columbus himself had shipped sugar from Madeira to Genoa in 1478, and the mother of his first wife owned a sugar estate on that island. He brought sugar cane with him to Española in 1493, and the cane grew well in American soil. But the growth of the sugar industry was painfully slow until Charles V intervened, ordering that sugar masters and mill technicians be recruited from the Canaries, and authorizing loans to build sugar mills on Española. There were thirty-four mills on the island by the late 1530s and sugar was one of the two staples of the island's economy (the other being cattle ranching) until the latter part of the sixteenth century.[12]

One of the causes for this late sixteenth-century decline of the sugar industry in the Spanish Antilles was competition from the mainland. Wherever the sun was hot and the rainfall sufficient, the Spanish planted cane. It became a common crop early after the conquests of Mexico and Peru in the lowlands and deeper valleys of those regions. Sugar cane poked up its profitable shoots all over the Spanish empire, from the Gulf of Mexico to the Río de la Plata. Asunción, for instance, boasted two hundred sugar mills in the early seventeenth century. The empire had a superabundance of sugar. Said Bernabé Cobo, "there must not be a region in all the universe where so much is consumed, and with all this many ships carry it to Spain."[13]

But the greatest producer of sugar in the Atlantic world in the sixteenth century, while American, was not Spanish-American. Portugal, by virtue of her possession of Madeira and São Tomé off the coast of Africa, was already the top producer of sugar when the sixteenth century opened, and sugar cane was sent to Portuguese Brazil soon after. By 1526 duty was being paid on Brazilian sugar at the Lisbon Customs House. The next century was the age of sugar in Brazil, and Brazil was the largest sugar supplier of the Atlantic world. In 1585 the settlement of Olinda alone had sixty-six sugar mills. Depending on which expert you read, by 1610 Brazil had either four hundred mills producing 57,000 tons of sugar annually, or only two hundred and thirty mills producing 14,000 tons annually.[14] The wealth created by selling such quantities of sugar in Europe persuaded the English and French of the Lesser Antilles to plant cane in the seventeenth century, which—in time—meant economic decline for the sugar plantations of Brazil.

Sugar, although of immeasurable commercial importance, is not the staff of life. Like other future plantation crops—tobacco, cotton, coffee—it brought wealth to management, but insufficient nourishment in itself to labor. Unless the standard European food plants could be grown in quantity in America, the growth of European settlement in the New World would be very slow.

The crux of the problem was temperature. Spain lies in the temperate zone. The great bulk of the Spanish empire lay between the tropics of Cancer and Capricorn. No farmer would ever be able to grow the staples of an Iberian diet at sea level in the tropical latitudes. He would have to follow Cortés and Pizarro into the mountains and find a substitute for a higher latitude in a higher altitude.

For the sake of brevity, let us consider only the plant foods most basic to Spanish cuisine—wheat, wine, and olive oil. Most of the early Spanish farms in the highlands of New Spain (Mexico) raised wheat, in accordance with the policy of the viceroys. The government had to be constantly vigilant to assure that New Spain would produce sufficient supplies of wheat and other foods to feed itself, for close attention to farming was simply not a Castilian virtue; but by 1535 Mexico was exporting wheat to the Antilles and Tierra Firme, by midcentury bread in Mexico City was "as good cheape as in Spain," and by the last quarter of the century Atlixco Valley alone was producing 100,000 fanegas (156,200 bushels) of wheat a year.[15]

The topography and climate of Peru are at least as varied as Mexico's, and they enable her to produce a great variety of crops. Rice, sugar, and bananas were growing in her wet lowlands within a generation of her conquest, and her temperate valleys near Lima and her highlands were producing wheat in quantity by the 1540s. The area around Arequipa, said the conquistador Cieza de León produces "excellent wheat . . . from which they make excellent bread." In time,

Peru became one of the chief sources of wheat for the hotter, wetter parts of the empire, especially for Panama and Tierra Firme.[16]

It is accurate to say that the Spaniards raised wheat nearly everywhere in the settled areas of their American possessions that climate permitted. We find wheat being harvested in Río de la Plata, New Granada, Chile, and even in the highlands of Central America within a few years of their colonization. Thomas Gage observed three kinds of wheat being grown in rotation in the mountain valleys of Guatemala in the seventeenth century.[17] An examination of any of the standard geographical accounts of Spain's empire in its first century— the *Relaciones Geograficas de las Indias,* the works of Juan López de Velasco or Vazquez de Espinosa or the first volume of Antonio de Herrera's monumental history—indicates that by 1600 the Spanish colonist could almost always obtain wheat bread, unless he were very poor or an inhabitant of the hot lowlands—and even the latter could have his wheat if he had the price to import it.

In contrast to wheat, wine is by no means one of the staffs of life, but few *hidalgos* have ever accepted the truth of that statement. If the Spaniard is to eat, he must have wheat; if he is to drink, he must have wine. But Spain's New World empire was lacking in grapes from which good wine could be made. (There is a story that one Spanish priest of more logic than orthodoxy drew the conclusion that if God had not Himself made it possible for the Indians to make sacramental wine, then He obviously had no intention that they ever be made Christians.)[18] The early records of the Spanish empire are filled with notations that grape vines would not grow here, showed promise there, and produced plentifully somewhere else. The vines would not grow in the Antilles or the hot, wet lowlands; and Mexico, though more temperate, produced little wine, and that of poor quality, "because generally the grapes doe not ripen with perfection."[19] Not until the conquistadors reached Peru did Spain acquire an area where vines would prosper. The year of the first Peruvian vintage was 1551. A hundred years later she was producing wine enough to satisfy not only her own enormous thirst, but also for export.[20]

Grapes also did well in many areas to the south of what is now Peru. Chile, for example, with its "temperature like unto Castile, in whose opposite altitude it falleth almost all . . . ," Tucumán and, generally, the Río de la Plata area grew grapes for wine, as well as all the other plants of Spain. In 1614 the diocese of Santiago, Chile, produced 200,000 jugs of wine. "Jug" is a wildly vague measure, but we can at least be sure that 200,000 jugs is a lot of wine.[21]

The Spanish, like the other people of the Mediterranean littoral, had to have bread, wine—and oil, olive oil. If possessed of these three, the Spaniards of the *Siglo de Oro*—the Golden Century—like the ancient Hebrews, had the basic plant food ingredients of what they felt was a civilized diet. The olive tree needs water, but not in the quantities that fall in most parts of the Greater Antilles and Caribbean coast. Few olive trees grew in Mexico, and the total yield of olives and oil there was insignificant in the sixteenth and seventeenth centuries.

The areas of the Americas settled by the Spanish in the sixteenth century which most closely resemble the dry Mediterranean lands where the olive trees grow best are the coastal valleys of Peru and Chile. The thought that olive trees might prosper there must have occurred to many of the earliest settlers, but the first olive trees were not planted until 1560. The long delay undoubtedly stemmed from the fact that the plants had to be brought all the way from Europe: there were none or too few in the usual halfway houses of Española or Tierra Firme to spare for Peru. And so it was in 1560, long after the Peruvian debut of wheat and vines, that Antonio de Rivera, one of the first settlers of Lima, returned from Spain with a number of olive seedlings. Only two or three, however, had survived the journey. Their value was so immense that he posted a number of slaves and dogs to guard them. It was no use: one was stolen and spirited off some five hundred leagues south to Chile. These seedlings, whether legitimately or illegitimately acquired, were the beginning of what quickly became a considerable olive oil industry in the irrigated valleys of South America's arid Pacific coast.[22]

The other Spanish food plants—vegetables and fruit trees—were sown wherever there was settlement and the slightest probability of their growing to fruition. A knowledge of Latin American geography and of what type of climate is good for a given food plant will generally allow an accurate guess as to where the Spanish raised the crop.

Not all or probably even most of the plants brought to America in the sixteenth century were for human consumption or were brought intentionally. A few of the forage grasses and clovers may have been consciously imported in the sixteenth century—they certainly were later—but most of the plants that came to America between 1492 and 1600 that do not produce food for humans or, at least, flowers for the pleasure of human senses, crossed the Atlantic as informally as did the smallpox virus. Their seeds arrived in folds of textiles, in clods of mud, in dung, and in a thousand other ways. The spread of these proletarians of the plants was doubtlessly quite rapid, as the Europeans followed and extended the Indian practice of burning over grasslands, and European livestock overgrazed large areas, opening the way for the heartier immigrant grasses and weeds. The fact that Kentucky bluegrass, daisies, and dandelions, to name only three out of hundreds, are Old World in origin gives one a hint of the magnitude of the change that began in 1492 and continues in the twentieth century. Today an American botanist can easily find whole meadows in which he is hard put to find a single species of plant that grew in America in pre-Columbian times.[23]

The Indians found most European food plants little more desirable than European weeds. Again and again in the accounts of the various colonies, English as well as Latin, we read that the Indians were not taking the opportunity to cultivate Old World crops. In Spanish America, where the white population often did not raise enough food for its own needs, the Indians were forced to raise wheat and other European crops, either under direct European direction or in order to make tribute payments in kind, but they rarely added these to their own diets. The Europeans destroyed the Indian's civilizations, and even drove his gods into Christian vestments, but in many of the most elemental ways, the Indian remained Indian.[24]

A great exception to this rule was his enthusiastic acceptance of Old World livestock, as we shall see presently.

The contrast between Old and New World fauna amazed Renaissance Europe, as we noted in Chapter 1. The difference between the two sets of domesticated animals on either side of the Atlantic was even more stunning than the general contrast. The Indian as farmer was as impressive as any in the world, but he was very unimpressive as a domesticator of animals. In 1492 he had only a few animal servants: the dog, two kinds of South American camel (the llama and alpaca), the guinea pig, and several kinds of fowl (the turkey, the Muscovy duck, and, possibly, a type of chicken). He had no animal that he rode. Most of his meat and leather came from wild game. He had no beast of burden to be compared to the horse, ass, or ox. Except in the areas where the llama lived, and except for the minor assistance of the travois-pulling dog, the Indian wanting to move a load moved it himself, no matter how heavy the load or how far it had to be moved. The classic case in point is that of the pre-Columbian peoples of Meso-America, who built great temples and carried on trade over hundreds of miles of broken terrain *in spite of the fact* that the fastest and strongest animal available for service there was man himself.[25]

A sensational preview of the impact that Old World livestock would have on the American mainland took place in Española and, shortly after, in the other Antilles. One who watched the Caribbean islands from outer space during the years from 1492 to 1550 or so might have surmised that the object of the game going on there was to replace the people with pigs, dogs and cattle. Disease and ruthless exploitation had, for all practical purposes, destroyed the aborigines of Española by the 1520s. Their Arawak brothers in Cuba, Puerto Rico, and Jamaica followed them into oblivion shortly after. The Bahamas and Lesser Antilles were not occupied by the Spanish, but as the Indians of the larger islands disappeared, slavers sailed out to the smaller islands, spread disease and seized multitudes of Arawaks and Caribs to feed into the death camps that Española, Cuba, Puerto Rico, and Jamaica had become. Thus, within a few score years of Columbus's first American landfall, the Antillean aborigines had been almost completely eliminated.[26]

As the number of humans plummeted, the population of imported domesticated animals shot upward. The first contingent of horses, dogs, pigs, cattle, chickens, sheep, and goats arrived with Columbus on the second voyage in 1493. The animals, preyed upon by few or no American predators, troubled by few or no American diseases, and left to feed freely upon the rich grasses and roots and wild fruits, reproduced rapidly. Their numbers burgeoned so rapidly, in fact, that doubtlessly they had much to do with the extinction of certain plants, animals, and even the Indians themselves, whose gardens they encroached upon.[27]

Of the imported animals, the pigs adapted the quickest

to the Caribbean environment. At the end of 1498, Roldán, the Españolan rebel, alone owned 120 large and 230 small swine. Soon pigs were running wild in incredible numbers. In April of 1514 Diego Velásquez de Cuéllar wrote the King that the pigs he had brought to Cuba had increased to 30,000 (which figure is perhaps best translated from the sixteenth-century Spanish as "more pigs than I ever saw before in my life").[28]

The multiplication of cattle was similarly spectacular. When Roldán revolted in 1498, he and his followers "found herds of cattle grazing and killed all the steers they needed for their food and took what beasts of burden they needed for the road." Alonzo de Zuazo, reporting to his king in 1518, told of great numbers of cattle on Española, cattle which were breeding two and three times a year in the salubrious environment of the New World: if thirty or forty cattle stray away, he said, they will grow to three or four hundred in three or four years.[29] So great was the proliferation of the cattle that by the end of the century numbers of marooned sailors and other such stray humans in the un-colonized northern half of Española were living off the wild stock there. The story goes that these people smoked the meat of the animals on a wooden grate called a *boucan* and thus, when they went pirating in the seventeenth century, were called buccaneers.[30]

Horses were slower to adapt to the tropics, and their reproductive rate was less spectacular than that of swine or cattle, but increase in number they did; and in time they, too, were running wild and free over the savannas of Española.[31] The reaction of the other types of European live-stock to the Caribbean environment was similar in nearly every case: goats, dogs, cats, chickens, asses grew faster, brawnier, reproduced at unheard of rates, and often went back to nature.

This amazingly successful invasion by Old World livestock

took place not only in Española but in Cuba, Puerto Rico, Jamaica, and, a bit later, in certain coastal islands, especially Margarita, the Venezuelan island which was the original source of the great herds of the llanos.[32] By the time of Cortés's assault on the mainland, the Spaniards had created in the Caribbean a perfect base camp for that assault. When the conquistadors moved into the interior of Mexico, Honduras, Peru, Florida, and elsewhere, they carried smallpox and many other maladies, freshened by recent passage through the bodies of the Arawaks. The Spaniards rode on horses bred in the Antilles, and wardogs from the same islands trotted beside them. Their saddlebags were packed with cakes of Caribbean cassava. Behind the conquistadors, herded along by Indian servants, came herds of swine, cattle and goats—a commissariat on the hoof—all of which had been born in the islands. In the span of the first post-Columbian generation, the Spanish had created in the Caribbean the wherewithal to conquer half a world.

The three animals which played the leading roles in that conquest were the *hidalgo* (the Spanish nobleman), the pig, and the horse. The *hidalgo* led the way—that is clear—but it is difficult to say which of the other two was the more important. The Spanish historian Carlos Pereyra judged that, "if the horse was of real significance in the Conquest, the hog was of greater importance and contributed to a degree that defies exaggeration."[33]

It is necessary to define this hog. He was not the peccary, the tusked, piglike animal native to America which Acosta described as a small hog with a navel on its back. Nor was the pig that followed the conquistadors the fat, slow-footed creature we are familiar with today. Once ashore in America he became a fast, tough, lean, self-sufficient greyhound of a hog much closer to appearance and personality to a wild boar than to one of our twentieth-century hogs. This Spanish swine thrived in wet, tropical lowlands and dry mountains alike, and reproduced with a rapidity that delighted the pork-hungry Iberians.[34]

Swine took up so little space on board ship and were so self-sufficient and prolific once ashore that many of the earlier explorers took them along as deck cargo and deposited them on islands to multiply and provide food for future visitors. Thus Cabeza de Vaca in Río de la Plata country in 1542 found a message from his predecessor, Irala, which read:

> In one of the islands of San Gabriel a sow and a boar have been left to breed. Do not kill them. If there should be many, take those you need, but always leave some to breed, and also, on your way, leave a sow and a boar on the island of Martín Garcia and on the other islands wherever you think it good, so that they may breed.[35]

Sometime in the 1550s the Portuguese stocked Sable Island in the northwest Atlantic with swine and cattle, which, by the time Sir Humphrey Gilbert came along thirty years later, had "exceedingly multiplied." In 1609 Englishmen shipwrecked in the uninhabited Bermudas were able to live off the great herds of pigs there. In the same decade the *Olive Blossom* touched at Barbados and found no people there, not even Indians, but did find quantities of wild pigs. Tradition credits their presence there to the Portuguese of Brazil. The pigs of Barbados and the other Lesser Antilles became a vitally important source of food for the early seventeenth-century settlers.[36]

Great numbers of swine accompanied the conquistadors on the continental expeditions. They were at least as adaptable to new environments as the Spaniards, and made a fine ambulatory meat supply. To give a few examples, De Soto brought thirteen pigs with him to Florida in 1539, used them for food only in dire emergency, and thus had seven hundred at the time of his death three years later. In 1540 Gonzalo Pizarro collected, along with horses, llamas and dogs, more than two thousand pigs for an expedition in search of the Land of Cinnamon on the east side of the Andes.[37]

It follows from the above that pork was often the only familiar meat available to the first colonists of a given area. The swine needed little care, the native tribute of maize made ideal feed for them, and—if that failed—they could forage for themselves. By the end of the first decade after the conquest of Mexico, pigs were so plentiful and cheap that stockmen were no longer interested in them. Pigs came to Peru with Pizarro in 1531, and pork was the first European meat to be sold in any quantity in the Lima meat market; there was little competition from other European meats for some years.[38]

Swine herds were to be found wherever the Spanish settled or even touched, and the same was true in the Portuguese areas. The environment of coastal Brazil was not one most European livestock found healthy, but the pig thrived in poorer pastures than cattle, for instance, could tolerate. "The Swine doe like very well heere," wrote a visitor to Brazil in 1601, "and they beginne to have great multitudes, and heere it is the best flesh of all."[39] In the captaincies of the central south, Río de Janeiro and São Paulo, pork became a major item in the colonial diet. In fact, so salubrious did pigs find their new homes in the Americas that in many areas they dispensed with their swineherds and took up an independent existence, running as wild as ever their ancestors had.[40]

It is possible to imagine the conquistador without his pig, but who can imagine him without his horse? The conquistador came from the most equestrian society in Europe. Medieval Iberia was the one section of western Europe where horses were so plentiful and cheap that they were not the exclusive possession of the nobility. This not to say that every Sancho Panza owned a horse, but it does mean that the Iberians of all classes were more accustomed to viewing the world from horseback and more skilled as riders than any other European people with easy access to the Atlantic.[41] The languages of western Europe confirm this: *caballero* means knight, nobleman, rider, horseman, gentleman, sir or mister; *chevalier,* from the other side of the Pyrenees, also means knight or nobleman, but cannot be so easily stretched to also mean rider or mister.

The horse the caballero rode was as much an aristocrat in the equestrian flesh as his master was in equestrian skill. This horse was the product of crossbreeding the strong, fast horse of Iberia and the fine Arabians brought in by the Moors.[42] The offspring was the finest horse in Europe.[43]

The first horses to exist in America since the Pleistocene arrived with Columbus in 1493. The transatlantic voyage was not an easy one for horses. The body of water between Spain and the Canaries, where almost all the early expeditions stopped on the way to America, was named the *Gulfo de Yeguas,* the Gulf of Mares, and the belts of windlessness in the Atlantic tropics were named the Horse Latitudes because so many horses died and had to be thrown overboard in these areas. But the price for getting horses to America was worth paying, and numbers of them were loaded on vessels bound for Española. By 1501 that island had twenty or thirty, and by 1503 there were, at the very least, no fewer than sixty or seventy.[44]

The enormous value of the horse came not merely from the fact that he provided the conquistador with the services of an excellent beast of burden. In the early years he was chiefly valuable as an instrument of war. The sight of a man on horseback was so frightening to the Indians that one guesses that the combination was for them as terrifying as the obscene creatures of Hieronymus Bosch would have been to the Spaniards, if they had suddenly leaped into life from the painted canvas. The Indians of South America had never seen an animal as big as the horse. No Indian anywhere had ever seen an animal which, at one time, was as strong, fast and obedient to the orders of man. The Arawaks suspected that horses fed on human flesh, and a single man on horseback could and did terrify whole crowds of these Indians. If fear failed to dissolve Indian resistance, then, according to the macabre hyperbole of Las Casas, one horseman could skewer two thousand Indians in an hour.[45]

Again and again, the Spanish cavalry turned massacre of Europeans into massacre of Indians. Bernal Díaz, writing of the conquest of Mexico decades after the event, mentioned horse after horse, reciting their names, colors and characters with as much care and detail as he lavishes upon his human comrades. In his appraisal of the losses of *la noche triste* he established a hierarchy of importance that surprises no one familiar with the conquistador mentality: "It was the greatest grief to think upon the horses, and the valiant soldiers we had lost." Hernando Pizarro, who rode out to hurry along deliveries of Atahualpa's ransom, knew what was most important and what was not: when his horses lost their shoes and there were no iron replacements, he had them shod in silver.[46]

After the conquest, the horse played a role of a less spectacular but no less significant nature. The conquistador would never have been able to keep the vast sullen Indian populations under control if the horse had not enabled him to transfer information, orders and soldiers from one point to another swiftly. The horse was a very important carrier and hauler of freight, although often replaced in this role by asses, mules and even native llamas. The horse made possible the great cattle industry of colonial America, which, in the final analysis, affected much larger areas of the New World than did any other European endeavor in that period. A swineherd can operate effectively on foot: a *vaquero,* or cowboy, needs a horse.

The society of colonial Spanish-America was one of the

most equestrian in all history, and, to a very great extent, its existence depended on the adaptability of the Old World horse to New World conditions. The horse was slower than the pig to increase his numbers in the tropical zone, but even there his numbers did increase and a few joined the swine as free agents.[47] But it was not until the Spanish frontier reached the great grasslands that the vast herds of horses celebrated in American legend burst into the history of the New World.

The three greatest grasslands of the Spanish empire were the llanos of Venezuela and Colombia, the prairies that stretch from deep in Mexico north into Canada, and the pampas of Argentina and Uruguay. In the llanos the increase of the herds of horses was slow. The brutally hot climate and the annual alteration of flood and drought held down the number of horses and other livestock, although the day would come when Venezuela would be famous for its herds of wild horses and cattle.[48]

The area first settled and exploited by the Spanish in New Spain was the coast and highlands in the general latitude of Mexico City. Large sections of this area offer good grazing for livestock, but the area is by no means perfect for horses. As of 1531, New Spain was raising fewer than two hundred horses a year. Then, as the horses were completing their adaptation to the climate and available fodder, the Spanish frontier moved north, toward and into the plains where the enemies of the horse were few and the grass plentiful and green. By 1550 mounts were available for little more than the effort to rope them. Within a few years of that date, ten thousand horses were grazing in the pasture lands between Querétaro and San Juan del Río alone. As the opening of new mines drew Europeans and their animals further and further north, the increase in the number of horses reached the magnitude of a stampede. By the end of the century wild horses beyond counting were running free in Durango. With mounts so plentiful, all Mexicans—Spanish, mestizo and even Indian—swung into the saddle, and even Cervantes's Sancho Panza knew of the excellence of Mexican horsemanship.[49]

The horses continued north, urged on by the men on their backs or with no more stimulus than the smell of water and grass ahead. Nothing but the driest deserts, the snows of Canada, and the eastern woodlands stopped their advance. In 1777 Fray Morfi wrote that the area between the Río Grande and the Nueces River was so full of horses "that their trails make the country, utterly uninhabited by people, look as if it were the most populated in the world." The wild horses never attained such numbers beyond the Nueces in what is now the United States and Canada, but they ranged widely, preceded the Anglo-Saxon pioneer onto the Great Plains and provided him with his mount. It was the Spaniard who supplied the North American cowboy with his horse and, as we shall see, his longhorns, the tools of his trade, and even the vocabulary to go along with that trade: mustang, bronco, lasso, rodeo, chaps, lariat, buckaroo.[50]

The beginning of the saga of the horse in South America was also one of slow beginnings, but of an even more spectacular climax. In the llanos, as has already been said, the tropical climate kept the number of horses low, as it did in Brazil, although the latter did have enough to supply her own needs and to export a few to Angola in the sixteenth century.[51]

The horse first arrived in Peru with Pizarro in 1532; Atalhualpa's first emissaries to the Spanish returned to tell him of huge animals which ran like the wind and killed men with their feet and mouths. These animals were slow to breed in the higher, colder regions of Peru, but did prosper in the rich pasture lands, such as those around Cuzco and Quito.[52]

Within a few years the conquistadors and their mounts were moving south into Chile, which by the beginning of the seventeenth century had become famous for its fine horses. In the same period the first settlers were arriving in Paraguay, on the east side of the Andes; and we soon hear of herds of wild horses there.[53]

The horse found a home in Peru, Chile, and Paraguay; in the pampas of Río de la Plata he found a paradise. What happened when the horse reached what is today Argentina and Uruguay is best described as a biological explosion: horses running free on the grassy vastness propagated in a manner similar to smallpox virus in the salubrious environment of Indian bodies.

The most commonly accepted story of the origin of the horses and other European livestock of the pampas at the end of the sixteenth century is that they were all descended from the handful of animals brought by Pedro de Mendoza to Buenos Aires at the time of its founding in 1535. But this first settlement of Buenos Aires proved to be abortive, and there had only been a tiny number of livestock there. It seems unlikely that the huge herds that existed on the pampas only forty or fifty years later could have all traced their ancestry back to Buenos Aires. There were horses in Paraguay who could have drifted south, and horses in Chile who might conceivably have found their way through the Andean passes. Wherever they came from, they found the grass to their taste.

The first permanent settlers of Buenos Aires arrived in 1580 and found that they had been preceded onto the pampas by enormous herds of wild horses. The horses had "multiplied infinitely" in the grasslands of Río de la Plata, possibly producing more colts faster than ever before in the history of the earth.[54] Vazquez de Espinosa tells us, at the beginning of the seventeenth century, of wild horses in Tucumán "in such numbers that they cover the face of the earth and when they cross the road it is necessary for travellers to wait and let them pass, for a whole day or more, so as not to let them carry off tame stock with them. . . ." He speaks with awe of the plains of Buenos Aires "covered with escaped mares and horses in such numbers that when they go anywhere they look like woods from a distance."[55]

The pig provided the conquistadors with sustenance, but the importance of his role in the development of colonial America dropped off sharply after the first few years of colonization in any given area. The achievements of none of the great colonizing people who came to the New World would have been possible without the horse. But the horse is a means to an end. Few people have ever made their livings by raising horses for their meat and hides. Millions have done so, however, by using them in the business of herding other grazing animals, in order to sell *their* meat and hides.

The figure in the history of colonial America who is most characteristically Iberian is the rancher on horseback observing his herds of livestock, most often herds of cattle. When faced with the immense grasslands of America, the Englishman paused, called them deserts and tried to find a way around them. The Spaniard embraced the plains, the llanos, the pampas, drove his cattle onto them, and let the multiplying beeves make a good life for him. As a result, there were probably more cattle in the New World in the seventeenth century than any other type of vertebrate immigrant.[56]

The cattle supplied the Spaniard with all the meat he could consume: an Englishman reported in the 1550s that one could obtain in Mexico City a "whole quarter of an oxe, as much as a slave can carry away from the Butchers, for five Tomynes, that is five royals of Plate, which is just two shillings and six pence. . . ."[57] The great numbers of Spaniards and Indians who devoted themselves exclusively to mining could never have done so if great quantities of highly nourishing food had not been available nearby in the form of huge herds of cattle and other livestock. This is especially true of those working in mines in barren country, such as those at Zacatecas and Potosí.

But meat eaters formed only one of the markets for

American beef, and not the most important market. More cattle were killed for hides and tallow than for meat. It was an age in which leather served many of the functions for which we use fiber, plastics and metals today: armor, cups, trunks, rope. The demand for hides in America and Europe was immense, and so was the number of hides exported from America to Europe. The fleet that crossed to Spain in 1587 landed nearly 100,000 hides at Seville. ("Hides" are not necessarily all cowhides, but it seems that the great majority were.) With such large numbers of cattle being slaughtered, tallow became so plentiful in America that candles—apparently something of a luxury in Europe—were used by rich and poor, and even Indians, in America. Without cheap and plentiful candles, mining could never have been carried on as extensively as it was. The work underground was accomplished in artificial light, and, even though tallow was extremely cheap, in the early seventeenth century 300,000 pesos a year was spent on candles for the Potosí mines.[58]

Many of the Iberian colonists were already cattlemen when they arrived in America. Southern Iberia was the only part of western Europe in Renaissance times in which open range ranching was common. The techniques that would characterize ranching in America—the constant use of the horse, periodic round-ups, branding, overland drives—were all "invented" by medieval Iberians. And these people, as their descendants in America, lived and tended their herds on a frontier troubled by the constant raiding of mounted enemies. In Europe the hostile natives were Moors, in America they were Indians. All in all, we may guess that there was no group of Europeans better equipped—technologically, socially, and psychologically—to deal with the American environment than the ranchers of southern Iberia.

Not only did Iberia develop men fit for life on the American steppes, but also animals for these new grasslands. The Spanish horses we have already discussed. Spanish cattle were even more adaptable. Fast, lean, and armed with long horns, the Spanish cow makes a poor showing at the stockyards today, but in her heyday she made an excellent showing in a variety of climates and against a variety of carnivores from the cougars of the upper Missouri River to the anacondas of the Paraguay River.[59]

The Spanish found the Greater Antilles quite suitable for the most prestigious of peacetime vocations, which were, first of all, gold mining and, when the gold ran out, ranching. In Spain the biggest herds of cattle had rarely exceeded eight hundred or a thousand. In the 1520s Oviedo spoke of many herds of five hundred or so on Española, and some of as many as eight thousand. The export of hides became, along with sugar, the chief support of Española, and even more exclusively the chief source of wealth of the other big islands. In 1587 alone Española sent 35,444 hides to Spain. So many were killed for their hides that "in some places the aire hath been corrupted with the aboundance of these stinking carcases." In the 1560s Española's income from her exports probably amounted to about 640,000 pesos annually from sugar and 720,000 from hides.[60]

Cattle were first brought to Mexico for breeding purposes in 1521. So few were they at first that their slaughter was forbidden, but within a decade there were scores of cattle ranches. The price of beef in Mexico City dropped 75 percent between 1532 and 1538. It seems that in the first years cattle lagged behind pigs and sheep in the matter of rapid propagation, but after a few decades left them both far behind. Cattle were soon grazing everywhere in Mexico, even on the hot Gulf coast. A traveller of 1568 records that over two thousand were driven through the town of Vera Cruz every morning "to take away the ill vapors of the earth."[61]

As the European population of Mexico built up and began to spread north, ranching went along with it. The penetration of Spanish cattle into the rich grass country of northern

Mexico in the sixteenth century set off one of the most bio-logically extravagant events of that biologically amazing century. In 1579 it was statéd that some ranches in the north had 150,000 head of cattle and that 20,000 was considered a small herd. Two ranches on what is now the border of Zacatecas and Durango branded 33,000 and 42,000 calves respectively in 1586. According to one witness who wrote in 1594, the cattle herds were nearly doubling every fifteen months. At the end of that century Samuel de Champlain, on a tour of Mexico for the French king, wrote with awe of the "great, level plains, stretching endlessly and every-where covered with an infinite number of cattle."[62]

Cattle were one of New Spain's greatest economic assets, and their hides figured significantly in her exports. In 1587, 64,350 hides were sent to Spain; that number, of course, does not include the very large number of hides kept in Mex-ico for local use.[63]

Wild cattle roamed freely in inestimable quantities far be-yond the colonists' horizons. When the Spanish began a seri-ous attempt to settle in southern Texas in the early eighteenth century, they discovered the wild cattle were there before them. These were the Hispanic ancestors of the famous Texas longhorns. Many of the English-speaking colonists who moved into Texas in the early nineteenth century con-sidered these cattle as native to the land (and, incidentally, as harder and more dangerous to catch than mustangs).[64]

Cattle did well in the savannas and mountains of Central America and Tierra Firme.[65] But, as we move south from Mexico, we find no cattle region to compare with its northern plains until we come to the llanos of Venezuela, six hundred miles east to west and two hundred north to south. The tem-perature is a good deal hotter on the average than that of the plains of Iberia, and the climate is a yearly cycle of drought and flood; so there could be no "biological explo-sions" of European livestock in the llanos. But the grass and the space attracted the Spaniard and his longhorns, anyway. In 1548 a Spanish stockman passed through with a small herd of cattle, bound for Bogotá. These were probably the first steers and cows in the llanos. In the latter half of the century the resistance of the Indians of these flatlands was broken, partly by force of arms and partly by smallpox and other diseases, and the adaptation of technology and animal to the difficult environment was made. By 1600 as many as forty-five ranches had been founded in the plains of Venezuela. A half century later something like 140,000 head of cattle grazed in the llanos. As in Mexico, the cattle tended to move into the interior ahead of the Europeans, being quicker to adapt than their owners. Sometimes these "strays" were driven along by African herdsmen, who had been brought to Venezuela to replace the dying Indians as servants of the Spanish, and who, like the cattle, moved beyond the frontier to excape their owners.[66]

The history of the llanos follows the same course as that of the plains of Mexico, only at a much slower pace. The sixteenth century was a period of bare beginnings, but the time would come two centuries later when cattle and horses, tame and wild, would number in the millions, and individual ranches would brand ten thousand head and more annually. Export of hides to Spain was beginning by the last decades of the 1600s, and took a prominent place in the economy of colonial Venezuela after the turn of the century. During the period 1620 to 1665 hides accounted for 75 percent or more of the total value of exports to Spain.[67]

In the rest of the continent south of Venezuela the story of cattle falls roughly into two categories; one, that of the Portuguese settlements in Brazil, where the climate was tough on cattle, as well as on men, and the increase of the herds was slow; and two, that of the Spanish settlements, where life was easier and propagation faster.

The story of the cattle of the Brazilian *sertão,* the back-country, is similar to that of their relatives in the llanos. The sertão produced no herds in the sixteenth century to compare with those of Mexico or, as we shall see, of the pampas; the chief limiting factor being, again, a difficult, truly tropical climate. This century was one of adjustment and adaptation for both man and animal. According to the record (which is very spotty for the earliest decades of Brazilian history), the first cattle came to Portuguese America with Martim Alfonso de Sousa between 1531 and 1533. Their number grew so slowly that they were too valuable to eat and were usually preserved to haul sugar cane to the mills and to turn the millstones to crush the cane. The sugar plantations expanded so rapidly that the natural increase of the cattle was not enough to answer the demand for animal power. Thus there was a concentrated effort to promote cattle raising in the coastal meadows of the northeast, not despite but because of the devotion of that area to sugar.

By 1590 pioneers moving north from Bahia had broken the back of Indian resistance in Sergipe, and soon herds of cattle browsed in its grasslands. At the mouth of the São Francisco River, whose valley was to become the great corridor into the interior, the Bahian cattlemen met the cattlemen moving south from Pernambuco, each group a vanguard of the sugar plantations spreading laterally along the coast.

Cattle also played a role in that part of sixteenth-century Brazil which did not dedicate itself to sugar. Far to the southwest of the main plantation areas cattle herds were slowly increasing in the area of São Paulo, and were becoming a fairly important element in the economy of the Paulistas. Thus by 1600 in two widely separated and different parts of Brazil, cattlemen were prepared for the first real penetration inland. Herds of five hundred and even a thousand were to be found here and there along the littoral. A breed of cattle and a breed of men tough enough to face the challenge of the Indians and the sertão were ready.[68]

Cattle were brought to Tierra Firme and Central America early in the sixteenth century, and their progeny arrived in Lima no later than 1539. The herds scattered here and there, wherever the grass was plentiful in the mountainous land. They adapted to the high altitudes more rapidly than horses. All in all, the course of events was not too different from that in New Spain, although on a much smaller scale: a rapid increase in numbers and the straying away of many head who soon became wild.[69]

Cattle, as was the case with horses, spread out from Peru with the Spaniards and south into Chile, and from there into and through the mountains. The cattle propagated rapidly in the green valleys of Chile, and in 1614 the residents of Santiago possessed 39,250 head, of which the annual increase was 13,500.[70]

In Paraguay and Tucumán the story of cattle is the same as that of horses: extremely rapid increase which, as the animals strayed south and west into even wider and greener pastures, accelerated. In 1593 there were already great numbers of wild cattle in the province of Corrientes. A few years later the plains of the Santa Cruz region were "full of cattle which today have run wild and cover the fields for a distance of every eighty leagues." In 1619 Governor Gondra of Buenos Aires reported that the number of cattle within the area under his jurisdiction was so great that if 80,000 a year were killed for their hides, natural increase would be sufficient to make up the loss.[71]

The herds of cattle continued to expand and to spread south toward Patagonia. The eyewitness reports of the size of the herds of the pampas reminds the student of United States history not so much of accounts of the Texas longhorns as of the buffalo. These myriads of cattle, domesticated and wild, provided Río de la Plata with an economic base. The chief export of the pampas in the colonial era was hides. This trade was already of some importance by the beginning of the seventeenth century and was to comprise the export of a million hides annually by the end of the eighteenth.[72]

Sheep ranching was even more important in Renaissance Spain than cattle ranching, and so it is not surprising that Columbus brought sheep with him in 1493, along with the other livestock. The number of sheep in the Americas eventually became immense, but they were slower to adapt than most of the other kinds of European livestock. They did not do well in the Caribbean islands or in hot, wet lowlands. As Bernabé Cobo noticed, lands not good for men were also unsuited for sheep. Nor did the sheep oblige the Europeans by running off into the wilderness to breed themselves into great herds and await the opportunity to make wealthy men of the first Spaniards to claim them. Sheep were much less capable of defending themselves against predators than swine, horses, or longhorns.[73]

Their inability to play the game of survival in the wilderness successfully did not change the fact that they were one of the basic elements of Iberian civilization. Mutton was a very common meat in the Spanish diet and remained so in the New World. Sheepskins were an important article of clothing in Europe and served the same purpose in the Americas. In the mining areas, dressed sheepskins were of special importance because mercury, so essential in the processing of silver ore, was stored in them. And, of course, sheep were the source of wool.[74]

Wool was the raw material used by the first real factory industry in America, the large textile mills in which Indians were driven, often to the detriment of their health, to produce woolen and other kinds of cloth. By 1571 New Spain had eighty mills and the viceroyalty of Peru lagged not far behind. By the seventeenth century the mills were producing woolens sufficient to fill the needs of the regions where the mills existed, plus a surplus for intercolonial commerce and even some for export to Spain.[75]

Some few sheep managed to eke out an existence in the hot Antilles in the early sixteenth century and so were available for shipment to the mainland shortly after the founding of the settlements there. Sheep came ashore in Panama as early as 1521 and, we may assume, at similarly early dates elsewhere in the Caribbean littoral. Cortés had such a high opinion of the potentialities of New Spain as a ranching area that he sent back to the Antilles for sheep and other livestock as soon as Aztec resistance was broken. But it was Antonio de Mendoza, the first viceroy (1535–1549), who looms as most important in the early annals of Mexican sheep herding. It was Mendoza who imported the superb sheep of Castile, the Merinos, and fostered their increase in New Spain—and who, incidentally, became one of the leading ranchers within his own jurisdiction.[76]

Despite the fact that sheep were not tough enough to manage on their own, they, like horses and pigs and cattle, propagated very rapidly in the relatively temperate interior plateaus and valleys of New Spain. It was estimated as of 1582 that 200,000 sheep were grazing on a range nine leagues square just to the north of San Juan de los Ríos. Antonio de Herrera tells a tale of "men that with two shag-haired sheep came to have above 40,000." The vastness of the sheep population soon gave rise to seasonal migrations; and no later than 1579, and probably a good deal earlier, 200,000 sheep and more flowed in a river of wool from Querétaro to Lake Chapala and western Michoacán every September, and back again in May, following the green grass. However, in spite of the size of the herds and their mobility, the sheep ranches were mostly concentrated in central Mexico and the northern plains were for the most part left to the tougher longhorns. An important exception was New Mexico, where sheep far outnumbered cattle until the coming of the Anglo-Saxons.[77]

Peru, no less than Mexico, was a land where sheep could thrive. One of the conquistadors, Captain Salamanca, imported sheep within four or six years of the conquest, and soon they were grazing in large numbers in the high meadows, alongside the cattle and the native stock. They delighted their owners, for they now were lambing twice in fourteen months.[78]

The effect of the sheep and other European livestock on the native herds was not so delightful. The European animals doubtlessly transmitted to the native stock a devastating selection of animal diseases. The llama and alpaca populations diminished as spectacularly as the Indian population after the conquest; and the reasons were largely the same: disease and brutal exploitation.[79]

The territory of the former Incan empire is a land broken and divided into so many compartments by the Andes that one cannot point to a single area as the main center of colonial ranching. Seemingly sheep grazed in every area where the presence of green grass, temperate climate and access to market combined. The reader will not be surprised to hear that the number of sheep rose immensely. Near the end of the sixteenth century José de Acosta wrote of Peru that "in former times there were men that did possesse three score and ten, yea, a hundred thousand sheep, and at this day they have not many lesse."[80]

Elsewhere in South America the history of sheep ranching contains few surprises. Some sheep herding went on in New Granada in the Andean foothills and highlands. The areas of Brazil settled by the Portuguese in the sixteenth century were much too tropical for sheep, except in the captaincies of the central-south—Río de Janeiro and São Paulo—where herds of sheep did exist by the end of the century. Sheep did exceedingly well in Chile, where the climate is temperate and the grass plentiful. In 1614 the district of Santiago alone contained 623,825 sheep, which produced in a year 223,944 lambs. The pampas were too hot and the Spaniards too few to provide sufficient shepherds for any large number of sheep. However in what is now northern Argentina, specifically in Tucumán, we hear of the presence of many sheep by 1600; and, eventually, Patagonia would become one of the chief sheep-herding centers of the western hemisphere.[81]

Much could be said of the other types of domesticated animals brought to the New World in the first century after Columbus, but the reader's patience is limited, so we will only mention a few briefly. Dogs existed in pre-Columbian America, but those which came with the conquistadors were much bigger and fiercer, so fierce, indeed, that they were used with great effectiveness against the Indians. They seem to have returned to nature as readily as the swine, and numbers of wild dogs appeared in Española, Peru, and, no doubt, many other areas. They ate what they could find: shellfish in Atacama on the Peruvian coast, crabs in Puerto Rico, and, in the areas where there were herds of cattle, the dogs lived as predators and were treated as wolves by the settlers.[82]

And there were cats, many of which followed the dogs back to nature. When Charles Darwin toured the La Plata region in the 1830s, he found the common cat in the rocky hills "altered into a large fierce animal." Goats came with the Europeans and by 1600 were to be found in large numbers just about everywhere the other grazing livestock were plentiful. Where conditions were right, they went wild, too. In Puerto Rico the "Goates live . . . securely, because they love cliffes of Rocks, or the tops of Hils, and therefore they are out of the ordinarie haunt of these murderous dogs." They went back to nature in the isolation of the Chilean islands.[83]

There is some confusion about domesticated fowls. The turkey and Muscovy duck were certainly present in pre-Columbian America, and some think that a type of chicken was also. The acceptance of a pre-Columbian American chicken probably also means acceptance of pre-Columbian trans-Pacific contacts with the areas where the chicken was first domesticated. Whatever the truth may be, there is no doubt that most of the chickens in America by 1600 were of European descent, plus a considerable number of guinea hens, of African origin.[84]

Who can imagine rural Latin America without the burro? Donkeys and mules are also importations from the eastern hemisphere. Although widely used as beasts of burden, they never became as plentiful as horses in the colonial era. Perhaps the presence of so many horses and oxen made the breeding of mules seem superfluous. Nevertheless, many large mule ranches existed, usually in the same areas where the other grazing animals prospered. Córdoba in Tucumán was especially noted for its mule ranches. These animals, too, went wild.[85]

If the reader's impression thus far is that the Iberian record of importing livestock was one of unblemished success, then that impression must be quickly corrected. By 1600 the Spanish and Portuguese were experimenting with animals brought in from Africa and Asia, as well as Europe, and some, such as the guinea hen, proved valuable additions to the fauna of the New World. Others, such as the camel, brought in to serve as a beast of burden in the Peruvian coastal deserts, did not. As in a similar experiment in the arid southwest of the United States two centuries later, the camels proved only theoretically valuable, for the equestrian Europeans were very unenthusiastic about them. A *don* could, with self-respect, admire a horse, or even a mule . . . but a camel? The camels were neglected and allowed to stray off. Escaped slaves—*los negros cimarrones*—who, no doubt, often knew more about camels than did the whites, killed the animals for food. The history of the camel of colonial Peru is only sixty years long. The last one of these unassimilable immigrants died in 1615.[86]

Not all the importations of fauna were intentional. The Iberian undoubtedly imported dozens, even hundreds, of kinds of insects and animals that he would have preferred leaving behind in the Old World. The Old World rat, as loyal a follower of man as the dog, hitched a ride across the Atlantic and became an important pest and carrier of disease in the ports of colonial America. This was probably the black rat, which is today more common in the tropics and on board vessels than the larger brown rat. Historically, the black rat has been the most important carrier of the bubonic plague, and as good a vehicle for typhus as any.[87]

There was some controversy as to whether the rats that tormented the sixteenth- and seventeenth-century Spanish-Americans were Old or New World in origin. Bernabé Cobo, knowing something of the science of genetics of his day, said that rats had always been everywhere because "it is a natural thing everywhere for these animals to be engendered from the rotting of the earth."[88]

Be that as it may, rats were not in the Bermudas before the coming of the Europeans, and when they arrived, set off one of the most spectacular ecological disasters of the age. The early seventeenth-century English colonists unintentionally brought a few with them and "the Lord sent upon the Countrey, a very grievous scourge and punishment, threatening the utter ruin and desolation of it." The rats spread to all the islands, honeycombed the earth with their burrows, nested in almost every tree, and nearly ate the colonists out of house and home: "for being destitute of food, many dyed, and we all became very feeble and weake, whereof . . . some would not; other could not stir abroad to seeke reliefe, but dyed in their houses."[89] Again and again it seemed the Lord would make the Europeans pay for the ecological sin of breaking out of Europe and taking their plants and animals with them.

It is impossible to doubt that the transfer of Old World foods and livestock to the Americas had an immense impact on the Indian. As already has been mentioned, the Indian was often slow to accept the new food plants, but the new domesticated animals were another matter. He could see little advantage in wheat over maize, but the Old World pig, horse, cow, chicken, dog, and goat were superior in nearly every way to anything the Americas had to offer.

The smaller Old World animals were more rapidly adopted by the Indians within or near the European areas of settlement than the larger. The Spaniards valued such animals less than the larger and considered Indian possession of them as no threat. These smaller animals were cheaper to obtain and less difficult for novice husbandmen to control. There was a geographically widespread precedent in America for the domestication of small animals, and, because of their smallness, they did not require their new owners to drastically alter their way of life. The Indians adopted Old World dogs, cats, pigs, and chickens into their economy and daily round of life in large areas of Spanish and Portuguese America within a generation or two of the conquest of their areas. Antonio de Herrera tells of a wise Indian who, when asked to name the most important things he and his fellows had received from the Castilians, put chicken eggs at the top of his list, because they were plentiful, "fresh every day, and good cooked or not cooked for young and Old." (The other items on his list were horses, candles, and lamps.)[90]

Examples of Indian horse, cattle, sheep, and goat herding in the areas under European control exist, but were not common. The keeping of such animals called for a radical change in the lives of the sedentary farmers, except in the highlands of Peru, where there was precedent for the herding of large animals. In New Spain only a few Indians acquired even small herds of sheep, and Indian ownership of herds of the fierce Spanish cattle was even rarer. In Peru, also, the Indian was rarely owner of large numbers of such animals.[91]

By and large, the bigger domesticated animals of the Europeans destroyed rather than enriched the Indians of the areas controlled by the Europeans. The spectacular rise in the population of domesticated animals in these areas was accompanied by an equally spectacular decline in the Indian population; and disease and exploitation do not entirely explain that decline. The Indians were losing out in the biological competition with the newly imported livestock. The peoples of the high Indian civilizations chiefly lived on a vegetable diet, and so anything radically affecting their croplands radically affected them. The Spanish, anxious to establish their pastoral Iberian way of life in their colonies, set aside large sections of land for grazing, a good deal of it land that Indians had formerly cultivated. And the livestock, in this new continent where fences and shepherds were so few, often strayed onto Indian fields, eating the plants and trampling them. As New Spain's first viceroy, Mendoza, wrote to his King about the state of affairs around Oaxaca: "May your Lordship realize that if cattle are allowed, the Indians will be destroyed." Many Indians went malnourished, weakening their resistance to disease; many fled to the hills and deserts to face hunger in solitude; some simply lay down and died within the sound of the lowing of their rivals. The history of this phenomenon is clear in Mexico, and we have good reason to believe that parallels are to be found elsewhere in the Americas.[92]

On the other hand, the impact of livestock on the Indians beyond the boundaries of European settlement often had a very positive affect. These Indians were by no means as numerous as those of Mesoamerica and Peru, and there existed among them plenty of room for the quadruped immigrants. Many of these Indians were already followers of a nomadic way of life, and the new arrivals multiplied the rewards of such a life. These Indians received the horses, cattle, sheep, and goats not as rivals but as immensely valuable additions to their sources of food, clothing, and energy.

The animals chiefly involved in this phenomenon were, in ascending order of importance, sheep, cattle, and horses. Sheep rarely went wild, and so they were available to the independent Indians only as loot to be seized by raiding or only if the Indian would become a shepherd. The latter seldom happened, but the exceptions are worth mentioning. By the end of the seventeenth century most of the tribes of the Chaco (in what is today Paraguay, Bolivia, and northern Argentina) were beginning to herd sheep. Another example is that of the Navaho people of New Mexico, who became owners of large herds of sheep a few decades later.[93]

Beyond every line of Spanish settlements in grass country were tribes who came to depend increasingly on the meat and hides of cattle. In New Spain the cattle immensely enriched the Yaquis, Tarahumaras, Pueblos, and other tribes, and—beyond the most northern frontier—the Athabascan people, of which the Navaho and Apache are best known. In the vast grasslands south and southeast of Peru the Spanish steer seemed to the Indians to be a gift from the gods. Just after the opening of the seventeenth century, Vázquez de Espinosa wrote that the plains of the Santa Cruz de la Sierra region were "full of cattle which today have run wild and cover the fields for a distance of over eighty leagues. . . . These Indians profit by the cattle, keeping them close to them and the poor Spaniards who lost them, far away." The Charrua of the Banda Oriental (Uruguay), and the Puelches, Aucás, Tehuelches, Ranqueles, and Araucanians of the Argentine pampas lived off the cattle and made tools, clothing, and shelters of their hide, bones, and sinew.[94]

For the most part, the people of these tribes and a score of others like them did not become true herdsmen, but obtained their cattle from the Spanish or the wild herds whenever there was need. The most prominent exception to this rule is the Goajiro people of the great peninsula that stands between the western shore of Lake Maricaibo and the Caribbean. The Goajiro, because of their position on the edge of the Caribbean, were among the earliest mainland people to have contact with the Spanish and their cattle. Cattle began grazing on the edges of their semiarid peninsula no later than the 1570s and perhaps as early as 1550 or so. We know next to nothing of the early post-Columbian history of the Goajiro, but we may guess that they became herders very soon after they first obtained cattle and other livestock— probably from the adjacent Riohacha region. This transformation must have taken place a very long time ago. In spite of the refusal of this fierce people to become either victims or wards of the white man, little trace of their pre-Columbian culture remains today. As of the middle of the twentieth century, the Goajiro, who themselves numbered no more than 18,000, possessed 100,000 head of cattle, 200,000 sheep and goats, 20,000 mules and horses, 30,000 donkeys, and numbers of pigs and chickens. As among the Masai of Kenya, cattle are the most important measure of wealth; their diet is almost completely composed of meat and milk products; the price of a bride is measured in cattle. The Goajiro are what all the Indians of the American grasslands might have become if only the livestock, but not the Europeans, had come to the New World.[95]

The Goajiro would never have been able to handle such large herds if they had not received horses along with the cattle. The fact that it is a compliment of the first rank to describe a woman's hair as being the color of a horse's mane reflects their love of horses.[96] The Goajiro are the last surviving example of those tribes of Indian centaurs whose culture was transformed and enriched by the horse.

The Indians began by being terrified of the horse, and if the Spanish had had their way, the Indians' wish to keep as far away from horses as possible would have been granted.[97] The Europeans were fully conscious of the advantage the horse gave them over their American subjects, and so tried to prohibit Indian ownership or use of horses. But the prohibition always failed: Indians were needed as vaqueros; Indian allies were ineffective in war unless mounted; and—above all—the horses reproduced so fast and strayed beyond European control in such numbers that it soon became as easy for many Indians to acquire mounts as Spaniards. Both the horses and diseases moved through the virgin lands of America faster than did the people who had brought them to the New World.

The story is similar for all the tribes of the great grasslands, from Alberta to Patagonia. Before the horse came, the steppe lands had few human inhabitants. The tough sod discouraged farming, and the plains animals were too fleet of foot to provide a dependable supply of food for large numbers of pedestrians. Then the horse gave the Indian the speed and stamina needed to take advantage of the opportunity to harvest the immense quantities of food represented by the buffalo herds of North America and the herds of wild cattle that propagated so rapidly in the grasslands of both Americas. The Indians stopped farming; the work was hard, boring, and unrewarding, compared to the nomadic life. The nomads found life more comfortable and richer than they had ever known before. By 1700 or 1750 the Pehuenches, Puelches, Aucás, Tehuelches, and Ranqueles of Río de la Plata were all in the saddle and ranging the pampas, encouraged and pushed from behind by those Araucanians who had cast aside much of their Andean culture to come down onto the flatlands to exploit the herds.[98]

In the area of similar topography and climate in North America the impact of the horse came later but was similar. By the late eighteenth century the Great Plains were full of redmen on horseback—the Blackfoot, Arapaho, Cheyenne, Crow, Sioux, Comanche. The Indians of the Great Plains and the pampas, tempted into similar extreme specialization by the horse, even grew to look alike. The pampa Indian lived on horseback from infancy, and his legs grew bowed and awkward. George Catlin's description of the North American plains Indian would do as well for his pampean brother:

> A Comanche on his feet is out of his element, and comparatively almost as awkward as a monkey on the ground, without a limb or a branch to cling to; but the moment he lays his hand upon his horse, his *face* even becomes handsome, and he gracefully flies away like a different being.[99]

The Indians took up an equestrian life because it was a rich life. The herds of horses were great wealth in themselves, and the meat, hides, bones and sinew of the plains animals to which the horse gave the Indian access improved his diet and added to the materials from which the aboriginal craftsman made articles of utility and beauty. The horse enabled the Indian to kill more animals than he needed for himself and his family, and the surplus could be traded for needles and blankets and firearms and whiskey. When the only beast of burden was the dog, no nomad could be rich. Now all this had changed. The horse enabled the nomad to move much heavier and larger items than ever before. The Blackfoot estimated that a horse could carry four times the burden of a dog twice as far in a day's march. The horse vastly increased the speed with which hunters could move and the distance which they could cover, and thus the area from which they could draw sustenance. The size of the nomadic band could and did grow.[100]

Increased wealth and larger nomadic units gave rise to greater social stratification: the rich became much richer and the poor only a little richer; and the egalitarianism of poverty began to disappear. The number of slaves increased, for they could be obtained more easily by equestrian warfare. For instance, the Guaná of the Chaco became agricultural slaves to the fierce Mbayá herders and horsemen.[101]

The increased number of prisoners-of-war came as result of the increased tempo of warfare. The horse immeasurably enhanced the Indian's ability to raid his fellow Indians and the European's frontier. Among some Indians, at least, the presence of the horse tended to make war more sanguinary, as static pedestrian tactics became obsolete and the cavalry charge common. The old stand-off weapons were disgarded in favor of those used in hand-to-hand combat of mounted warriors.[102]

In the long view of history, the greatest effect of the horse on the Indian was to enhance his ability to resist the advance of Europeans into the interiors of North and South America. Not only did the mounted Indian defend himself effectively, but he was sometimes tempted and often forced by the needs of his rapidly changing culture to raid the rich herds of the whites. The Chichimecs of Mexico were swinging up into the saddle before the end of the sixteenth century; as a result, their power in New Spain was not broken decisively for generations. The Navahos and Apaches were learning to ride and raid Spanish settlements by the last half of the seventeenth century, and were still resisting the white advance at the end of the nineteenth century.[103]

By 1700 all the plains tribes south of the Platte River and north of the Spanish settlements in Mexico were, to some degree, familiar with the horse. Horses were numerous among the Blackfoot tribes, well north of the Platte, in 1751. Horses with Spanish brands, obtained most likely by raids of the Mexican frontier and then traded from one tribe to another, were seen on the banks of the Saskatchewan River in 1784.[104] The Indians of the Great Plains—Sioux, Blackfoot, Comanche, Arapaho, Dakota, Crow—were off on horseback on one of the most spectacular adventures that any people has ever known. It lasted three or four generations, ending finally with the destruction of the buffalo herds, the catastrophic wars with the United States Army, and the final occupation of the prairies by the Old World peoples in the last half of the nineteenth century.

The story of the horse and the Indian in the Venezuelan llanos and the grasslands of Brazil was rather different from that in the plains of North America. The climate of these South American regions did not encourage the rapid growth of large herds of horses that could enable the Indian to become an expert mounted fighter before the arrival of the pioneer. The Portuguese slave hunters ran afoul of mounted Indians no later than the mid-seventeenth century, but only deep in the interior in or near Paraguay, and not close to the Portuguese settlements.[105]

It was only in the southern part of South America that the story of the horse and Indian paralleled that of those two in the North American prairies. As the Spanish and their herds penetrated into what is now Paraguay, the tribes of the Chaco saw their first large domesticated animals. By the middle of the seventeenth century Abipón, Mocoví, Mbayá, and Guaicurú and all were themselves acquiring herds of these animals, of which the horse was the most important. A century and a half later the Chaco was still under the control of bands of Indian cavalry, and was still a place in which no outsider could feel secure. The scarcity of non-Indian population was not entirely due to the unattractive climate; the military capabilities of the mounted aborigines were enough in themselves to discourage colonizers.[106]

South of the Chaco the first Indians to become horsemen were those of that complex of Chilean tribes called the Araucanians. They were making use of the horse in warfare before 1600, and soon after were plunging through the Andean passes down onto the Río de la Plata grasslands. Before this Araucanian avalanche lost momentum it moved nearly to the gates of Buenos Aires, and its influence was so great that the Araucanian tongue became in time the lingua franca of the Argentine plains.[107] The Pehuenches and other pampean tribes soon learned horsemanship from the Araucanians, and by the eighteenth century even the Telhuelche of Patagonia were on horseback.

In 1796 the area of Río de la Plata that was really under European control was no larger than it had been in 1590. Several factors had hampered the Spanish advance: there was no gold or silver to attract colonists, and Spanish mercantilism tended to strangle rather than encourage economic expansion in Argentina. The chief factor was that the Spaniards were hemmed in by troops of mounted warriors, who ravaged the frontier ranches and garrison villages, and then returned to the trackless plains before the Spanish could react.

As the Europeans moved into the interior in the nineteenth century, these mounted tribes were exterminated.[108] As in North America, the horse enriched the tribes of the grasslands and enabled them to resist the advance of the whites for a time. Then came the obliteration of those tribes and the advance of the white man.

By 1600 all the most important food plants of the Old World were being cultivated in the Americas. The akee, mango, and breadfruit, foods grown in the Caribbean today, were not brought there until the eighteenth century.[109] But aside from these and a few others, the important food plants were probably all growing on the mainland of the New World, or at least in the Antilles, by the time of Cortés's death.

This fact is not merely of antiquarian interest. The Indian slaves could continue to eat Indian foods, and the African slaves could be forced to, or both could be left to eat nothing at all. But the Europeans would come to the New World in great numbers only if a dependable supply familiar, European food was available. In the Americas the Europeans' demand for their own kinds of food was strengthened by social and racial prejudice. To this day the upper classes in wide areas of Mexico consider maize products as the food of Indians, and wheat bread the food of the upper class. Without the successful transportation of European agriculture to the western hemisphere, there would have been an appreciably smaller number of Europeans willing to make the same trip.

But we must give the Indian agriculturalist credit, even if the Spanish colonists did not. Wheat is neither superior nor inferior to maize; each has its advantages and its disadvantages. Among the root crops, the creations of New World horticulture are superior to those of the Old World; a lot more manioc and white and sweet potatoes are grown in Europe, Africa, and Asia than turnips and the types of yams that were indigenous to the eastern hemisphere.

There are many examples of how particular Indian plants are equal or superior to their Old World counterparts, but this would not alter the fact that the immigrant flora did vastly enrich the food-producing potentialities of America. For example, Maize and manioc are amazingly adaptable plants, but neither grows well in swampy soils. In the swamps of the hot lowlands rice produces greater yields than any pre-Columbian grain, and its protein content makes it a more valuable plant than manioc, which has practically none. In addition to rice, the dwellers of the hot, wet lowlands also received bananas, African yams, mangos, and several other food plants from the Old World. At the other American extreme, the mountaineers received wheat, barley, and European broadbeans, which grow at higher altitudes than maize, supplementing the potato and quinoa in the Andes.[110]

The arrival of Old World plants in the Americas doubled and even tripled the number of cultivatable food plants in the New World. That is important in itself. There is great advantage in having a large variety of food plants, for exactly the same reason that the sensible investor has a number of different investments. If one or a dozen fail, then the loss will be made up by returns from one or a dozen other sources. When blight withers the manioc, rice survives—not because it is a superior plant, but simply because it is a different plant and susceptible to a different set of diseases. When a whirlwind flattens maize before the ears develop, a crop of turnips is safe in its underground niche.

But more important than the plants brought to America by Columbus and his followers are the animals they brought. The Spanish were so active in bringing animals to the New World that all the most important domesticated species had arrived by 1500. What happened to them, especially to the horses and cattle, is a truly spectacular biological success story.

The impact of domesticated animals on the Indian has already been discussed. The impact on the European colonist was, in part, the same as that of the transfer of plants. The fields of America could now provide the colonist with meat as well as vegetables. Livestock as food sources became particularly important in the enormous steppe regions and savannas too dry, too hot, or too wet for crop cultivation. The dominant plant life in those regions was grass. The Indian had no device for turning grass into food for humans. The European had several such devices: cattle, sheep, and goats and the meat and milk they produced are among the most nourishing of all foods. The coming of the Europeans and their animals created a colossal increase in the quantity of animal protein available to man in America. By 1600 one of the cheapest foods in the American colonies was meat; the Spanish-American settlers were probably consuming more meat per man than any other large group of non-nomadic people in the world. In fact, the Europeans in America have only rarely experienced famine and, taking plant and animal foods together, have possibly been the best-fed people in the world, a fact that has motivated more people to migrate to the New World than all the religious and ideological forces combined.

The materials from which to make various tools and utensils—the fibers and hides of the animals—were a tremendous boon to man in the western hemisphere. The alpaca and llama were already providing the Indians with wool in 1492, but only in the Andean highlands. These animals were never as valuable to man in the Americas as sheep became within two or three generations of Columbus's death. The hide, bone, and sinew of cattle probably had no more uses than the hide, bone, and sinew of the large native domesticated animals, but by 1600 there were many more cattle than any native domesticated animal in large sections of America.

Animals also provided the New World with a new source of power. In the whole of the pre-Columbian Americas the only important sources of extrahuman energy were the dog and llama. Windmills and waterwheels were unknown, the dog was small and weak, and the llama was incapable of carrying any burden heavier than about a hundred pounds. The importation of the horse, ass, and ox brought about a revolution in the quantity of power available to man in the New World similar to that which Watt's steam engine brought to late eighteenth-century Europe.

Livestock provided not only much of the muscle with which exploitation of America was undertaken, but was in itself an important end-product of that exploitation, and a factor spurring Europeans to expand the areas being exploited. The importance of mining in the frontier history of the New World is well known, but mining led directly to the development of only a few areas. The agriculturalists did even less than the miners to advance the frontier. The farming frontier is one that almost always moves slowly. The champion European frontiersman of the New World was the cattleman. Again and again, the frontier of European civilization advancing into the interior of the Americas has been that of the cattle industry. This was particularly true in the great grasslands, which had no gold or silver for the miner, and often the wrong amount of rain for the farmer. The European's ability to settle and exploit the grasslands was proportional to his ability to pasture his livestock on them.

The story of Brazil is a case where cattle were crucial to the colonial expansion. Without cattle, there would not have been meat for those who labored to produce the sugar, gold, and diamonds, nor would there have been the power to turn the early sugar mills nor to carry the miners into the interior and their wealth back to the coast. As Caio Prado has put it, "quite apart from its role in the colony's subsistance, the contribution of cattle raising to the opening up and conquest of the Brazilian interior would be enough to place it among the most important chapters of its history."[111]

Cattle raising may have been chiefly responsible for the fact that there is one and not two Brazils. There were two separate and distinct Brazils in the sixteenth and early decades of the seventeenth century—one of the sugar millionaires in the northeast and the other of the bandeirantes hundreds of miles to the southwest at São Paulo. The northeast had little interest in the interior, and São Paulo, although famous for its matchless pioneers, raided rather than developed the interior. Then in the seventeenth century the demand for meat, tallow, hides, and beasts of burden persuaded cattlemen of both areas to move into the valley of the São Francisco River, and Portugal's first real penetration of the interior began. By 1700 or so the cattle ranches were so numerous that one could ride 1500 miles through the valley of this huge river and never have to spend a night out-of-doors. The two Brazils had been bound together with thongs of cowhide.[112]

Of those animals brought to the western hemisphere, the one which most affected sixteenth-century methods of cultivating the soil of the Americas was the ox. This docile, powerful animal could pull a plow through soil which had always been too heavy or too matted with roots for the Indian's digging stick. Regions which, of necessity, had been left fallow now could be put to work producing food. The ox and plow combination enabled a few men to cultivate very large areas of land—*extensive* cultivation—which became more and more important as the Indian population declined and with it the quantities of foodstuffs produced by the techniques of *intensive* cultivation.[113]

Cultivation of the soil with a plow is much more apt to lead to erosion and destruction of the soil than cultivation with a hoe or digging stick. It is quite likely that soil erosion in the New World accelerated after the arrival of the Europeans. As the number of sedentary Indian farmers increased over the centuries in the areas of the high pre-Columbian civilizations, erosion also increased, but not with such rapidity. The Indians did not have the plow and, more important, their animals were rarely so numerous as to destroy the ground cover. The European's animals were an even worse threat to the land than the plow, because the plow usually stayed in comparatively level land, where the danger of erosion was not immediate, but horses, cattle, sheep, and goats climbed the slopes and destroyed the fragile network of plants and their roots just where the danger of erosion was the greatest. Arroyos and barrancas began to scar the slopes, and trees encroached on the denuded savannas, and the weeds and coarser grasses spread in the steppes. The Europeans and their animals changed the rules of the battle for the survival of the fittest.[114]

Over a period of generations the civilizations of the Americas had accumulated immense treasures of gold and silver, which the conquistadors squandered in a few years. Over the millennia the grasslands of America had been accumulating immense riches in loam, plant and animal life, visible and invisible organisms. The squandering of those riches was already evident in the lifetime of Las Casas. He remarked that there had been a palatable grass, a fine thatch, which he had known as a young man in Española, but which had disappeared—destroyed, he guessed, by the rapidly in-

creasing livestock herds. In the 1570s López de Velasco remarked that the pastures of that island were diminishing in
size as the guava trees encroached along their edges. The
disappearance of the Arawak farmers, who had worked constantly to keep the jungle out of their gardens, was probably
also a factor in this case. By the 1580s overgrazing in Mexico
was becoming apparent, and Father Alonso Ponce saw cattle
starving in certain areas. Today the presence of large numbers of palmettos or scrub palms in the regions of Mexico
where the sheep once grazed in open grasslands is probably
due to the fact that the sheep destroyed the other, more
palatable plants. Cattle do not crop their grass quite so
closely as sheep, but when kept in large herds they have a
deleterious affect on the land. The coastal savanna of Sinaloa
was giving way to scrub growth within a century of the fall
of Tenochtitlán.[115]

The history of this phenomenon is best known for Mexico,
but there is sufficient evidence to suggest that a similar sequence of events—expansion of livestock herds and then decline in the size and quality of the grasslands—occurred elsewhere, or at least began to occur elsewhere in the Americas
in the sixteenth and seventeenth centuries. The accounts of
the earliest colonists indicate that the savannas of Central
America today are much smaller than they were during
Balboa's lifetime. (Here the decline in Indian population was
probably more important than the spread of livestock.) No
number of animals could bring the forest to the steppes of
Río de la Plata, but in the 1830s Darwin found scores, perhaps hundreds, of square miles of Uruguay impenetrable because they were overgrown with the prickly Old World
cardoon (*Cynara cardunculus*). "I doubt," he said, "whether
any case is on record of an invasion on so grand a scale
of one plant over the aborigines." Usually such invasions are
so successful only if the original ecology of the area has been
shattered—as, for instance, by widespread overgrazing. As

for the llanos, no one claims that they are today what they once were, when the seasonal floods were less violent because the ground cover was still thick enough to keep the water from spilling precipitously into the rivers, and the colts could run for hundreds of miles shoulder-deep in the fresh grass at the end of the wet season.[116]

The awesome initial increase of the herds lasted only a few score years in any given area. There were many factors which slowed the fantastic increase: indiscriminate slaughter of the livestock by Spaniard and Indian alike; wild dogs, other predators, insects, and pathogenic organisms coming in from elsewhere or adapting themselves to European animals as sources of food and as hosts. But the most important reason is probably this: when the hoarded riches of the grasslands were gone, the increase of the herds halted or proceeded at a pace now more arithmetical than geometrical. Martin Eriques reported from Mexico in 1574 that the "Cattle are no longer increasing rapidly; previously, a cow would drop her first calf within two years, for the land was virgin and there were many fertile pastures. Now a cow does not calve before three or four years."[117]

This wild oscillation of the balance of nature happens again whenever an area previously isolated is opened to the rest of the world. But possibly it will never be repeated in as spectacular a fashion as in the Americas in the first post-Columbian century, not unless there is, one day, an exchange of life forms between planets.

NOTES

1. Bernabé Cobo, *Obras*, 1:420.

2. Jean de Léry, *Journal de Bord de Jean de Léry,* ed. M. R. Mayeux, 52–53; Joseph de Acosta, *The Natural and Moral History of the Indies,* 1:233.

3. Acosta, *The Natural and Moral History,* 169, 232; Juan López de Velasco, *Geografía y Descriptión Universidad de las Indias,*

114 | THE COLUMBIAN EXCHANGE

39, 40, 47, 98; Gonzalo Fernández Oviedo y Valdés, *Natural History of the West Indies*, trans. Sterling A. Stoudemire, 15, 17.

4. Caio Prado, Jr., *The Colonial Background of Modern Brazil*, trans. Suzette Macedo, 191; Samuel Purchas, ed. *Hakluytus Posthumus or Purchas His Pilgrimes*, 14:550; López de Velasco, *Geografía*, 566; Pero de Magalhães, *The Histories of Brazil*, trans. John B. Stetson, 2:158–159; André Thevet, *The New Founde Worlde, or Antarctike*, trans. Thomas Hacket, 92r.

5. Richard Hakluyt, ed., *The Principal Navigations, Voyages, Traffiques and Discoveries of the English Nation*, 9:391; Jorge Juan and Antonio de Ulloa, *A Voyage to South America*, trans. John Adams, 33. The Spanish never learned to like maize as well as did the English of the thirteen colonies: see Peter Kalm, "Peter Kalm's Description of Maize, How It is Planted and Cultivated in North America, Together with the Many Uses of This Crop Plant," trans. Esther L. Larsen, 3.

6. Marcos Jiménez de la Espada, ed., *Relaciones Geograficas de Indias–Perú*, 1:382; Pedro de Cieza de León, *The Incas of Pedro de Cieza de León*, 271.

7. Percy W. Bidwell and John I. Falconer, *History of Agriculture in the Northern United States, 1620–1860*, 97–98.

8. Acosta, *Natural and Moral History*, 1:265.

9. Christopher Columbus, *Journals and Other Documents on the Life of Christopher Columbus*, trans. Samuel Eliot Morrison, 143; Ferdinand Columbus, *The Life of the Admiral Christopher Columbus by His Son Ferdinand*, trans. Benjamin Keen, 127.

10. Purchas, *Hakluytus Posthumus*, 14:440; Girolamo Benzoni, *History of the New World*, trans. W. H. Smyth, 90–91.

11. Oviedo, *Natural History*, 100, 102; Cobo, *Obras*, 1:421.

12. Noel Deerr, *The History of Sugar*, 1:115–133; Mervyn Ratekin, "The Early Sugar Industry in Española," 1–14.

13. Cobo, *Obras*, 1:405–406; François Chevalier, *Land and Society in Colonial Mexico*, trans. Alvin Eustis, 74; Antonio Vazquez de Espinosa, *Compendium and Description of the West Indies*, trans. Charles Upson Clark, 41, 42, 173, 221, 320–321, 323, 338, 390, 455, 471, 497, 553, 597, 601, 613, 621, 643, 683, 688, 731.

14. Deerr, *History of Sugar*, 1:102–104.

15. Arthur P. Whitaker, "The Spanish Contribution to American Agriculture," 4; Hakluyt, *Navigations*, 9:357; Chevalier, *Land and Society*, 50, 51, 59, 60, 61; Charles Gibson, *The Aztecs Under Spanish Rule*, 322, 324.

16. Cobo, *Obras*, 1:407; Emilio Romero, *Historia Económica*

del Perú, 98; Cieza de León, *Incas*, 18, 42, 97, 317, 350; Purchas, *Hakluytus Posthumus*, 14:531.

17. Thomas Gage, *A New Survey of the West Indies, 1648*, 219–220.

18. Henry Steele Commager and Elmo Giordanetti, eds., *Was America a Mistake? An Eighteenth Century Controversy*, 30.

19. Purchas, *Hakluytus Posthumus*, 14:439.

20. Romero, *Historia Económica*, 123–125; Acosta, *Natural and Moral History*, 1:168, 267; Cieza de León, *Incas*, 43, Jiménez de la Espada, *Relaciones Geograficas*, 1:176, 251, 348, 394, 2:48, 49, 57, 287, 294–295; Julian H. Steward, ed., *Handbook of South American Indians*, 2:356–357.

21. Vazquez de Espinosa, *Compendium and Description*, 678, 733; Purchas, *Hakluytus Posthumus*, 14:539, 546–547; Emilio A. Coni, "La Agriculture, Ganadería e Industrias Hasta el Virreinato," 4:364–365.

22. Cobo, *Obras*, 1:393–395; Purchas, *Hakluytus Posthumus*, 14:464, 522; Vazquez de Espinosa, *Compendium and Description*, 171, 390, 394, 426–427, 454–455, 471, 495, 503, 512, 518, 520, 727; López de Velasco, *Geografía*, 516.

23. Edgar Anderson, *Plants, Man and Life*, 8, 12; Bidwell and Falconer, *History of Agriculture*, 19–20, 159–160; Henry N. Ridley, *The Dispersal of Plants Throughout the World*, 638; William L. Thomas, Jr., ed., *Man's Role in Changing the Face of the Earth*, 730–731.

24. Kalm, "Description of Maize," 102; Alonso de Zorita, *Life and Labor in Ancient Mexico*, trans. Benjamin Keen, 251; Charles Gibson, *Spain in America*, 119; Steward, *Handbook*, 2:354, 357, 358; Jiménez de la Espada, *Relaciones Georgraficas*, 2:277; Homer Aschmann, "The Head of the Colorado Delta," 251.

25. Frederick E. Zeuner, *A History of Domesticated Animals*, 436–439; Carl O. Sauer, *The Early Spanish Main*, 59, 71, 115.

26. Sauer, *The Early Spanish Main*, 193–194.

27. Ibid., 59; F. Columbus, *Life of the Admiral*, 109; C. Columbus, *Journals*, 217.

28. C. Columbus, *Journals*, 217; F. Columbus, *Life of the Admiral*, 209–210; Sauer, *Early Spanish Main*, 189.

29. F. Columbus, *Life of the Admiral*, 194; Jiménez de la Espada, ed., *Relaciones Geograficas*, 1:11.

30. Alan Burns, *History of the British West Indies*, 292; Clarence H. Haring, *The Buccaneers in the West Indies in the XVIII Century*, 57.

31. Cobo, *Obras*, 1:382; Jiménez de la Espada, *Relaciones Geograficas*, 1:11; Oviedo, *Natural History*, 10–11.

32. Hakluyt, *Navigations*, 11:238; Purchas, *Hakluytus Posthumus*, 14:454; Vazquez de Espinosa, *Compendium and Description*, 119; John J. Johnson, "The Introduction of the Horse Into the Western Hemisphere," 600.

33. Quoted in Richard J. Morrisey, "Colonial Agriculture in New Spain," 26.

34. Sauer, *Early Spanish Main*, 189; Bidwell and Falconer, *History of Agriculture*, 31. A similar story can be told of the English swine in seventeenth-century New England.

35. Quoted in Madaline W. Nichols, "The Spanish Horse of the Pampas," 125.

36. Hakluyt, *Navigations*, 8:63; Purchas, *Hakluytus Posthumus*, 19:23; Bryan Edwards, *The History, Civil and Commercial, of the British West Indies*, 317; Burns, *History of the British West Indies*, 115.

37. Sauer, *Early Spanish Main*, 189; Frederick W. Hodge and Theodore H. Lewis, eds., *Spanish Explorers in the Southern United States, 1528–1543*, 171, 235; John J. Johnson, "The Spanish Horse in Peru Before 1550," 32.

38. Chevalier, *Land and Society*, 84–85; Cobo, *Obras*, 1:385; Benzoni, *History of the New World*, 252; Romero, *Historia Económica*, 98–99.

39. Purchas, *Hakluytus Posthumus*, 14:500.

40. Prado, *Modern Brazil*, 231–232; Cobo, *Obras*, 1:386; Vazquez de Espinosa, *Compendium and Description*, 20, 118, 746; Oviedo, *Natural History*, 50; Ramon Paez, *Wild Scenes of South America or, Life in the Llanos of Venezuela*, 143; Acosta, *Natural and Moral History*, 1:16.

41. Charles J. Bishko, "The Peninsular Background of Latin-American Cattle Ranching," 507.

42. The Moors taught the Spanish more than a little about horses: Garcilaso de la Vega recorded that Peru was won *a la gineta*, which is to say, by men riding with short stirrups in the style of the Muslims. Quoted in R. B. Cunningham Graham, *The Horses of the Conquest*, 18.

43. Johnson, "Introduction of the Horse," 589.

44. Ibid., 589, 592, 593, 594, 597–598.

45. C. Columbus, *Journals*, 241; F. Columbus, *Life of the Admiral*, 129; Johnson, "Introduction of the Horse," 599; Cobo, *Obras*, 1:379.

46. Graham, *Horses*, 55ff, 68; Johnson, *Greater America*, 27.

47. Cobo, *Obras*, 1:382.

48. Graham, *Conquest*, 136; López de Velasco, *Geografía*, 138–148; Antonio de Herrera Tordesillas, *Historia General de los Hechos de los Castellanos en las Islas y Tierra Firme del mar Océano*, 1:42ff. The evidence of the last two sources is strictly negative.

49. Chevalier, *Land and Society*, 85, 94; J. Frank Dobie, *The Mustangs*, 96; Miguel de Cervantes Saavedra, *Don Quixote*, trans. Samuel Putman, 571.

50. Dobie, *The Mustangs*, 96, 100, 108; Gibson, *Spain in America*, 192–193.

51. Purchas, *Hakluytus Posthumus*, 14:500; Magalhães, *Brazil*, 2:150.

52. Johnson, "Spanish Horse in Peru," 25, 33; Cobo, *Obras*, 1:382.

53. López de Velasco, *Geografía*, 516, 531–532; Cobo, *Obras*, 1:382; Vazquez de Espinosa, *Compendium and Description*, 675; Coni, "La Agricultura," 4:360; Julio V. González, *Historia Argentina*, vol. 1, *La Era Colonial*, 127; Harris Warren, *Paraguay, An Informal History*, 77, 127–128.

54. Herrera, *Historia General*, 1:183; Nichols, "Spanish Horse," 119–129.

55. Vazquez de Espinosa, *Compendium and Description*, 675, 694; Hakluyt, *Navigations*, 11:253.

56. Cobo, *Obras*, 1:382.

57. Hakluyt, *Navigations*, 9:357.

58. Chevalier, *Land and Society*, 107; Cobo, *Obras*, 1:383; Vazquez de Espinosa, *Compendium and Description*, 625.

59. Bishko, "Peninsular Background," 494, 497–498.

60. Ibid., 500; Oviedo, *Natural History*, 11; Acosta, *Natural and Moral History*, 1:62–63, 271; Ratekin, "Early Sugar Industry," 13. See also Benzoni, *History of the New World*, 92; López de Velasco, *Geografía*, 98, 111, 120, 127, 137; Purchas, *Hakluytus Posthumus*, 14:440, 16:91; Vazquez de Espinosa, *Compendium and Description*, 41, 47; Hakluyt, *Navigations*, 11:239; Morrisey, "Colonial Agriculture," 25; Dolores Mendez Nadal and Hugo W. Alberts, "The Early History of Livestock and Pastures in Puerto Rico," 61–64.

61. Donald D. Brand, "The Early History of the Range Cattle Business in Northern Mexico," 132–133; Chevalier, *Land and Society*, 85, 92; Hakluyt, *Navigations*, 9:361–362.

118 | THE COLUMBIAN EXCHANGE

62. Chevalier, *Land and Society*, 63, 92, 93, 94; Brand, "Range Cattle Industry," 134.

63. Acosta, *Natural and Moral History*, 1:271.

64. J. Frank Dobie, "The First Cattle in Texas and the Southwest Progenitors of the Longhorns," 181–182.

65. J. H. Parry and P. M. Sherlock, *A Short History of the West Indies*, 86; Vazquez de Espinosa, *Compendium and Description*, 244, 314; López de Velasco, *Geografía*, 358; Purchas, *Haklutus Posthumus*, 14:487, 490, 494.

66. Taylor M. Harrell, "The Development of the Venezuelan Llanos in the Sixteenth Century," 1–5, 59, 65, 70, 72, 162, 168, 172–172, 197; C. Langdon White, "Cattle Raising: A Way of Life in the Venezuelan Llanos," 123.

67. Paez, *Wild Scenes*, 74ff, 280; Alexander Walker, *Columbia: Being a Geographical, Statistical, Agricultural, Commercial and Political Account of that Country*, 2:154–156; Purchas, *Hakluytus Posthumus*, 14:455; Vazquez de Espinosa, *Compendium and Description*, 91; Eduardo Arcila Farias, *Económica Colonial de Venezuela*, 77–78.

68. Rollie E. Poppino, "Cattle Industry in Colonial Brazil," 219–226; Magalhães, *Histories*, 2:150; Purchas, *Hakluytus Posthumus*, 16:500.

69. Oviedo, *Natural History*, 79; Carl L. Johannessen, *Savannas of Interior Honduras*, 36–37; López de Velasco, *Geografía*, 350, 359, 383; Purchas, *Hakluytus Posthumus*, 14:498; Vazquez de Espinosa, *Compendium and Description*, 205, 220–221, 227, 351, 376, 633, 644; Romero, *Historia Económica*, 99, 118; Jiménez de la Espada, ed., *Relaciones Geograficas*, 2:213.

70. López de Velasco, *Geografía*, 516–533; Vazquez de Espinosa, *Compendium and Description*, 733.

71. Vazquez de Espinosa, *Compendium and Description*, 647, 675, 690; González, *Historia Argentina*, 1:131–133.

72. Vazquez de Espinosa, *Compendium and Description*, 691; Ricardo Levene, *A History of Argentina*, trans. William S. Robertson, 117.

73. Cobo, *Obras*, 1:386; López de Velasco, *Geografía*, 20. Also see Bidwell and Falconer, *History of Agriculture*, 28, for a similar analysis of the early history of sheep in New England.

74. Chevalier, *Land and Society*, 107; Juan and de Ulloa, *Voyage*, 223; Vazquez de Espinosa, *Compendium and Description*, 541.

75. Vazquez de Espinosa, *Compendium and Description*, 133, 135, 136, 173, 363, 368, 393, 400, 475, 491, 493, 616, 732, 746; William H. Dusenberry, "Woolen Manufacture in Sixteenth-Century New Spain," 223–234.

76. Edward N. Wentworth, *America's Sheep Trails*, 23; Dusenberry, "Woolen Manufacture," 223; Whitaker, "Spanish Contribution," 4–5.

77. Morrisey, "Colonial Agriculture," 27; Purchas, *Hakluytus Posthumus*, 14:469; Chevalier, *Land and Society*, 95; Dobie, "Cattle in Texas," 173.

78. Cobo, *Obras*, 1:386; Jiménez de la Espada, *Relaciones Geograficas*, 2:213.

79. Romero, *Historia Económica*, 117; Cobo, *Obras*, 1:367.

80. Romero, *Historia Económica*, 118; Cobo, *Obras*, 1:387; Purchas, *Hakluytus Posthumus*, 14:533; López de Velasco, *Geografía*, 20; Acosta, *Natural and Moral History*, 1:270.

81. Vazquez de Espinosa, *Compendium and Description*, 733; Magalhães, *Histories*, 2:150; Purchas, *Hakluytus Posthumus*, 16:500; Prado, *Colonial History*, 232; Carlos Pereyra, *La Obra de España en America*, 171.

82. Oviedo, *Natural History*, 11; López de Velasco, *Geografía*, 20–21; Acosta, *Natural and Moral History*, 1:272; Vazquez de Espinosa, *Compendium and Description*, 667; Cobo, *Obras*, 1:388–389; Purchas, *Hakluytus Posthumus*, 16:92.

83. Vazquez de Espinosa, *Compendium and Description*, 49, 117–118, 396, 530, 727, 733, 748; Oviedo, *Natural History*, 11; Cobo, *Obras*, 1:387–388, 390; Charles Darwin, *The Voyage of the Beagle*, 120.

84. Cobo, *Obras*, 1:390–391, 420; Purchas, *Hakluytus Posthumus*, 16:500–501; F. Columbus, *Life of the Admiral*, 234; Benzoni, *History of the New World*, 252; Steward, *Handbook*, 6:394; Sauer, *Early Spanish Main*, 212.

85. Cobo, *Obras*, 384; Hakluyt, *Navigations*, 9:390–391; Acosta, *Natural and Moral History*, 1:272; Vazquez de Espinosa, *Compendium and Description*, 678; George Laycock, *The Alien Animals*, 149–154. It may be of interest to the reader to know that many still are wild. As of 1957 about 13,000 wild burros existed in the United States.

86. Acosta, *Natural and Moral History*, 1:272; Cobo, *Obras*, 1:420–421; Frank Lammons, "Operation Camel, An Experiment in Animal Transportation, 1857–1860," 20–50.

87. Vazquez de Espinosa, *Compendium and Description*, 339; "Rats," *Encyclopaedia Britannica*, 18:989–990; Hans Zinsser, *Rats, Lice and History*, 141–158.

88. Cobo, *Obras*, 1:350–351.

89. Purchas, *Hakluytus Posthumus*, 19:180–182.

90. Herrera, *Historia General*, 2:34–35.

91. Cobo, *Obras*, 1:383; Gibson, *Aztecs Under Spanish Rule*, 345–346; Gibson, *Spain in America*, 193–194.

92. Lesley Byrd Simpson, *Exploitation of Land in Central Mexico in the Sixteenth Century*, frontispiece; Chevalier, *Land and Society*, 94; Zorita, *Life and Labor*, 9, 109, 268–271; Steward, *Handbook*, 2:23.

93. Steward, *Handbook*, 1:265; Gibson, *Spain in America*, 194.

94. Gibson, *Spain in America*, 193; Steward, *Handbook*, 1:192; González, *Historia Argentina*, 1:69–70; Vazquez de Espinosa, *Compendium and Description*, 647.

95. López de Velasco, *Geografía*, 148; Steward, *Handbook*, 4:20, 369, 371; Gustaf Bolinder, *Indians on Horseback*, 42, 94.

96. Bolinder, *Indians*, 26; Walker, *Columbia*, 1:545–551.

97. Steward, *Handbook*, 2:427; Robert M. Denhardt, "The Role of the Horse in the Social History of Early California," 17; Dobie, *Mustangs*, 25.

98. González, *Historia Argentina*, 1:68–70; Steward, *Handbook*, 1:250, 2:756, 763–764; Alfred J. Tapson, "Indian Warfare on the Pampa During the Colonial Period," 5.

99. Ruth M. Underhill, *Red Man's America*, 153; Tapson, "Indian Warfare," 5; Walter P. Webb, *The Great Plains*, 65.

100. John C. Ewers, *The Horse in Blackfoot Indian Culture with Comparative Material from Other Western Tribes*, 308.

101. Steward, *Handbook*, 1:203.

102. Ewers, *Horse in Blackfoot Indian Culture*, 109–110; Clark Wissler, "The Influence of the Horse in the Development of Plains Culture," 17.

103. Chevalier, *Land and Society*, 103; Harold E. Driver, ed., *The Americas on the Eve of Discovery*, 19; Jack D. Forbes, *Apache, Navaho and Spaniard*, 167, 191; Edward H. Spicer, *Cycles of Conquest*, 547; Ewers, *Horse in Blackfoot Indian Culture*, 3.

104. Ewers, *Horse in Blackfoot Indian Culture*, 4, Wissler, "Influence of the Horse," 5–6.

105. Richard M. Morse, ed., *The Bandeirantes*, 110.

106. Steward, *Handbook*, 1:201–203, 312; Tadeo Haenke, *Viaje Por el Virreinato del Río de la Plata*, 57; R. B. Cunningham Graham, *Conquest of the River Plate*, 127.

107. Steward, *Handbook*, 2:764.

108. Tapson, "Indian Warfare" 1, 5, 11; Steward, *Handbook*, 1:14–15, 139; 2:763–764; Nichols, "Spanish Horse," 129.

109. Parry and Sherlock, *West Indies*, 148–149. It was the need for a fast growing plant that would produce food in quantity for

slaves of the British West Indian plantations that sent Captain Bligh and H.M.S. *Bounty* off to Tahiti to collect breadfruit plants in 1787.

110. *Food Composition Tables for Internation Use: Food and Agricultural Organization Nutritional Studies No. 3*, 9, 10; Steward, *Handbook,* 2:54, 356.

111. Prado, *Colonial Background,* 214.

112. Poppino, "Cattle Industry," 246.

113. Morrisey, "Colonial Agriculture," 24.

114. Johannessen, *Savannas,* 109–111; Harrell, "Venezuelan Llanos," 24; Sauer, *Early Spanish Main,* 287–288.

115. Sauer, *Early Spanish Main,* 156; López de Velasco, *Geografía,* 98; Simpson, *Exploitation of Land,* 22–23; Brand, "Range Cattle Industry," 138. Also see Sherburne F. Cook, *The Historical Demography and Ecology of Teotlalpán* and *Soil Erosion and Population in Central Mexico.*

116. Sauer, *Early Spanish Main,* 285–288; Johannessen, *Savannas,* 109–111; White, "Cattle Raising," 127–128; Darwin, *Voyage of the Beagle,* 119–120.

117. Chevalier, *Land and Society,* 102, 104–105. See also Mendez Nadal and Alberts, "Livestock and Pastures," 62.

The Early History of Syphilis: A Reappraisal 4

The New World gave much in return for what it received from the Old World. In the writings of Desiderius Erasmus, one can find mention of nearly every significant figure, event, crusade, fad, folly, and misery of the decades around 1500. Of all the miseries visited upon Europe in his lifetime, Erasmus judged few more horrible than the French disease, or syphilis. He reckoned no malady more contagious, more terrible for its victims, or more difficult to cure . . . or more fashionable! "It's a most presumptuous pox," exclaims one of the characters in the *Colloquies*. "In a showdown, it wouldn't yield to leprosy, elephantiasis, ringworm, gout, or sycosis."[1]

The men and women of Erasmus's generation were the first Europeans to know syphilis, or so they said, at least. The pox, as the English called it, had struck like a thunderbolt in the very last years of the fifteenth century. But unlike most diseases that appear with such abruptness, it did not fill up the graveyards and then go away, to come again some other day or perhaps never. Syphilis settled down and became a permanent factor in human existence.

122

Syphilis has a special fascination for the historian because, of all mankind's most important maladies, it is the most uniquely "historical." The beginnings of most diseases lie beyond man's earliest rememberings. Syphilis, on the other hand, has a beginning. Many men, since the last decade of the fifteenth century, have insisted that they knew almost exactly when syphilis appeared on the world stage, and even where it came from. "In the yere of Chryst 1493 or there aboute," wrote Ulrich von Hutten, one of Erasmus's correspondents, "this most foule and most grevous dysease beganne to sprede amonge the people." Another contemporary, Ruy Díaz de Isla, agreed that 1493 was the year and went on to say that "the disease had its origin and birth from always in the island which is now named Española." Columbus had brought it back, along with samples of maize and other American curiosities.[2]

The most popular theory of the origin of syphilis since the third decade of the sixteenth century has been the Columbian theory, but popularity has not saved it from disputation. In fact, the matter of the origin of syphilis is doubtlessly the most controversial subject in all medical historiography. It would take months of labor merely to assemble a full bibliography of the subject.

Until the most recent decades there were only two widely accepted views of the provenance of syphilis: the Columbian theory and its antithesis, which stated that syphilis was present in the Old World long before 1493. Now the Unitarian theory has appeared, which postulates that venereal syphilis is but one syndrome of a multi-faceted world-wide disease, treponematosis. But before we examine this newest challenge to the veracity of Ulrich von Hutten and Díaz de Isla and the other Columbians, let us deal with the older argument: was venereal syphilis present on both sides of the Atlantic in 1492 or only on the American?

The documentary evidence for the Old World seems clear.

No unequivocal description of syphilis in any pre-Columbian literature of the Old World has ever been discovered. Description of diseases which might be the pox have been uncovered, but they might also be descriptions of leprosy, scabies, or something else. It is especially noteworthy that, in spite of Chinese worship of the ancients and the tradition of quoting from the classics whenever possible, no Chinese writer has ever described syphilis as being mentioned in ancient literature. Galen and Avicenna and other medical writers of ancient and medieval times knew nothing of germ theory or antibiotics, but they were accomplished clinicians and could describe the surface symptoms of a disease as well as any modern physician. If a disease is not mentioned in their writings, we may assume that it had a different character in their time or that they never saw it.[3] This assumption is particularly safe when we are searching for mention of a disease which spreads as widely as syphilis does in nearly every society exposed to it.

The physicians, surgeons, and laymen of the Old World who wrote about venereal syphilis in the sixteenth century recorded, with few exceptions, that it was a new malady; and we have no reason to believe they were all mistaken. From Díaz de Isla to Wan Ki—Spaniards, Germans, Italians, Egyptians, Persians, Indians, Chinese, and Japanese—agreed that they had never seen the pox before.[4] It is very unlikely that they were all mistaken on the same subject at the same time.

Even if no direct statements on the newness of syphilis to the inhabitants of the Old World existed, there is enough linguistic evidence to support that contention. The variety of names given it and the fact that they almost always indicate that it was thought of as a foreign import are strong evidence for its newness. Italians called it the French disease, which proved to be the most popular title; the French called it the disease of Naples; the English called it the French disease, the Bordeaux disease, or the Spanish disease; Poles called it the German disease; Russians called it the Polish disease; and so on. Middle Easterners called it the European pustules; Indians called it the disease of the Franks (western Europeans). Chinese called it the ulcer of Canton, that port being their chief point of contact with the west. The Japanese called it Tang sore, Tang referring to China; or, more to the point, the disease of the Portuguese. A full list of the early names for syphilis covers several pages, and it was not until the nineteenth century that Girolamo Fracastoro's word, "syphilis," minted in the 1520s, became standard throughout the world.[5]

Another indication of the abrupt appearance of the pox is the malignancy of the disease in the years immediately after its initial recognition in Europe. The classic course of a new disease is rapid spread and extreme virulence, followed by a lessening of the malady's deadliness. The most susceptible members of the human population are eliminated by death, as are the most virulent strains of the germ, in that they kill off their hosts before transmission to other hosts occurs. The records of the late fifteenth and early sixteenth centuries are full of lamentations on the rapid spread of syphilis and the horrible effects of the malady, which often occurred within a short time after the initial infection: widespread rashes and ulcers, often extending into the mouth and throat; severe fevers and bone pains; and often early death. The latter is a very rare phenomenon in the initial stages of the disease today, and most who do die of syphilis have resisted the disease successfully for many years. Ulrich von Hutten's description of syphilis in the first years after its appearance indicates a marked contrast between its nature then and its "mildness" today:

> There were byles, sharpe, and standing out, hauying the similitude and quantite of acornes, from which came so foule humours, and so great stenche, that who so ever ones smelled it, thought

hym selfe to be enfect. The colour of these pusshes [pustules] was derke grene, and the slight therof was more grevous unto the pacient then the peyne it selfe: and yet their peynes were as thoughe they hadde lyen in fire.

This extreme manifestation of the disease, he tells us, "tarryed not long above the vii yere. But the infyrmytie that came after, which remayneth yet is nothynge so fylthy."[6]

The most convincing of all evidence for the abrupt arrival of the French disease in the Old World in approximately 1500 is the physical remains, the bones of the long dead. No one has ever unearthed pre-Columbian bones in the Old World which display unequivocal signs of syphilitic damage. Elliott Smith, the famous paleopathologist, tells us that "after examining something like 30,000 bodies of ancient Egyptians and Nubians representing every period of the history of the last sixty centuries and from every part of the country, it can be stated quite confidently that no trace whatever, even suggesting syphilitic injuries to bones or teeth, was revealed in Egypt before modern times." It is nearly certain that if syphilis were present in pre-Columbian Europe, and likely that if it were present in any of the high civilizations of the Old World engaged in long-distance commerce before 1493, one of the bodies examined by Smith would have shown syphilitic lesions.[7]

Several anti-Columbian theorists have brushed aside all the above arguments by hypothesizing that syphilis had existed in the Old World prior to the 1490s, but in a *mild* form. Then, in the 1490s the causative organism mutated into the deadly *Treponema pallidum,* and syphilis began to affect the deep body structures and became a killer. This hypothesis cannot be disproved and it comfortably fits all the facts, but it cannot be proved, either. Microorganisms simply do not keep diaries, so the only way we can "prove" the validity of the mutation theory is by the process of elimination. We must disprove all the other hypotheses, which brings us to a direct consideration of the Columbian theory.

Where did syphilis come from? If it came from America, then we may be nearly certain that it came in 1493 or shortly after. Let us consider the physical evidence first. Is there a contrast here between the Old and New Worlds? The answer becomes more and more unequivocally affirmative as the archeologists and paleopathologists disinter from American soil an increasing number of pre-Columbian human bones displaying what is almost surely syphilitic damage. According to one researcher, the deformation of the forehead bones in some of these skeletons is as unambiguously syphilitic in origin as a positive Wassermann reaction.[8]

Documentary evidence supporting the Columbian theory is quite impressive: some of the most trustworthy physicians and historians of the sixteenth century insisted that Columbus must bear the blame for bringing the pox to Europe. But the certainty with which they spoke must be weighed against the fact that none of them insisted on the American origin of syphilis until a generation after the first Columbian voyages. One would think that if a relationship existed between the sensational discovery of the New World and the sensational new disease, that relationship would have been emphasized over and over again in the 1490s and early 1500s. No mention of the connection between the two, however, appears until guaiacum, a decoction of a West Indian wood, became widely popular as a sure cure for the French disease. According to the logic of the time, God always arranges for a disease and its remedy to originate in the same locality. "Our Lorde GOD would from whence this euill of the Poxe came, from thence would come the remedy for them." To reverse the logic, if American guaiacum cured syphilis, then syphilis must be American. What could be more sensible? Many historians have judged, therefore, that the source of the Columbian theory is guaiacum, and not the actual origin of syphilis in the West Indies.[9]

An illustration from the sixteenth-century *Lienzo de Tlaxcala, a picture story of the conquest of Mexico. The significance of the horses in the Spaniards' success is obvious.*

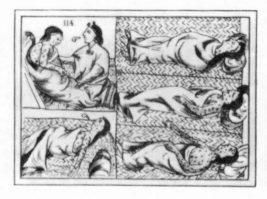

Smallpox strikes the Indians of Mexico during the Cortés invasion. The illustration is from Fray Bernardino de Sahagun's sixteenth-century General History of the Things of New Spain.

The preparation and use of guaiacum in the treatment of syphilis, from an engraving by Jan Van der Straet. This illustration of a sickroom interior shows the stages in the preparation of an infusion for the treatment. Impression in the Wellcome Institute of the History of Medicine.

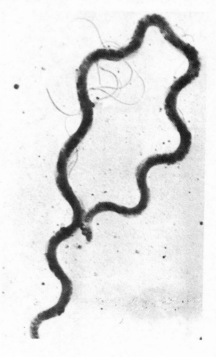

An electron photomicrograph of Treponema pallidum, *the spirochete that causes veneral syphilis.*

Albrecht Durer's The Syphilitic *(1496).*

A figure of maize made near the middle of the sixteenth century. It illustrates the confused understanding of the plant at that time. Reprinted with permission of The Macmillan Company, from Indian Corn in Old America *by Paul Weatherwax. Copyright 1954 by The Macmillan Company.*

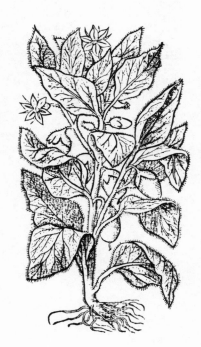

The tomato plant. From Mattheoli's Commentaires *(1579).*

*Slaves packed on a ship for the voyage to America. From
Thomas Clarkson's* Abstract of Evidence *(1791).*

The Immigrants, *a nineteenth-century rendition of the difficult conditions of transatlantic migration.*

Van Gogh's The Potato Eaters *illustrates the importance of the plant in the diet of the lower classes.*
COURTESY AMSTERDAM, VAN GOGH MUSEUM (VINCENT VAN GOGH FOUNDATION)

Indians of Incan times working in the potato fields. From Poma de Ayala's seventeenth-century work, Nueva Coronica y Buen Gobierno.

Portrait of John Gerard holding a leaf and flower of the potato plant. From the frontispiece of his Herbal *(1597).*

Irish famine sufferers searching for potatoes. From The Illustrated London News *(1597).*

An early European attempt to reconstruct the appearance of a buffalo from the accounts of those who had seen them in America. From André Thevet's Les Singularitéz de la France Antarctique, autrement Amerique *(1557).*

Even more discomforting for the Columbians is the fact that neither syphilis nor anything resembling it is mentioned at all in the documentation of the Columbian voyages written prior to the first epidemic of the pox in Europe. It certainly would have been advantageous to Columbus to omit any such mention from his reports, but it is strange that one of the other eyewitnesses did not do so. Nor do we find any contemporary reports of syphilis in Spain or Portugal in the months and years between the return of the ships of the 1492 and 1493 voyages to America and the first recorded epidemic of syphilis in Europe, which began in Italy in 1494 or 1495. Such reports do exist, but they were written years after the alleged events.

But we cannot be sure that syphilis was not prevalent simply because it is not mentioned in contemporary documents. The documentation is too sparse. For example, we know little or nothing about what happened aboard the *Pinta* on the first voyage, for she spent much of the time in the West Indies and the last half of the return trip far beyond the sight and knowledge of Columbus, the only chronicler of that voyage. Nor do we know much about the condition of the Indians—who may well have been latently syphilitic—brought back to Europe in 1493 and 1494. Furthermore, it was to the interest of many involved in Columbus's schemes, some in high places, to suppress negative reports about the New World. There may be an even simpler explanation for the absence of the mention of the pox from the early documentation. Many of the documents of this period have been lost forever. Others undoubtedly still lie buried in European archives, unread for four hundred years.[10]

Let us examine the written evidence supporting the Columbian hypothesis. The first mention of Europeans with syphilis in the New World is found in the biography of Columbus by his son, Ferdinand. It is a work of immense value, but unfortunately we have only an Italian translation of it. The original Spanish version is lost, and we cannot be

sure that the Italian translation is absolutely accurate. Be
that as it may, Ferdinand tells us that when his father arrived
in Española on his 1498 voyage he found that "Part of the
people who had left were dead, and of the survivors more
than one hundred and sixty were sick with the French sickness." This unfortunately proves nothing beyond the fact that
the colonists were a very active lot, because syphilis was already widespread in Europe by 1498.

Also contained in this book is the "Relation of Fray
Ramon Concerning the Antiquities of the Indians, Which He,
knowing Their Language, Carefully Compiled by Order of
the Admiral," written, according to Ferdinand, in the mid-
1490s. This relation tells practically all we know of the
cosmogony of the Arawak people of Española. Their great
folk hero, according to the good friar, "had great pleasure"
with a woman, "but soon had to look for many bathhouses
in which to wash himself because he was full of those sores
that we call the French sickness." Humans are very slow to
change their folklore, and so it seems unlikely that the
Arawaks would have altered their legends so as to give a
new disease to their Achilles, their Beowulf, so soon after
the arrival of the Europeans.[11]

The two most important historians of the early Spanish
empire, Bartolomé de Las Casas and Gonzalo Fernández de
Oviedo y Valdés, both state that Columbus brought syphilis
back from America to Europe. Their accounts differ somewhat in detail, and taken together, are not clear as to which
of the first fleets returning from America first brought
syphilis to Europe. The difference in detail does not necessarily indicate a lack of veracity: such an importation would
be very difficult to pinpoint chronologically. Both Las Casas
and Oviedo were certainly qualified by personal experience
and access to those who sailed with Columbus to make their
statements on the origin of the pox. Las Casas was in Seville
in 1493 when Columbus came to that city with his report

on his discoveries and with his Indian captives. Las Casas's father and uncle sailed with Columbus in 1493, and he must have known many other participants in the early voyages, as well. Las Casas himself came to the New World in 1502, and spent most of the rest of his life working for and with the Indians.

Oviedo was attached to the Spanish court in the 1490s, and met Columbus even before his 1492 epochal voyage. Oviedo was quite friendly with the great explorer's sons and with members of the Pinzón family, which figured so importantly in the first voyages to America. A number of his friends, whom he asked to bring back detailed reports, sailed with Columbus in 1493. Oviedo was even on hand in Italy for the initial European syphilis epidemic, about which he wrote, "Many times in Italy I laughed, hearing the Italians speak of the French disease, and the French call it the disease of Naples; and in truth both would have had the name better, if they called it the disease of the Indies." In 1513 he sailed to the Indies, where he spent most of the rest of his life. No one can claim that Las Casas and Oviedo did not have full opportunity to know all there was to know about the alleged American origin of the pox.

Las Casas personally asked the Indians if they had known the disease before the coming of the Europeans, and was told, that they had indeed suffered from it beyond all memory. Both the historians report the medically significant fact that the disease was much less dangerous for the infected Indians than for the Spaniards, a contrast one would expect if the former race had had long contact with the malady and the latter none at all.[12]

The third charter member of the Columbian theory school was a physician, Ruy Díaz de Isla, who claimed in a book first published in 1539 that he had treated some of Columbus' men who had contracted syphilis in 1492 in America, and that he had observed its rapid spread through Barcelona.

He did not know what the disease was at the time, but later realized that he had been witness to the arrival of syphilis. He called it *Morbo Serpentino,* for, as the snake "is hideous, dangerous and terrible, so the malady is hideous, dangerous and terrible."

One must either accept Díaz's account and become a Columbian, or one must reject it completely. It is certain that he was no quack. He was one of the most accomplished clinicians of his time, and even his most vehement twentieth-century detractor, R. C. Holcomb, admitted that "he was the greatest syphilographer of his time. His historical errors do not affect my opinion of him as a surgeon in the slightest." Indeed, it took scientists immeasurably better equipped than Díaz four hundred years to properly appreciate his shrewd guess that a high fever, such as that caused by malaria, tends to arrest syphilis.[13]

At the present stage of research we have no documents specifically confirming what Díaz tells us. Perhaps one day we will. It is lucky that we even have his book, which apparently caused little stir when it first appeared. Then, in contrast, for instance, to the writings of Paracelsus, it almost completely disappeared from scholarly concern until Jean Astruc consulted it in the eighteenth century. Again it dropped out of sight, for all practical scholarly purposes, until rediscovered by Montejo y Robledo in the 1850s. It is a very rare book today, and but for microfilm, few researchers would ever have a chance to read it. All in all, the saga of Díaz's book is a very good object lesson for any who would place a great deal of confidence in negative evidence when dealing with the documentation of the sixteenth century.[14]

The only evidence we have which even tends to directly corroborate Diaz's statements was taken down a generation after the initial voyage to the West Indies, and pertains to the obscure death of the commander of the *Pinta,* Martín

Alonso Pinzón. In his original manuscript, but not in the published book, Díaz says that one of the seamen who returned from America in 1493 suffering from syphilis was "a pilot of Palos called Pinzón." At least two members of the Pinzón family of Palos sailed with Columbus in 1492, and all authorities agree that Martín Alonso died very shortly after his return to Spain. Díaz tells us that the ailing sailors attributed their new illness to "the tolls of sea, or other causes according as they appeared to each one." In testimony taken a generation later, witnesses of the return of the *Pinta* to Palos agree that Martín Alonso was sick upon arrival and that he died shortly after of an illness brought on by the exhaustion and hunger he had undergone during the voyage. This testimony corroborates in part what Díaz says. Even though he may have misinterpreted the facts, he did have them.[15]

The documentary evidence for the Columbian provenance of venereal syphilis is obviously shaky. We cannot say, moreover, that the evidence provided by the paleopathologists is utterly decisive, but when the two are combined—when archivists and gravediggers join hands to claim that America is the homeland of *Treponema pallidum*—it becomes very difficult to reject the Columbian theory. Or, at least, it would be very difficult to do so if the argument on the history of syphilis was still being fought over the same ground as it was a generation ago. But the scene of battle has changed. All the arguments, pro and con, touched on in this paper thus far may not be wrong so much as merely irrelevant!

Is venereal syphilis a separate and distinct disease, once endemic to only one part of the world, or is it merely a syndrome of a disease which has always been worldwide, but happens to have different symptoms and names in different areas? Those who accept the Unitarian theory, as it is called, claim that that which is called syphilis, when transmitted venereally, is really the same malady as the nonvenereal illnesses called yaws in the tropics, bejel in the Middle East, pinta in Central America, irkinja in Australia, and so on. The manner in which this ubiquitous disease, named "treponematosis" by the Unitarians, manifests itself in man is somewhat different in different areas, because of climatic and cultural differences, but it is all one disease. If this is true, then all the squabble about deformation of forehead bones here and not there, ulcers on the sex organs now and not then, and on and on, is completely irrelevant. As E. H. Hudson, the foremost champion of the Unitarian theory, puts it, "Since treponematosis was globally distributed in prehistoric times, it . . . is idle to speak of Columbus' sailors bringing syphilis to a syphilis-free Europe in 1493."[16]

Perhaps the best way to present the Unitarian theory is to summarize Hudson's version of that theory. His arguments are not accepted universally even by the Unitarians, but they will serve to introduce the reader to the basic ideas of the proponents of this hypothesis. The organism which causes treponematosis is an extremely delicate one. It needs the moisture and the warmth of the body of a host to survive for more than a few minutes, and normally it is carried by man alone among the animals.[17] Thus it is very sensitive to differences in climate and human habits, and, in its Darwinian adaptations to these differences, appears as "different" diseases. Hudson theorizes that man first acquired the treponema causing these maladies in moist, hot sub-Saharan Africa, where the climate allowed it to live on the surface of the body, many thousands of years ago. The disease was originally manifested as yaws, an infection which, initially, at least, affects only the surface layers of the body. Then, as man migrated into drier areas, the organism retreated into the bodies of its hosts, and became a kind of nonvenereal syphilis, a disease of childhood, transmitted by close contact under very unhygienic conditions. This manifestation is called bejel in the Middle East. As cities developed and the general level of civilization rose, more careful personal hygiene, cleaning of eating utensils, separation of sleeping individuals, and so on, robbed the treponemas of most of their avenues of transmission from human to human and threatened their existence everywhere on the surface of the bodies of their hosts. Therefore, they retreated even deeper into the human body, into the bones and arteries and nervous system, and utilized the only avenue of transmission left open to them by modern man: the one extremely intimate contact with another human which modern man has not given up and in which he indulges many times over, sexual intercourse. Venereal syphilis appeared.[18]

A great deal of scientific evidence has accumulated to support the Unitarian theory. The syndromes of the several "different" diseases of the trepanematosis group are not sharply contrasted one from the other. Rather, there seems to be a continuum of at least partial similarity from the surface lesions of pinta, on one extreme, to the deep body structure damage caused by venereal syphilis, on the other extreme. The recognition of these similarities is not new. Sixteenth-century Europeans in America were certainly acquainted with venereal syphilis, and may also have seen yaws among the Indians. The latter had a disease they called "pians," characterized by pustules and often, but not always, transmitted venereally. Some Europeans called it the French disease and some did not, even when Europeans ·contracted it through intercourse with Indian women. Thomas Syndeham, the great British physician of the seventeenth century, believed venereal syphilis to be a variation of yaws, brought to both Europe and America on the slave ships. In the book *Every Man His Own Doctor or Poor Planter's Physician,* popular in Britain's American colonies around 1730, the suggested cure for yaws is also recommended for syphilis, "because the Symptoms are much the same, [and] it is very probable, the one was the Graft of the other."[19]

The organisms which cause the various treponematoses have different names—*Treponema pallidum, Treponema pertenue, Treponema carateum*—but they cannot be differentiated under a microscope. The antibodies created within the body of the host by one treponema serve to immobilize the others, too, so acquired immunity to one of the treponematoses seems, in many, many cases, to confer immunity to all of them. All, or at least very many, of the victims react positively when given the Wassermann test, which was specifically created as a test for venereal syphilis alone. At present, the only way to differentiate between the several allegedly different treponemas is by infecting laboratory animals with them, and then checking the symptoms. The symptoms thus created are different, but by no means is the contrast a sharp one. And the symptomatic differences observed in one animal (e.g., rabbits) are not always identical to those found in another (e.g., hamsters).[20]

All this is very disconcerting for the Columbians, but not necessarily disastrous for their hypothesis. The scientific evidence certainly indicates a very close relationship between the various treponemas, but it has not been proved that they are all the same. The great majority of experts either withhold final decision on the matter or continue to consider them as separate kinds of organisms. Perhaps our current means of differing between these organisms are too crude, and one day soon a more discriminating test will be invented. After all, smallpox and cowpox are closely related maladies symptomatically, immunity to one is immunity to both, and the organisms that cause these diseases appear to be nearly identical under the electron microscope. But no one would claim that the two illnesses are the same.[21]

If we accept the Unitarian theory we have two possible explanations for the appearance of venereal syphilis in

Europe during the lifetime of Columbus. One, the practice of improved hygiene in the cities had risen to such a level as to bring about, by the process of elimination of the less adaptable treponemas, a venereal strain of treponematosis. This seems unlikely because it would have been a gradual process, and the contemporaries agreed upon the abrupt appearance of venereal syphilis. Two, in the 1490s the treponemas living in the bodies of Europeans suddenly mutated, producing a new and deadly version of an old disease. This explanation fits nearly all the facts we have, but, as said before, it is not susceptible to proof or disproof.

In fact, such is the paucity of evidence from the fifteenth and sixteenth centuries that the Unitarian theory is no more satisfactory than the Columbian. We simply do not know much, and may never know much about the world distribution of the treponemas in the 1490s. The field is nearly as wide open for theorizers today as in that terrible decade when many Europeans blamed the pox on the conjunction of Saturn and Mars and on "the unholsom blastes of the ayre."[22]

There are only two things of which we can be sure. One, the only pre-Columbian bones clearly displaying the lesions of treponematosis or one of that family of diseases are American. The infections which affect only the surface or viscera would, of course, leave no trace on bones, no matter how deadly the disease, but that does not necessarily prove that pinta did exist in the Old World in 1492. It only means that we do not know and perhaps never will. Two, several contemporaries did record the return of venereal syphilis with Columbus. Their testimony cannot be shrugged off. They may have been confused, but they were not fools or liars.

The Columbian theory is still viable. Even if it is unequivocally proved that all the treponematoses are one, the Columbians can simply claim that treponematosis was exclusively American in 1492. There is no unquestionable evidence that any of the treponematoses existed in the Old World in 1492. For instance, sub-Saharan Africa is usually thought of as the homeland of yaws, but we really do not know this as a fact. We know practically nothing about the medical situation in Africa in Renaissance times.[23]

It is not impossible that the organisms causing treponematosis arrived from America in the 1490s in mild or deadly form, and, breeding in the entirely new and very salubrious environment of European, Asian, and African bodies, evolved into both venereal and nonvenereal syphilis and yaws. If this is true, then Columbus ranks as a villain with the serpent of the Garden of Eden.

A less presumptuous theory is that the treponematoses were one single disease many thousands of years ago. Then, as man changed his environment and habits, and especially when he crossed the Bering Straits into the isolation of the Americas, the differing ecological conditions produced different types of treponematosis and, in time, closely related but different diseases.[24]

To illustrate how difficult it is to definitively solve the riddle of the origin of venereal syphilis, let us examine briefly the history of another disease carried from one hemisphere to the other. This disease affected plants, not people, and traveled from the Old to the New World, rather than vice versa. The chestnut trees of the United States are closely related to those of Asia. The American and Asian chestnuts are both often hosts to Endothia fungi native to their areas, and suffer no damage from those fungi. But in the 1890s the Asian variety, *Endothia parasitica,* arrived in the United States, and by the mid-1930s the American chestnut, which had been one of the dominant trees of the eastern deciduous forests—the tree beneath which Longfellow's smithy labored—was gone. Only a few examples of it remain in the United States.[25]

Imagine how difficult it would be to recreate the history of this epidemic if it had taken place four hundred years ago. Who could say with certainty that a given piece of disinterred wood was four hundred and fifty, four hundred, or only three hundred and fifty years old? Who could say with certainty that the tree which had produced this piece of wood had been exactly what kind of chestnut tree, which had died of exactly what kind of fungus? The ambiguities and possibilities for error are so many that even science can offer only tentative answers. We might find ourselves turning with at least equal confidence to the record of history. The men who lived four hundred years ago knew more about their world than we do.

The field is still wide open for those who wish to theorize about the origin of syphilis. It seems logical to believe that if deadly diseases crossed the Atlantic from east to west, then there must have also been a similar countercurrent. The most likely candidate for the role of America's answer to the Old World's smallpox is venereal syphilis. The theory of the origin of the treponematoses offered in this chapter squares with all Darwin tells us about evolution, and allows the American Indians and Columbus the dubious honor of incubating and transporting venereal syphilis. It is this hypothesis which, in the current state of medical and historical research, seems to hold the most promise as a vehicle for future inquiry and speculation.

Having finished with the polemics of syphilis, let us turn to the first century of its recorded history. By the fifteenth century, treponematosis had evolved into several related maladies in the desert-isolated jungles, isolated plateaus, different islands, and continents of the world. Then came one of the greatest technological advances: European innovations in shipbuilding, seamanship and navigation spawned the generation of Columbus, Da Gama, and Magellan. All the races of mankind found themselves in direct contact for the first time since the days of Adam. A great mixing of peoples, cultural influences, and diseases began.

The various treponematoses spread out from their hearthlands, mixing and changing under new ecological conditions in a way that will probably always confound medical historians. The evidence that comes down to us from that time is sparse and confused. The Europeans bemoaned the arrival of venereal syphilis. The Ceylonese became the reluctant hosts of the organism causing yaws, which, according to tradition, was introduced following the arrival of the Europeans.[26] (If this expanded version of the Columbian hypothesis is kept in mind, perhaps other evidences of the wanderings of the treponematoses may be discovered.)

Europeans drew the world together by means of ocean voyages. Their great travelers were sailors. The epidemiology of syphilis has a special characteristic: it is usually transmitted by sexual contact and spreads when a society's or a group's allegiance to marital fidelity fails. Sailors, by the nature of their profession, are men without women, and therefore, men of many women.[27] If we may assume that the nature of sailors in the sixteenth century was not radically different than in the twentieth, then we can imagine no group of the former century more perfectly suited for guaranteeing that venereal syphilis would have worldwide distribution. Whether Columbus's sailors or his Indians brought it across the Atlantic makes little difference. European sailors carried it to every continent but Antartica and Australia before Columbus was in his grave.

Venereal syphilis arrived in Barcelona in 1493, according to Díaz de Isla, but we have no other news of it in Spain for several years. Why? First, because of the paucity of documentation. Second, because syphilis spreads by venereal contact, and not by touch, breath, or insect vectors, as do the traditional epidemic diseases of smallpox, typhus, plague, and so on. In a stable society its spread will be steady but not extremely fast. Let us play an artificial little game to illustrate this point. Imagine 1,000 people, one of whom is syphilitic. He infects two others, who infect two others each, in turn. The number of the diseased goes up steadily: 1, 2, 4, 8, 16, 32, and so on. In the early stages the disease's advance is rapid, but the victims are few and below the threshold of society's attention. The disease's spread does not accelerate, it is passed on from one to another no more rapidly than before, but 32 becomes 64, 64 leads to 128, 128 is suddenly 256—and society abruptly decides that its existence is threatened by epidemic, long after the initial arrival of syphilis.

Venereal syphilis will only spread with the rapidity of plague or typhus when a society is in such chaos that sexual morality breaks down. Such a sad state of affairs is usually the product of war. Women are without protection or food, and have only their bodies to sell. The men of the armies have a monopoly of force, most of the wealth and food—and no women.

The first recorded epidemic of syphilis took place in Italy in the mid-1490s. In 1494 Charles VIII of France, in pursuit of his claims to the throne of Naples, crossed the Alps into Italy with an army of about 50,000 soldiers of French, Italian, Swiss, German, and other origins. The campaign was not one marked by full-scale battles, but the army, trailing its column of the usual camp followers, engaged in the usual practices of rape and sack anyway. The Neapolitans, retreating toward their city, laid the countryside to waste. Charles, once ensconced in Naples, discovered that the Italians, appalled by his success, were putting aside their personal conflicts and forming a coalition against him. Ferdinand and Isabella, anxious to prevent the establishment of French hegemony in Italy, were sending Spanish troops. Charles packed his bags and marched back to France, and the whole process of battle, rape, and sack was repeated in reverse.[28]

Syphilis, hitherto spreading slowly and quietly across Europe, flared into epidemic in Italy during this invasion, just as the epidemiology of the malady would lead one to expect. It is probable that there was also a rapid spread of typhus, another traditional camp follower. It was in Italy that the truth of Voltaire's epigram was first demonstrated: "Depend upon it, when 30,000 men engage in pitched battle against an equal number of the enemy, about 20,000 on each side have the pox."[29]

Charles arrived back at Lyon in November 1495, where he disbanded his army; and its members, with billions of treponemas in their blood streams, scattered back to their homes in a dozen lands or off to new wars. With the dispersal of that army, the lightning advance of syphilis across Europe and the rest of the Old World became inevitable.[30]

Syphilis had already appeared in Germany by the summer of 1495, for in August Emperor Maximilian of the Holy Roman Empire issued a mandate at Worms calling it the "evil pocks" and blaming it on the sin of blasphemy. In the same year Swiss and Frenchmen recorded its arrival with horror. The pox reached Holland and England no later than 1496. Greece knew it in the same year, and Hungary and Russia in 1499.[31]

By the turn of the century, from London to Moscow great numbers of Europeans "be vexed with the frensshe pockes, poore, and nedy, leyenge by the hye wayes stynkynge and almoost roten above the ground . . . [suffering] intollerably withe puscules & dolorus burnings o the armis shulders nek & leggs or the shynnes as the bones shuld part from the flesh." Europe was in the terrible grip of an epidemic of venereal disease.[32]

The epidemic rolled on into Africa, where "If any Barbarie be infected with the disease commonly called the Frenche pox, they die thereof for the most part, and are seldom cured"; and appeared in the Middle East as early as

1498, with a similar result. The Portuguese, among the earliest to receive the infection, probably carried it farthest, around the Cape of Good Hope. It appeared in India in 1498 and sped on ahead of the Portuguese to Canton by 1505. In a decade it advanced from the Caribbean to the China Sea, at once a tribute to man's nautical genius and social idiocy.[33]

We are lucky in our attempt to trace the early history of syphilis in that shame was not attached to the disease at the beginning. One of the common symptoms of early syphilitics was biographical in nature. As if to illustrate the frankness of the age, Ulrich von Hutten, the great humanist, wrote a gruesomely detailed tract on his own sufferings, gratuitously mentioning that his father had the same disease, and dedicated the whole to a cardinal![34] Our knowledge of early syphilis is limited only by the diagnostic abilities of the sixteenth century.

The plentiful documentation enables the venerologist of an antiquarian bent to trace not only the history of the epidemic but the history of its remedies and of the character of the disease itself. The best analysis of the latter is by Jean Astruc. Although he died just over two hundred years ago, he is still probably the greatest venerologist who ever lived, and his writings on the early history of the French disease are the best secondary study on the subject to date. He breaks down the early history into five stages.

1) 1494–1516. In this period the first sign of the disease in a patient was small genital ulcers, followed by a widespread rash of various character. (This rash is vividly illustrated in all the early depictions of the disease, including one by Albrecht Dürer, dated 1496).[35] As the disease spread through the victim's body, palate, uvula,

jaw, and tonsils were often destroyed. Large gummy tumors were common, and the victim suffered agonizing pains in muscles and nerves, especially at night. General physical deterioration followed and often culminated in early death.

2) During the period 1516 to 1526 two new symptoms were added to the syphilis syndrome: bone inflammation, characterized by severe pain and eventual corruption of the bone and marrow; and the appearance in some sufferers of hard genital pustules, resembling warts or corns.

3) A general abatement of the malignancy of the disease marked the period 1526 to 1540. The number of pustules per sufferer decreased, and we hear more of gummy tumors. Inflammed swelling of the lymph gland in the groin became common. Loss of hair and teeth became common, but this may have been caused by mercury poisoning, mercury having been used as a remedy.

4) From 1540 to 1560 the diminution of the more spectacular symptoms of the malady continued. Gonorrhea, which by this time and for centuries afterward was confused with syphilis, became "the most common, if not perpetual symptom" in the early stages of syphilis.

5) Between 1560 and 1610 the deadliness of the malady continued to decline, and only one new symptom was added: noise in the ears.

By the seventeenth century syphilis was as we know it today: a very dangerous infection, but not one that could be called explosive in the nature of its attack on the victim. Astruc was so encouraged by the record of the declining virulence of the malady that he looked forward with hope, if not with complete confidence, to its final disappearance.[36]

If one wished to create a disease to encourage the proliferation of quacks and quack remedies, one could do no better than syphilis; and this was particularly true in the sixteenth century. The disease was new and no traditional remedies for it existed. Its symptoms were hideous, persuading sufferers to try any and all cures. Syphilis is a malady characterized by periods of remission and latency: "it seemeth to edyfye and fortyfye a castell, there to reste a longe season" and so if the quack does not kill with his cure, he can often claim success—for a time, at least. The quacks cured by searing the pustules with hot irons, and prescribed an unbelievable assortment of medicines to swallow and to apply, the latter including even boiled ants' nest, along with the ants. Ulrich von Hutten, whom one healer warned not to eat peas, for "there growe certayne worms in them with wynges," knew of another so skilled "that in one day he killed iii husbandmen. . . ."[37]

The two most popular remedies for syphilis in the sixteenth century were mercury and guaiacum. The first came into use very soon after the appearance of the pox, both in Europe and Asia. It was already on hand as the most important ingredient in the Arabic ointment, *Ugentum Saracenium,* which had been used successfully in treatment of scabies. Syphilis also produced skin sores, and so the ointment was quickly enlisted against it. It was effective, and in fact it proved to be the only generally effective means of arresting syphilis for the next four hundred years. Before the middle of the sixteenth century, mercury was being rubbed on, applied to the body in plasters and swallowed in pills.[38]

Unfortunately, mercury was overused, and in many cases the cure was successful but the patient died of it. The humoral theory of disease, which dominated European thinking at the time, taught that illness came as the result of an imbalance among the four humors. Syphilis could be cured if the body could be obliged to bleed, defecate, sweat out, and spit out the excess of the offending humor: phlegm, in this case. The most obvious symptom of mercury poisoning is the constant dribbling of saliva, even to the amount of several pints a day. What, though the sixteenth-century physician, could be more desirable? The body is purging itself of that which is making it sick. Out came the offending excess, often along with gums, teeth, and assorted interior fragments of the body. William Clowes, a Tudor surgeon of some wisdom, vividly describes the plight of one poor mercury victim as follows: "A great and an inordinate flux of vicious and corrupt humours passed out of his mouth, with much acrimony, burning heat and sharpness, by reason of the putrefaction of his gums, with a horrible stinking savour and a fever accompanying the same." "Many had lever dye," said Ulrich von Hutten, "than so to be eased."

Although mercury remained the only effective means of treating the pox for several hundred years, patients from London to Canton were inclined to agree with the Scot whose unintentional slip of the pen rendered its name "quack-silver."[39] Many other remedies were tried in its place—China root, sassafras, sarsaparilla, and so on—but only one displaced mercury as the cure, if only for a time. This was guaiacum, a decoction of the wood of a tree of the West Indies, which became the most popular panacea of the 1520s. The wood had much to recommend it. It came from America, as did the disease; and this is, of course, the way a thoughtful God would arrange things. It was a very impressive wood, extremely hard and so heavy that "the leaste pece of its caste into water, synketh streyght to the bottom," which indicated that it must have additional miraculous properties. A decoction of it caused the patient to perspire freely, a very desirable effect, according to humoral theory. Among its proponents were Girolamo Fracastoro and Ulrich von Hutten, two of the greatest writers of the day—a high recommendation for the wood in that age of humanism. And it at least did not injure the patient. Benvenuto Cellini, in spite of the advice of physicians, used it to treat himself for a self-diagnosed case of the pox; and if it did not cure him of what he probably did not have, at least it did not kill him, either.[40]

The prevalence of syphilis and the wood's effectiveness not only against it but also against "goute in the feete, the stone, palsey, lepre, dropsy, fallyng evyll, and other diseases," drove its price to dizzy heights. Like a poor man's soup bone, the sawdust of guaiacum was boiled up again and again for those not lucky enough or wealthy enough to buy the first decoction. Counterfeit guaiacum flooded the market and pieces of the wood were hung in churches to be prayed to by the most impecunious syphilitics. And all, all were cured.

Or were they? Murmurs, soon rising to shouts, of the wood's ineffectiveness began to be voiced in the 1530s. Philippus Paracelsus, for one, proclaimed the wood worthless, and mercury the real hope of the syphilitic. The fad of the Holy Wood from the New World returned a few generations later, and the use of it never quite died out—it was not removed from the British Pharmacopoeia until 1932—but its reputation as *the cure* had evaporated. Europe returned to China root, sassafras, prayer, and, especially, mercury.[41]

The effects of the guaiacum fad were what one would expect: desperate optimism and finally the death of men and women who might otherwise have received at least partly successful treatment. There are few lines in all literature more pitiful than those of Ulrich von Hutten on his "cure." With little left of his few remaining years but a return of pain, he wrote:

> And lo through the helpe of Guaiacum, I am bolde nowe to lyve, and to drawe breath agayne. Whiche mynd god gyve to all good menne, that they never ceasse to hope and trust. As for me, I repent my selfe in nothynge, and yf by any meanes long lyfe myght be graunted unto me, I have great hope that I shulde lyve hole, sounde, and lusty.[42]

In an age in which the Pope had to rescind an order expelling all prostitutes from Rome because of the loss of public revenue that resulted, the new venereal disease inevitably spread to every cranny of Europe and became, like smallpox or consumption, one of the permanently resident killers. The English doctor, William Clowes, stated in the 1580s that one out of every two he had treated in the House of St. Bartholomew had been syphilitic, and that "except the people of this land do speedily repent their most ungodly life and leave this odious sin, it cannot be but the whole land will shortly be poisoned with this most noisome sickness."[43]

However, *Treponema pallidum* brought some good in its train, though those who benefited from it were few. Physicians, surgeons and quacks found a source of wealth in the pox. The story goes that the physician Thierry de Héry once knelt before a statute of Charles VIII, explaining that "Charles VIII is good enough saint for me. He put 30,000 francs in my pocket when he brought the pox to France."

The Fuggers of Augsburg, the greatest banking family of the day, also turned the spread of the French disease into money. They became the chief importers of guaiacum in Europe and were among the most enthusiastic promoters of the Columbian theory of the origin of the pox. At least one doctor, mentioned by Ulrich von Hutten, took a not unwise view of guaiacum and its successes, calling it "a vayne thing, and nothing worthe; but that the marchauntes fayned it to doo these things."[44]

For many for whom the pox was not a matter of profit, it became a subject for humor. When man is both helpless and foolish in the presence of horror, as is often the case in matters pertaining to venereal disease, he finds solace in jokes. There was a great deal of joking about the French disease in the sixteenth century. Cervantes mentions it in a satirical treatment of one scholar's criticism of another's work: My rival, says the pedant, "forgot to tell us who was the first man in the world to have a cold in his head, or the first to take unctions of mercury for the French disease, all of which I bring out most accurately, citing the authority of more than twenty-five books."[45] Rabelais, as one would expect, touches on the subject of syphilis many times, once even using it as a means of self-praise:

> What shall I say of those wretched devils plagued by pox and gout? How often they have appeared before us saturated with quicksilver ointment, salves and grease. Their faces shone like a larder keyhole . . . their teeth danced in their heads like a keyboard of an organ or spinet under the fingers of a maestro . . . they foamed at the gullet like a boar at bay in the toils of a pack of bloodhounds. . . . What did they do in this crisis? Their sole consolation was to have somebody read them a few pages of this book."[46]

Erasmus mentions syphilis a number of times. In one of his *Colloquies* he announces to the world that "unless you're a good dicer, an infamous whoremonger, a heavy drinker, a reakless spendthrift, a wastrel and heavily in debt, decorated with the French pox, hardly anyone will believe you're a knight."[47] It almost seems that this description inspired Shakespeare to create his bacchanalian knight, Sir John Falstaff. Sir John feared himself to be afflicted with the dreadful French disease and, like so many since, sent off a urine specimen to be tested. He was informed that the doctor said that "the water itself was a good healthy water; but, for the party that owed it, he might have more diseases than he knew for." Sir John decided to turn his illnesses to good use: "A pox of this gout! or a gout of this pox! for the one or the other plays the rogue with my big toe. 'Tis no matter if I do halt; I have the wars for my colour, and my pension shall seem more reasonable. A good wit will make use of anything: I will turn my diseases to commodity." On his deathbed, in which he laid himself not long thereafter, he spoke mournfully of women and said "they were devils incarnate."[48]

To most, however, the pox was no subject for laughter, but an unmitigated disaster. It was no respecter of rank, and thus had a direct and dismal effect on political and church history. Díaz de Isla claimed to know "of kings, dukes, and grand señores, who had died of the disease," and no one familiar with the history of the sixteenth century would contradict him. Two dynasties whose members were not noted for monogamous behavior died out in that age, the House of Valois and the House of Tudor. As usual, little can be proved, but the inability of queens to give birth to living children makes one suspect that syphilis played a role in the demise of these families, and thus in the political turmoil of their realms. There is little doubt that Francis I, famous for having "lost all save life and honor" in the battle of Pavia, lost both in the end to the pox. And there is little doubt that one and possibly two of the husbands of Mary Queen of Scots, and, therefore, possibly the woman herself, had the disease. In 1500 Cesare Borgia, refused to give an audience because he was suffering from an "ulcer" and "a sore in the groin"; and three years later his "face was disfigured with red blotches and pimples." Do these bits of information refer to the primary and then the secondary symptoms of syphilis, and, if he had it, how did his illness affect his policies? Is it true that Pope Julius II would not allow his foot to be kissed because it was disfigured with syphilitic sores? The truth does not matter: the Protestants believed all such reports.[49]

The pox's full impact, however, can never be measured if we restrict ourselves to economics, literature, politics, and religion. *Treponema pallidum* was chiefly a social villain, one of the most evil of the whole age of Erasmus, Shakespeare, and Francis I. The fear of infection tended to erode the bonds of respect and trust that bound men and women together. The prostitute's chance of Christian forgiveness faded. "If I were judge," roared Luther, "I would have such venemous syphilitic whores broken on the wheel and flayed because one cannot estimate the harm such filthy whores do to young men."[50] And those less obviously offensive suffered, also, from the terror engendered by the new plague. The sick and the stranger found closed doors where once they had found hospitality. Friendships were altered by a new coolness, as men began in some degree to limit their contacts with any who might conceivably have been touched by the pox.

We find little bits of information indicating the change. Public baths went out of style, for it was widely realized that many as innocent of promiscuity as newborn babes had contracted the French disease in such places. The use of the common drinking cup fell out of style.[51] The kiss, a customary gesture of affection between friends as well as lovers, came under suspicion. In *Henry V,* Shakespeare tells us why. Nell, taking leave of the men off to the wars in France, kisses Bardolph goodbye. Nym, although her former lover, refuses the invitation to follow him to her lips. He deprives himself, perhaps for the good reason that Bardolph's face "is all bubukles, and welks, and knobs, and flames o' fire." "Bubukles" is a combination of the words carbunkles and *bubos,* the name the Spaniards gave to syphilis and the English gave to syphilitic swellings. When next we hear of Nell, it is that she is "dead i' the [ho]spital Of the malady of France."[52]

What was the effect of syphilis on general human contact? Consider that one of the crimes—false or no—of which Cardinal Woolsey was accused in his arraignment before Parliament in 1529 was that he, "knowing himself to have the foul and contagious disease of the great pox . . . came daily to your grace [Henry VIII], rowning in your ear, and blowing upon your most noble grace with his perilous and infectious breath, to the marvellous danger of your highness."[53]

Erasmus summed up the whole diffuse but powerful influence of the pox on the manners of the time in a perky dialogue between one Petronious and his friend, Gabriel:

Pet: At least so deadly a disease as this should have been treated with the same care as leprosy. But if this is too much to ask, no one should let his beard be cut, or else everybody should act as his own barber.

Gab: What if everyone kept his mouth shut?

Pet: They'd spread the disease through the nose.

Gab: There's a remedy for that trouble, too.

Pet: What is it?

Gab: Let them imitate the alchemists: wear a mask that admits light through glass windows and allows breath through mouth and nose by means of a tube extending from the mask over your shoulders and down your back.[54]

It is obvious that in no area did syphilis wreak more havoc than in relations between men and women. No civilization has ever satisfactorily solved the problem of sex. Even if there were no such thing as venereal disease, the sex relationship would still produce distrust, fear, and pain, as well as confidence, love, and comfort. Add to the normal emotional difficulties of the sex relationship not just the possibility of the pains of gonorrhea but the danger of a horrible and often fatal disease, syphilis. Where there must be trust, there must now also be suspicion. Where there must be a surrender of self, there must now also be a shrewd consideration of future health. Generosity of spirit and body may lead one to the ludicrous fate of the syphilitic Englishman of the late sixteenth century whose lover insisted that "but for only him and her husband she was as good a maid as she was born of her mother."[55]

Gabriello Falloppio, in his book of syphilis, *De Morbo Gallico* (1564), suggested that after sexual intercourse a man should carefully wash and dry his genitals. The age of the canny lover had arrived.[56]

NOTES

1. Desiderius Erasmus, *The Colloquies of Erasmus,* trans. Craig R. Thompson, 401, 405.

2. Ulrich von Hutton, *Of the Wood Called Guaiacum,* trans. Thomas Paynel, 1; Ruy Díaz de Isla, *Tractado llamado fructo de todos los sanctos: contra el mal Serpentino,* iii. The passages in the Díaz book which pertain to the American origin of syphilis are reproduced in Ivan Bloch, *Der Ursprung des Syphilis,* 306–307. Bloch's book is the most famous secondary source on the American origin of Syphilis. The equivalent for Old World origin is Karl Sudhoff's "The Origin of Syphilis," in his *Essays in the History of Medicine.*

3. K. Chimin Wong and Lien-teh Wu, *History of Chinese Medicine,* 218; William A. Pusey, *The History and Epidemiology of Syphilis,* 12.

4. P. Huard, "La Syphilis Vue par les Médecins Arabo-Persans, Indiens et Sino-Japonais du XVe et XVIe Siècles," 9–13.

5. Ibid., passim; Wong and Wu, *Chinese Medicine,* 217; Cyril Elgood, *A Medical History of Persia and the Eastern Caliphate,* 378; Pusey, *Syphilis,* 7–8; Bloch, *Ursprung des Syphilis,* 297–305; G. L. Hendrickson, "The 'Syphilis' of Girolamo Fracastoro with Some Observations on the Origin and History of the Word 'Syphilis,' " 544; Díaz de Isla, *Tractado,* iii.

6. Girolamo Fracastoro, *Fracastor, Syphilis or the French Disease, A Poem in Latin Hexameters,* trans. Heneage Wynne-Finch, 8; F. S. Morton, *Venereal Diseases,* 27, 87; Pusey, *Syphilis,* 11; von Hutten, *Guaiacum,* 2–2r.

7. Bruce Barrack, "Syphilis and Yaws," 510; Folke Henschen, *The History and Geography of Diseases,* trans. Joan Tate, 124–126.

8. Henschen, *History and Geography of Diseases,* 124; Saul Jarcho, "Some Observations on Diseases in Prehistoric America," 14–15; James E. Anderson, "Human Skeletons of Tehuacan," 497; Henry E. Sigerist, *A History of Medicine,* vol. 1: *Primitive and Archaic Medicine,* 55–56; C. W. Goff, "Syphilis," 279–294.

9. Nicolás Monardes, *Ioyfull Newes Out of the Newe Founde Worlde,* trans. John Frampton, 10r; Robert S. Munger, "Guaiacum, the Holy Wood from the New World," 196, 197, 226; Samuel Eliot Morison, *Admiral of the Ocean Sea, A Life of Christopher Columbus,* 2:199–200; Charles C. Dennie, *A History of Syphilis,* 30.

10. For a masterly consideration of this evidence, consult Morison, *Admiral of the Ocean Sea,* 2:193–218.

162 | THE COLUMBIAN EXCHANGE

11. Ferdinand Columbus, *The Life of Admiral Christopher Columbus by His Son Ferdinand*, trans. Benjamin Keen, 155, 191.

12. Bartolomé de Las Casas, *Historia de las Indias*, 5:349; Gonzalo Fernández Oviedo y Valdés, *Historia General y Natural de las Indias*, 1st ed., 1:55; Gonzalo Fernández Oviedo y Valdés, *Natural History of the West Indies*, trans. Sterling A. Stoudemire, xi, xii, 88–90. Carl O. Sauer, *The Early Spanish Main*, 38–39.

13. Díaz de Isla, *Tractado*, iii; Richmond C. Holcomb, Letter to the Editor, 515; Dennie, *History of Syphilis*, 16.

14. Richmond C. Holcomb, "Ruiz Díaz de Isla and the Haitian Myth of European Syphilis," 277–280.

15. Morison, *Admiral of the Ocean Sea*, 2:204, 248; Bloch, *Ursprung des Syphilis*, 307; Emiliano Jos, "Centenario de Fernando Colón (Enfermedad de Martín Alonso)," 99–100.

16. E: H. Hudson, "Treponematosis in Perspective," 738.

17. Morton, *Venereal Diseases*, 69; C. J. Hackett, "On the Origin of Human Treponematoses," 21.

18. Hudson, "Treponematosis in Perspective," 735–748; E. H. Hudson, "Treponematosis and Man's Social Evolution," 885–901; E. H. Hudson, "Treponematosis and African Slavery," 43–52.

19. Ed. Jeanselme, *Traité de la Syphilis*, 227–228; Max Isenberg, "Syphilis in the Eighteenth and Early Nineteenth Centuries," 456; John E. Lane, "A Few Early Notes on Syphilis in the English Colonies of North America, 217–218; Dennie, *Syphilis*, 66, 68; Jean de Léry, *Journal de Bord de Jean de Léry*, ed. M. R. Mayeux, 376–378; André Thevet, *The New Found Worlde, or Antarctike*, trans. Thomas Hacket, 70–71.

20. Hackett, "Human Treponematoses," 8, 18–19; Abner I. Weisman, "Syphilis: Was It Endemic in Pre-Columbian America of Was It Brought Here from Europe?" 297; Thorstein Guthe, "The Treponematoses as a World Problem," 68; Philip H. Manson-Bahr, *Manson's Tropical Diseases*, 512; Morton, *Venereal Diseases*, 42–43, 69.

21. A. J. Rhodes and C. E. van Rooyen, *Textbook of Virology for Students and Practitioners of Medicine* (1962), 156, 167, 173–174.

22. von Hutten, *Guaiacum*, 2r–3.

23. Barrack, "Syphilis and Yaws," 515.

24. This pattern of divergent evolution has affected more than one of man's parasites. For example, body lice, certainly ancient companions of man, have become adapted to the differences among the races. Oriental, Caucasian, African, and American Indian lice are all different. See Thomas A. Cockburn, "The Origin of the Treponematoses," 221–228.

25. W. D. Billings, *Plants and Ecosystems*, 35.

26. Hackett, "Human Treponematoses," 16.

27. A United States Public Health Service publication of 1948 states that eighty seafarers, selected at random, admitted to sexual intercourse with 615 persons in 112 ports in forty-five different countries. See Eduard H. Hermans, "Interrelationship of Syphilis Incidence and Maritime Activity," 132.

28. *The Cambridge Modern History*, vol. 1, *The Renaissance*, 108–117; *The New Cambridge Modern History*, vol. 1, *The Renaissance*, 350–354.

29. Voltaire, *Candide and Other Stories*, trans. Joan Spencer, 125; Morison, *Admiral of the Ocean Sea*, 2:197–198.

30. Fracastoro, *Fracastor*, 4.

31. Ibid., 4–5, 9; Pusey, *Syphilis*, 5.

32. John Fisher, *The English Works of John Fisher*, ed. John E. B. Mayor, 240; E. L. Zimmermann, "An Early English Manuscript on Syphilis," 468.

33. Holcomb, "Ruiz Díaz de Isla," 355; Huard, "La Syphilis Vue Par Les Médecins," 10; Fracastoro, *Fracastor*, 5.

34. Fracastoro, *Fracastor*, 208; von Hutten, *Guaiacum*, passim.

35. Pusey, *Syphilis*, 6, 7, 10.

36. R. S. Morton, "Some Aspects of the Early History of Syphilis in Scotland," 176–177; Jean Astruc, *A Treatise of Venereal Diseases*, part 1:95–99, 104.

37. von Hutten, *Guaiacum*, 3r, 4, 6r; E. L. Zimmermann, "Extra-genital Syphilis as Described in the Early Literature (1497–1624) with Special Reference to Focal Epidemics," 771–772.

38. Fracastoro, *Fracastor*, 22–25.

39. William Clowes, *Selected Writings of William Clowes*, ed. F. N. L. Poynter, 65; von Hutten, *Guaiacum*, 6; Morton, "Syphilis in Scotland," 177; Wong and Wu, *Chinese Medicine*, 219.

40. von Hutten, *Guaiacum*, 9; Benevenuto Cellini, *The Memoirs of Benvenuto Cellini*, trans, Anne MacDonell, 122–123.

41. Munger, "Guaiacum," 212, 213–218; Fracastoro, *Fracastor*, 27.

42. von Hutten, *Guaiacum*, 51.

43. Preserved Smith, *The Age of the Reformation*, 507; Clowes, *Selected Writings*, 74.

44. R. S. Morton, "St. Denis, Patron Saint of Syphilitics," 285; von Hutten, *Guaiacum*, 19r; Munger, "Guaiacum," 209–210, 227; Henry E. Sigerist, *Civilization and Disease*, 76–77.

45. Miguel de Cervantes Saavedra, *Don Quixote*, trans. Samuel Putnam, 652.

46. François Rabelais, *The Five Books of Gargantua and Pantagruel*, trans. Jacques Le Clerq, 162.

47. Erasmus, *Colloquies*, 428–429.

48. William Shakespeare, *King Henry IV*, Part II, act 1, sc. 2; William Shakespeare, *King Henry V*, act 2, sc. 3.

49. Holcomb, "Ruiz Díaz de Isla," 359. Henschen, *History and Geography of Diseases*, 127; Morton, "Syphilis in Scotland," 179; James Kemble, *Idols and Invalids*, 86; Will Durant, *The Renaissance, A History of Civilization in Italy from 1304–1476* A.D., 441. It seems unlikely that that most famous of rakes, Henry VIII, had syphilis. See J. F. D. Shrewsbury, "Henry VIII: A Medical Study," 141–185.

50. Martin Luther, *Luther's Letters of Spiritual Counsel*, ed. and trans. Theodore Tappery, 293.

51. Zimmermann, "Extragenital Syphilis," 757–780; Erasmus, *Colloquies*, 150, 402.

52. Shakespeare, *King Henry V*, act 2, sc. 3, act 3, sc. 6, act 5, sc. 1.

53. Shrewsbury, "Henry VIII," 175.

54. Erasmus, *Colloquies*, 411.

55. Clowes, *Selected Writings*, 91–92.

56. B. E. Finch and Hugh Green, *Contraception through the Ages*, 4.

New World Foods and Old World Demography | 5

The fact that Old world diseases devastated the aboriginal peoples of America and the fact that venereal syphilis in Europe, Asia, and Africa has killed millions and crippled the reproductive capacities of legions seem relatively unimportant when placed alongside the statistics on population growth of the post-Columbian era. It is this latter phenomenon, and not the other two, which is the most impressive single biological development of this millennium. In the last three hundred years the number of human beings on this planet has quadrupled, doubling between 1650 and 1850 and then once again in the last century. The best current quantitative estimation of the world's population history for the past three centuries is listed in Table 1.

It is provocative to those engaged in an examination of the biological consequences of the voyages of Columbus and his generation to note that this population growth has occurred since 1492. Rapid worldwide human population growth probably occurred only twice before in all history: once when man, or protoman, first developed tools and again when man invented agriculture. And then it happened again,

TABLE 1
WORLD POPULATION
(in millions)[1]

	1650	1750	1800	1850	1900	1950
Africa	100	95	90	95	120	198
Asia						
(excluding USSR)	327	475	597	741	915	1,320
Latin America	12	11	19	33	63	162
North America	1	1	6	26	81	168
Europe and USSR	103	144	192	274	423	593
Oceania	2	2	2	2	6	13
Total	545	728	906	1,171	1,608	2,454

after the century in which Europeans made highways of the oceans. Is there a connection between Christopher Columbus and the population explosion?[2]

The answer for the New World is probably yes. The number of humans in the Americas has probably increased since the fifteenth century. It seems that for every Indian who died, a European or an African has disembarked and proceeded to found a family. The transfer of Old World plants and, especially, Old World animals vastly enhanced America's capacity to feed this growing population of alien humans.

But how is it that the Old World was able to supply so many millions of emigrants to the New? She did so not by depopulating her own lands: in fact, in the case of Europe, her population was growing so rapidly that the people she sent to America can, by and large, be defined as surplus population. One of the more important factors in the imigration of so many people from the Old to the New World was the population pressure existing in the former. This enables us to focus our question more sharply: is there a connection between Columbus and the population explosion in the Old World?

The causes of the increase are usually given as follows: a decrease in the number and severity of wars; advances in medical science and hygiene; the establishment of stable governments over large areas; improvement in transportation, which permits rapid transfer of food from areas of surplus to areas of famine; and an increase and improvement of food supply. There are others which have also been suggested, but the above are the most widely circulated. How valid are they? Birth and death rates are the result of such myriad factors that demographers agree that all of the given reasons for population expansion are, if taken one by one, invalid. Some, however, have less general validity than others, whatever their significance may be in specific cases. It seems likely that wars, by and large, have increased, rather than decreased, in their destructiveness in the last three hundred years. It is certain that few of the mothers and babies since 1650 have enjoyed the benefits of hygienic surroundings or decent medical treatment. Stable governments probably do enhance population increase, but what about China's rapid population growth in the nineteenth and twentieth centuries, a period on which chaos became increasingly the rule rather than the exception within that empire? Improved transportation certainly helps to limit the number and duration of famines, but it is hard to believe that this is a factor of major importance; and it is certainly true that world population growth began to accelerate generations before the engine—steam, gasoline, or other fuel—replaced human and animal muscle in transportation.

The one factor that will promote population growth and that has been nearly universally influential over the past three hundred years is the increase and improvement of the food supply. We have come full circle, all the way back to Thomas Malthus. Of course, his theory that population increase follows upon increase in food supply is a grossly oversimplified explanation of an extremely complicated matter, but he was basically right about that phenomenon in preindustrial societies, a category which included the entire human race of his time a century and a half ago. In such societies starvation and malnutrition are usually significant checks on the population growth: therefore, an increase in the food supply will produce an increase of people.

For example, in eighteenth-century Sweden, the nation for which we have the most reliable vital statistics prior to 1800, "Not only marriage but crude birth rates and married and unmarried fertility rates rose following adequate harvest and declined in years following harvest failures; whereas death rates showed an equally strong tendency to rise after a failure and decline in periods of abundance."[3]

The most obvious way in which a people can improve food production is by raising more of its standard crops. But this is not always easy; often most of the land suitable for the traditional crops is already planted with them, and often an increase in the sowing of traditional crops will only bring on an increase in the pests and diseases that prey on them.

An entirely new food plant or set of food plants will permit the utilization of soils and seasons which have previously gone to waste, thus causing a real jump in food production and, therefore, in population. But before we accept this statement as gospel, let us acknowledge that we are taking much for granted. How can we be *sure* that a population which simultaneously switches from wheat to maize and increases in size could not have accomplished the increase without every having heard of maize? Perhaps the switch to maize came not because of its greater productivity but because the people in question simply liked the way it tasted. Perhaps the increase in population stemmed from a dozen or a hundred factors having nothing whatever to do with maize.

But let us proceed. Hypotheses about past events are not susceptible to scientific proofs, and the historian can never hope to have a hypothesis certified as anything better than reasonable. He must lope along where scientists fear to tread. It seems reasonable to say that human beings, in matters of diet, especially of the staples of diet, are very conservative, and will not change unless forced. No coercion is as generally effective as hunger. And when hunger is assuaged—even by the products of alien seed—babies are conceived, are born, thrive, and live to have their laps full of grandchildren.

All the basic food plants are the products of careful cultivation and breeding practiced by the neolithic farmer. Although he never saw or heard of genes, he produced wheat, barley, rice, maize, potatoes, manioc, and other foods—the chief supports of human life on this planet—from wild species so unpromising that only the professional botanist can see the resemblance between today's plant and its ancestor.

We do not know whether agriculture was invented several times in different places in the Old and New Worlds, or only once, and that in the Old World. We do know that the Atlantic and Pacific oceans acted as excellent insulators before the sixteenth century, tending to restrict cultivated plants, if not necessarily agricultural techniques, to the continents of their origins. Because of the oceans, two different patterns of agriculture grew up in the eastern and western hemispheres. Unfortunately for those addicted to precision, research over the past few decades has made it increasingly obvious that these two worlds were not hermetically sealed, and that prehistoric men did find ways across the great waters for themselves and at least a few or their cultigens. The sweet potato, for instance, a plant of American origin, was cultivated in New Zealand long before the arrival of the Europeans. The old thesis that only the Vikings got from one hemisphere to the other and back before 1492, and that neither they or anyone else carried anything of importance in either direction, is crumbling. But the claim that there were *almost* entirely different groups of food plants cultivated in the Old and New Worlds in pre-Columbian times is still acceptable to historians, archeologists and paleo-botanists. There is no doubt whatsoever that no crop of one hemisphere was a significant source of food for large numbers of people of the other hemisphere before 1492.[4]

The great Russian botanist Nikolai Ivanovich Vavilov, in the course of his research on the geographical origins of various cultigens, made up a list of the 640 most important plants cultivated by man. Roughly speaking, five hundred of them belonged to the Old World and one hundred to the New.[5] Driven by the fact that America provided so few domesticated animals for food, the Indian produced some of the most important of all food plants. He also gave humanity such nonfoods as tobacco, rubber, and certain cottons, but let us restrict ourselves to a list of his most valuable food crops.[6]

Maize	Pumpkin
Beans of many kinds (*Phaseolus vulgaris* and others)	Papaya
	Guava
Peanuts	Avocado
Potato	Pineapple
Sweet potato	Tomato
Manioc (also called cassava and tapioca)	Chile pepper (*Capsicum annuum* and others)
Squashes	Cocoa

The botanists' assurance that these foods are of American origin is supported by the testimony of the etymologists: all but three of the listed names are derived from American Indian words. Collectively these plants made the most valuable single addition to the food-producing plants of the Old World since the beginnings of agriculture.[7]

Of these crops, maize, potatoes, sweet potatoes, beans, and manioc have been most abundantly cultivated and eaten in the last four hundred years. The others have had great significance in restricted areas, but have never become staple foods for as large a part of the human race as the five above.

If maize were the only gift the American Indian ever presented to the world, he would deserve undying gratitude, for it has become one of the most important of all foods for men and their livestock. Ears of ancient wild maize, recently unearthed in Mexico, enable us to measure the achievement of the American Indian agriculturalist. The mature ear of wild maize was about as thick as a pencil and an inch long. The food value of the whole ear was probably less than a single kernel of twentieth-century maize.[8]

Many types of maize existed when the European arrived in America and many more exist today. As a result, maize will produce good crops in an extreme variety of climates. Its advantage over equivalent Old World plants is that it will prosper in areas too dry for rice and too wet for wheat. Geographically, it has fitted neatly between the two. Its supremely valuable characteristic is its high yield per unit of land which, on world average, is roughly double that of wheat. For those to whom famine is a reality, maize has the additional benefit of producing food fast. Few other plants produce so much carbohydrate, sugar, and fat in as short a growing season.[9]

Despite the fact that the potato does not grow well in the tropics, it is one of the crops raised in greatest quantity by man. Only wheat competes with it as the most important plant food of the temperate zones, and the potato produces several times as much food per unit of land as wheat or any other grain. Furthermore, it can be, and so often has been, cultivated very successfully in tiny plots of poor land in a great variety of temperate zone climates, at altitudes from sea level to well over 10,000 feet, and by the most inept farmers using the most primitive tools.[10]

Although there are few parts of the world where the sweet potato is the primary crop, its unusually high yield—three to four times that of rice, for instance—and its resistance to drought and tolerance of poor soils make it a vitally important secondary crop throughout a wide band of the warmer lands. A good example is to be found in Indonesia, which produced 13.4 million metric tons of rice in 1962–1963—and also over three million metric tons of sweet potatoes.[11]

The bean was one-third of the alimentary trinity that supported Meso-American civilization when the Spaniard arrived—the other two members being maize and squash—and plays a role of similar, if not equal, importance in the diets of millions throughout the world today. The bean family contains over one thousand species—some New, some Old World in origin—and since most writers and statisticians have been satisfied that "beans is beans," it is difficult to make precise statements of the importance of *American* beans. The most important single kind of bean is the eastern hemisphere's soybean, but the lima, sieva, Rangoon, Madagascar, butter, Burma, pole, curry, kidney, French, navy, haricot, snap, string, common, and frijole bean are all American. Often called the "poor man's meat," American beans are especially rich in protein, as well as in oils and carbohydrates.[12]

When the European arrived in America, the American beans already existed in varieties suitable to almost every climate, and they were so obviously superior to many Old World pulses that they quickly spread to Europe, Africa and Asia.[13] Because they have often been a private garden crop rather than a field crop, they have escaped the official censuses; when they are listed in censuses, they are often grouped under the general heading "Pulses" with a number of other kinds of beans. Their importance defies exact statistical description, but that importance is still there. Any world traveler will tell you that the visitor-from-far-away may be treated to gormet delights for his first few meals in a strange new country, but eventually he will find himself confronted—in Norway, Siberia, Dahomey, and Australia—with a plate of beans—American beans.

Of all the more important American foods, manioc is the least known to the inhabitant of the temperate zone. He knows it best by the name tapioca, under which title it arrives on his table as dessert. To add to the confusion, it is also known as manihot or cassava. To the North American and European manioc is a specimen of rare and exotic flora, but it is as important a contribution to the food supply of the tropics as maize or potatoes is to the temperate zones.[14]

The manioc plant is a large shrub which is usually harvested when no more than five to twelve feet high, although it can grow to eighteen feet. Its young shoots and leaves can be and often are eaten, but it is chiefly valuable for its roots, which, at harvest, are usually one to two feet in length and two to six inches in diameter and weight one to five kilograms or more.[15] From the eater's point of view (though not necessarily from the botanist's), there are only two kinds of manioc, sweet and bitter. Sweet manioc can be eaten fresh, but bitter manioc contains lethal quantities of prussic acid and must be processed before eating. The basic process of changing it from a poison into a food has not changed since it was developed by the American Indian, so let us draw on Roger Barlow's description of it, presented to Henry VIII over four hundred years ago. The Indians, Barlow wrote, take the manioc root,

> and rubbe it on a stone and so it turneth to curdes, which thei take and put in a long, narowe bagge made of ryndes of trees, and so press out the liquor and gather it in a vessell, and when the iuce is out ther resteth in the bagge the floure as fyne and white as the snowe, wherof thei make cakys and bake them upon the fier in a panne, and after this be bakyn it is a very good brede, holsome and medecinable, and will endure a yere without corruptyng. And likewise thei take the

licour and seethe it over the fyre and after that it is a good
drynke and of grete sustenaunce and strength, but and if one
shuld drinke of it before it were boiled over the fire, and litle
quantite as wold into a nuttys shelle, thei suld die incontynent.[16]

Manioc prospers from sea level to seven thousand feet and
in soil too poor to support almost any other important crop:
in parts of the Bas-Congo it is claimed that manioc will yield
five tons per hectare of land too infertile for maize. It ignores
drought and pests that destroy other crops. Although it is
composed chiefly of starch and contains little protein or fat,
it has significant amounts of certain vitamins and other nutri-
ments. And, above all, it generally will produce more food
by weight per unit of land than any other tropical plant.[17]

All that manioc asks of man and nature is a frost-free climate, dirt that is neither saline nor swampy, and from twenty
to two hundred inches of rain a year! No wonder it has become one of the staple crops of the tropics. Since Columbus
first saw it, it has spread around the waistband of the globe.
Between thirty degrees north and thirty degrees south it fills
bellies from Sumatra to the Congo to its homeland, Brazil.[18]

The last few pages make it apparent that a switch from
Old World to New World crops often means an improvement
in food supply. The improvement, when it exists, is not always simply quantitative but often qualitative. Attempts to
ferret out information on the quantities of various foods
raised in the world can often lead to egregious errors, because
our statistics are poor. Attempts to discover the average
world *quality* of foods can lead to what amounts to science
fiction, but perhaps if we only ask a single simple question
about the most easily measured nutritional quality and
do not allow ourselves to become too confident about the
validity of the answer, we can obtain useful data. What is
the average yield in calories per hectare of the world's major
plant foods? (This question implies a disregard for the vital
role that proteins, vitamins, minerals, etc., play in man's ali-

mentation. However, it is crudely true that if man's caloric intake is sufficient, he will somehow stagger to maturity, and he will reproduce.) The answer to the question is provided in Table 2 (beans are purposely omitted because Old and New World varieties are grouped together by statisticians and nutritionists alike), which also shows the magnitude of the contribution of the American Indian agriculturalist.

But let us not substitute numerals for reason. The above statistics serve to describe an utterly mythical entity: the average world hectare under the influence of the average world weather. The variety of soils and climates in this world is enormous. There are vast areas of the globe where it would be much more calorically fruitful to plant oats than maize or potatoes, no matter what the averages say. But it is just that variety that made American food plants such a valuable addition to the cultigens of the Old World. Indian plants increased the variety of plants which the Old World farmer could try to match to the variety of soils and weather in order to coax nourishment out of nature.

TABLE 2
VARIETIES OF OLD AND
NEW WORLD STAPLES[19]
(in millions of calories per hectare)

Chief American Crops		Chief Old World Crops	
Maize	7.3	Rice	7.3
Potatoes	7.5	Wheat	4.2
Sweet potatoes		Barley	5.1
and yams[a]	7.1		
Manioc	9.9	Oats	5.5

[a] Food and Agricultural Organization documents group sweet potatoes and yams together. The caloric value for sweet potatoes is higher than for yams, and more sweet potatoes are raised than yams, so I feel justified in including this statistic.

As the Old World farmer expanded the area under his cultivation and tried to increase production per unit of land, he discovered that he had an enemy who grew stronger and stronger as the generations passed: the problem of diminishing returns. Even the steppes of Russia do not have an endless capacity to produce wheat. For generations the Chinese have had no large undeveloped areas suitable for rice cultivation, unless they leveled mountains. The great advantage of the American food plants is that they make different demands of soils, weather and cultivation than Old World crops, and are different in the growing seasons in which they make these demands. In many cases the American crops do not compete with Old World crops but complement them. The American plants enable the farmer to produce food from soils that, prior to 1492, were rated as useless because of their sandiness, altitude, aridity, and other factors. In many areas, because of their different requirements for sunlight or rainfall or other factors, they have enabled the farmer to eliminate the fallow season when the soil yields no food for man or his animals, thus employing unused labor power to good purpose and enormously increasing production. Arthur Young's note on the importance of maize in southern France in the 1780s illustrates this point:

> Where there is no maize, there are fallows: and where there are fallows, the people starve for want. For the inhabitants of a country to live upon that plant, which is the preparation for wheat, and at the same time to keep their cattle fat upon the leaves of it, is to possess a treasure.[20]

Let us turn now to the various areas of the Old World where American crops are important sources of food, to see if the record of history discloses when they became important, and if the population began to grow at about the same time. Our claims for the validity of our findings will be modest: we know that even if both trends began simultaneously, a cause and effect connection between the two cannot be taken as fact. We know that the agricultural and demographic histories of most of the areas under examination have yet to be written, much less correlated. We know that we are *not* demographers and have none of their skills and special knowledge: we will be sketching out a hypothesis—that is all. We know that we will be attempting the patently absurd—a bird's eye view of Europe, Africa, and Asia since 1492! But the big questions are really the only ones worth considering, and colossal nerve has always been a prerequisite for such consideration.

It would seem that the logical place to turn to first for evidence of the influence of American food on the Old World would be Europe, for the Europeans were the first from the eastern hemisphere to establish permanent contact with the New World. It is true that some American foods have been so thoroughly adopted by the Europeans that one cannot imagine what their national diets must have been like before Columbus. What would Mediterranean dishes be like without chiles, or the eastern European diet without paprika, that condiment derived from the chile pepper? Who can imagine the Italian chef deprived of the tomato?

The American crops of primary importance in Europe have been beans, maize, and, above all, potatoes. The bean, as usual, defies the searcher for precise information. The assumption that it was cultivated in Europe in the sixteenth century, spread rapidly and became an important part of the diet by the eighteenth century, is almost certainly correct, but information on where and when the bean became important and how important it became is hard to come by. The haricot bean was in Europe at least by 1542, for in that year the botanists Tragus and Leonard Fuchs described and sketched it. It was probably grown in appreciable quantities in France by the end of the century; otherwise, why would the Englishman, Barnaby Googe, write of it as the "French bean" in 1572? String beans and lima beans were among the chief products of seventeenth-century Spain. John Locke, traveling on the Continent in 1678, suggested: "Take the leaves of kidney beans . . . and put them under your pillow or some convenient place about your bed. They will draw all the puneses [bedbugs] and keep you from being bit."[21]

The saga of the bean in Europe is obscure, but we can be sure that its cultivation was widespread in the eighteenth century. A Gallic botanist summed up its significance in a book published in the first year of the French Revolution, describing the common American pulse (*Phaseolus vulgaris*) as "cultivated almost everywhere because of the use that is made of its fruits in the cuisine."[22]

The bean spread to almost all the latitudes of Europe, but the impact of maize was and is restricted almost entirely to the southern half of that continent because this plant thrives only where granted several months of good hot weather. Today it is a crop of great importance in a band stretching across Europe from Portugal through northern Italy, Yugoslavia, the Danube valley, and into the Caucasus. But the Europeans were slow to take it up, possibly because Europe entered a cold period in the 1550s that lasted until the eighteenth century, and most certainly because most Europeans did and still do agree with John Gerard, who wrote in 1597:

> We have as yet no certaine proofe or experience concerning the vertues of this kinde of Corne, although the barbarous Indians which know no better are constrained to make a vertue of necessitie, and think it a good food: whereas we may easily judge that it nourisheth but little, and is of a hard and euill digestion, a more convenient food for swine than for man.[23]

Indeed, Hungarians, whose biggest single crop is maize, feed it almost exclusively to livestock, a policy which most European maize growers have tended to follow from the first.[24]

Yet millions of Europeans have lived on a diet based on

maize in the last four hundred years, and continue to do so today. Maize was grown here and there in sixteenth- and seventeenth-century Europe, but its importance as a staple over large areas generally dates from no earlier than the end of the latter century. John Locke, in the south of France in the 1670s, observed "plots of Maiz in several parts, which the country people call *bled d'Espagne,* and, as they told me, serves the poor people for bred." In the eighteenth century it continued to spread, becoming a basic element in the southern French diet, and, to hazard a guess, perhaps figured in the renewed growth of the French population after the decline that marked the first decades of the century. The name for maize that the "country people" gave Locke suggests that maize was important in Iberia at least as early as his continental exile. Arthur Young, the agricultural expert and journalist, saw it again and again in the fields of northern Spain a hundred years later, and travelers in Portugal in the same era noted that it was *the* staple of the peasant there. During the seventeenth century Spain's population had declined; in the eighteenth it began to increase. Maize was cultivated very early in the Po Valley—some say even *before* Columbus—and when Goethe made his famous Italian journey in the 1780s he discovered that polenta, a kind of corn meal mush, was the staple of the north Italian peasant's diet. Maize must have played some sort of role, at least in the north, in Italy's recovery from the population decline that occurred in the second half of the seventeenth century. Even the few wisps of information presented in this paragraph indicate that no one should make final judgments on the demographic history of the Mediterranean peoples in the eighteenth century without inquiring into the effect of the increase in maize production.[25]

Maize is more important in southeastern than southwestern Europe today, Yugoslavia and Rumania being among the biggest maize producers in the world.[26] Its importance in the Balkans and environs seems to date from no earlier than the beginning of the eighteenth century. Geographers and travelers, writing about the Balkans in the seventeenth century, make little or no mention of maize. Then, as population pressure began to rise in the eighteenth and nineteenth centuries, the cultivation of maize and other American crops, such as squash and potatoes, began to expand. The case of Hungary is a good example. As the Turks were driven out of Hungary, thousands of immigrants entered and a slow transition from a society of cattle grazers to one of farmers took place. By the end of the eighteenth century the chief product of the eastern half of Hungary was maize. Chiefly because of Hungary, the Hapsburg empire was Europe's leading maize producer in the nineteenth century.[27]

Maize and other American food plants were known and raised at least to some extent all over the Balkans by 1800. Then, in the nineteenth century, population grew very rapidly in the Balkans, a phenomenon which was both a cause and an effect of the cultivation of American foods, among other factors. Many of the peoples—the Serbs are a clear example—followed the example of the Hungarians, changing from pastoralist to agriculturalists and, in the process, they took up maize as a staple food.[28]

Rumania is a classic case for anyone searching for Old World examples of the importance of American foods. Maize may not even have been introduced into Rumania until the eighteenth century; certainly it had no importance there before that century. Yet, by the last decades of the nineteenth century, Rumanians were almost as devoted to and dependent on maize as Mexicans. Rumanians raised wheat and maize, the former to export, the latter to eat. Maize, which pairs so well with wheat in crop rotation, enabled Rumania to become one of Europe's breadbaskets. Mamaliga, a maize porridge, became and remains the Moldavian peasant's staff of life, "the principle or sole item of every meal." And when the same peasant celebrates, he drinks spirits made from maize, even as the Tennessee mountaineer.[29]

No other Balkan nation adopted maize so wholeheartedly as Rumania, but by 1900 it and other American plants were established as important crops throughout the peninsula. At the end of the nineteenth century one expert on the Balkans described the typical Macedonian village as consisting of "unpicturesque houses, surrounded by fields of maize, and gardens rich in such unromantic vegetables as the pumpkin."[30] Potatoes also abounded, especially in the mountains, but maize was, over all, the single most important American crop. This remains true, although the dependence on maize as food for humans is decreasing, along with population pressure. Strong echoes of the past remain, however. Joel Martin Halpern, in his book, *A Serbian Village,* notes that the poorer peasants of Orašac still eat maize rather than wheat bread, and, on their few hectares, raise maize rather than wheat because of the former's superior yield. The vegetable gardens of Orašac, by the way, with their peppers, snap beans, tomatoes, potatoes, pumpkins and squash, would make an Aztec's mouth water.[31]

Maize has had an important influence on population growth in southern Europe, but it cannot be credited with being one of the primary causes of the general European demographic expansion of the last two hundred years, which has had such awesome effects on world history. That population explosion is the result of many factors, not the least of which has been medical advance. Another factor of no minor significance has been Europe's love affair with the common American potato.[32]

Sixteenth-century European documents mentioning the potato are of very little help to us because the same word was often used to indicate potatoes and/or sweet potatoes. This, however, is of no great significance because neither had any importance except as novelties and aphrodisiacs! Said

Shakespeare's Falstaff in a moment of passion, "Let the sky rain potatoes." A few years later a lesser playwright put these words in the mouth of one of his characters: "I have fine potatoes, Ripe potatoes! Will your Lordship please to taste a fine potato? 'Twill advance your wither'd state, Fill your Honour full of noble itches."[33]

For long after the initial century of acquaintance, the mass of Europeans looked upon the potato with fear and contempt. Many, for instance, were sure it caused leprosy. Others thought it a very dreary, plebian sort of food. Diderot's *Encyclopedia,* that monumental production of the eighteenth century avant-garde, declares that no matter how the potato is prepared, "this root is insipid and mealy. It cannot be classed among the agreeable food stuffs, but it furnishes abundant and rather wholesome nutrition to men who are content to be nourished. The potato is justly regarded as flatulent, but what are winds to the vigorous organs of peasants and laborers?"[34]

Threats of rot and gas could not forever conceal from Europeans the significance of the fact that potatoes could produce more "wholesome nutrition" from the average piece of land in the northern half of Europe than any other crop. It was the Irish, of course, who first wholeheartedly adopted the potato. It came to their island sometime in the last years of the sixteenth century, and within a hundred years the Irish were known as "mighty lovers of potatoes." In 1724 Jonathan Swift, with typical bitterness, described his countrymen as "living in filth and nastiness upon buttermilk and potatoes." The moist, cool atmosphere and deep, friable soils of Ireland are perfect for the potato, and the Irish, condemned by foreign rule to the depths of poverty, could have asked God for no better gift than the potato. As the crop spread in Ireland, the population grew, which made further spread of the tuber almost compulsory, for no other plant could feed so many Irishmen on such small plots of earth.

One-and-a-half acres, planted with potatoes, would provide enough food, with the addition of a bit of milk, to keep a family hearty for a year. It was not exceptional for an Irishman to consume ten pounds of potatoes a day and very little else. On this diet the Irish, without benefit of medical science, hygiene, industrialization, or decent government, increased from 3.2 million in 1754 to nearly 8.2 million in 1845, not counting the 1.75 million who emigrated before 1846. Then came the potato blight, the failure of the Irish staple, and one of the worst famines of modern times. The Irishmen who had lived by the potato died by the potato.[35]

In few other parts of Europe were the conditions of demography, soil, and weather such as to produce such total commitment to the potato as in Ireland; however, the commitment elsewhere became, in time, at least comparable. As population expanded and industrialization drew more and more people into the cities, the potato assumed greater and greater importance in the diet of the eighteenth- and nineteenth-century English peasant and laborer.[36] The number of articles in English journals on potatoes, potato bread and potato cultivation increased noticeably as even the English upper classes became conscious of the population pressure. Typical is an 1803 article in *The Annual Register* entitled, "Observations on the Means of Enabling a Cottager to Keep a Cow by the Produce of a Small Portion of Arable Land." It called for the planting of three-and-one-quarter acres of land in potatoes, turnips, a grain crop, and clover in rotation. The "potatoes shall go for the maintenance of the cottager and his family" and the rest for the cow and to sell for cash income.[37]

On the Continent the peasant, it seems, was more hesitant about the potato, but the tuber's advantages and the pressures to extract more nourishment from the land had the same effect in many areas as in the British Isles. The potato spread, roughly speaking, from west to east, with the French and Germans (the latter more wholeheartedly than the former) taking up its cultivation a generation or so after the English. On the continent the adoption of the potato was more a matter of conscious government policy than in Great Britain. The potato was served at the royal table in France, and Marie Antoinette wore its flowers as a corsage to advertise its virtues. In Prussia Frederick the Great urged its cultivation. After the famine of 1772 in Hungary, the government ordered that potatoes be grown, despite the fact that they were practically unknown in that land. Again and again, as in Hungary, we find potato production spurting upward after famines, in spite of the fact that the peasants "attributed every possible mischief to potatoes." By the end of the eighteenth century the potato was already under cultivation in eastern Europe. In the first years of the next century Alexander von Humbolt accurately referred to that "beneficent plant" as already indispensable for a large part of the people of the colder lands of Europe.[38]

In the nineteenth century, while potato production climbed precipitously in western and central Europe, the Slavs of eastern Europe also wholeheartedly adopted the plant. A famine and epidemic in 1765 persuaded Catherine the Great of the potential importance of the tuber to Russia, and her government launched a campaign to encourage its cultivation. However, the potato did not become a major crop in central Russia until after the crop failures of 1838 and 1839. Russia was one of the world's top producers of potatoes by 1900. In the last forty years of the last century, her potato production went up over 400 percent. Some of these potatoes went for industrial use, but most went to feed Russians, the number of which increased by 70 percent in the same period. Today Russia leads all other nations by a wide margin as a producer of potatoes.[39]

Even if Russian production is excluded entirely, it is still true that in mid-twentieth century half the world's potatoes were spaded out of the soil of Europe. The European could well add to his liturgies the prayer first heard by white men in Peru in the sixteenth century:

> O Creator! Lord of the ends of the earth! Oh, most merciful! Thou who givest life to all things, and hast made men that they might live, and eat and multiply. Multiply also the fruits of the earth, the papas [potatoes], and other food that thou hast made that men may not suffer from hunger and misery.[40]

The importance of American foods in Africa is more obvious than in any other continent of the Old World, for in no other continent, except the Americas themselves, is so great a proportion of the population so dependent on American foods. Very few of man's cultivated plants originated in Africa—only 50 out of 640, according to Vavilov—and so Africa has had to import its chief food plants from Asia and America. This has been especially true in the rain forest areas, for practically none of the jungle food crops is native to Africa.[41]

Those Africans who owe most to the American Indian are the Eastern Nigritic people, who populate an area, very roughly speaking, from Nigeria east to the center of the continent, and who raise maize, manioc, peanuts, various squashes, pumpkins, and sweet potatoes. Nearly everywhere else in Africa, American crops are of *at least* secondary importance, and the total African production of these foods is enormous. One authority claims that Africa produces 5 or 6 percent of the world's maize, 25 percent of her peanuts, and—by an estimation perhaps too enthusiastic—50 percent of her manioc and 50 percent of her sweet potatoes and yams. (The statisticians have paired these last two in a geographically improper fashion).[42]

These proportions are higher now than in the past, but American foods have played an important role in Africa for a long time. Tropical Africa lies in the same latitudes as

South America, and so crops transferred from one to the other had a minimum of adaptation to undergo. Furthermore, the trans-Atlantic slave trade, which was initiated by men of the Columbus generation, promoted a significant transfer of flora from the Americans to Africa sooner than from the former to Europe. To illustrate, easily preserved food was needed in quantity to feed the human cargoes on their way to the New World. What better way to provide for this need than to plant maize, so easily preserved from corruption by drying, on the slave coasts of Africa?

The bean, tomato, sweet potato, various cucurbita, cacao, and peanut play and have played very important roles in Africa. The last two are especially important as export crops. But maize and manioc rank as the most important of American foods consumed in Africa. Maize was under cultivation in West Africa at least as early as the second half of the sixteenth century, and perhaps even earlier.[43] The chief grains of Africa before the sixteenth century were probably millet and sorghums, which yield considerably less than maize in the wet tropics; and so maize spread rather rapidly in the rain forest areas. The seventeenth-century Dutchman, Olfert Dapper, declared that there was an abundance of maize in the Gold Coast and "it grows profusely. They bake it, with or without mixing it with millet." Its tall green stalks were also to be seen to the south, on the Congo and Angola coasts, and the people of the interior were adopting it in the same century. Oral tradition indicates that maize first came to the Bushongo people of the south-central Congo basin in the seventeenth century.[44]

By 1900 maize could be found almost everywhere in Africa, except for Uganda, exceeding in production all other grains but rice in the jungles, the savanna regions, and along the rivers; and successfully competing with millet and sorghums in many of the drier areas. The Boers, as they trekked north from Cape Colony in the early nineteenth century, found the South African Bantu already planting and harvesting maize. Today maize, or "mealies" as it is called in South Africa, is the staple of the Bantu diet. South Africa is one of the world's greatest producers of maize and about seventy percent of its total crop area is devoted to that American plant. In our century cultivation of maize has continued to spread, and maize has become, for the first time, a mainstay of diet for most of eastern and central tropical Africa.[45]

Even more impressive than the spread of maize in the last hundred years has been that of manioc. The latter's ability to grow in nearly any kind of soil, its resistance to African pests, and its enormous productivity in weight of food produced per unit of land have endeared it to the African farmer. An especially admirable quality is its resistance to drought, a common phenomenon in the grasslands that compose most of sub-Saharan Africa. In the mid-twentieth century manioc is a staple or supplemental food to the people of almost every area south of the Sahara and Ethiopia and north of the Zambezi.[46] So common has it become that West Africans, according to a recently returned Peace Corps worker, insist that the plant is native to Africa.

It is not. It originated in South America and was probably brought by the Portuguese to the Congo and Angola in the sixteenth century and around the Cape to Madagascar and Mozambique in the eighteenth. Manioc was much slower to spread than maize, possibly because of ignorance of or lack of faith in the process for leeching out its poison. Except for the Congo, manioc was not a staple crop in any widespread area of Africa before 1850. However, despite the Africans' hesitation, it did spread into the interior and was grown throughout most of its present range by 1900. In our century African production of manioc has shot upward. Nigeria, for instance, raises more manioc than any other food.[47]

The rapid rise in African population following 1850 (see

Table 1) not only coincides with the spread of political stability and modern medical techniques—alleged characteristics of the growth of the European colonial empires—but also with the accelerated spread of maize, manioc and the other American foods. As for the influence of these crops before 1850, we might hypothesize that the increased food production enabled the slave trade to go on as long as it did without pumping the black well of Africa dry. The Atlantic slave traders drew many, perhaps most, of their cargos from the rain forest areas, precisely those areas where American crops enabled heavier settlement than ever before.

There is no area in which the story of American foods is as obscure and yet as vital to the understanding of world history as in the Middle East. Maize and other American plants seem to have arrived in the Middle East in the sixteenth century.[48] Whenever they arrived in the Middle East, we can be sure that the people of that area played a very important role in their dissemination to other parts of the world. There is little documentary or archeological proof for this as yet, but there is an impressive body of linguistic evidence. Early European names for maize, some of which still prevail, are *granoturco, blé de Turquie, Turkisher Korn, Turkie wheat,* and *trigo de Turquia.* Many names for maize in the Indian subcontinent—*Mecca, Makka, Makkaim makaī, mungari*—indicate either that it is a food from Mecca, meaning God, or, more likely, that it originally reached India from some Islamic region. Careful examination of the words for maize in the languages and dialects of Africa yields strong evidence that the plant came to the Africans not only directly across the Atlantic but also from Egypt via the Lake Chad region and from Arabia via Zanzibar, Madagascar and Mozambique. When Napoleon was in Egypt at the end of the eighteenth century the Egyptians were calling maize "wheat of Turkey" or "wheat of Syria." If the Old

World beginnings of maize are as Middle Eastern as these bits of evidence seem to indicate, then perhaps so are the beginnings of other American crops suitable to the climates of the Middle East.[49]

Dr. Leonhard Rauwolf, a sort of proto-botanist who journeyed through the Middle East in the 1570s, wrote an account of his adventures in which he tells us of kidney beans, French beans, and Indian millet (maize) "six, seven or eight cubits high" on the banks of the Euphrates and in the fields around Aleppo and Jerusalem. A specimen of maize that he collected in the Euphrates valley in 1574 exists today in a Leyden herbarium.[50]

Indeed a claim that American food plants did not find their way to the Middle East before 1600 would deserve little support. They were present in all the other chief divisions of the Old World by that date: why not in the Middle East? The Ottoman Empire was the most important Middle Eastern and Mediterranean power in the sixteenth century, drawing all things to it, just as all things today are drawn to Russia or the United States. The Ottoman Empire was undergoing rapid population growth, which inclines any people to experiment with new crops. The expansion of the Ottomans into the Balkans and their control and influence over the Asian and Sudanese caravan routes enabled any item newly popular with the Turks, including food plants, to spread far and wide very rapidly. However, the fact that European travelers in the Middle East in the seventeenth and eighteenth centuries made little, if any, mention of maize and other American crops confuses and undermines any generality we may dare to make.[51]

Today the American crops are of only secondary importance in the Middle East, except for Egypt, where the mass of the *fellaheen* are clearly dependent on maize to keep them from famine. Maize may have reached Egypt very early in the sixteenth century, but it did not become a staple crop until the eighteenth century. By the last decades of that century it was already an important source of food, and its importance has increased ever since.[52]

The population figures for Egypt in the first three quarters of the nineteenth century are very poor, but we can be sure that there was a steady rise which has continued and even accelerated since. In 1882 Egypt had 6.7 million people; in 1907, 11.2 million; in 1935, 16 million; and, in 1964, 28.9 million.[53] There has been some territorial expansion of Egypt in this time, but most of the population rise has come from natural increase stemming not only from medical advances but also from the expansion of maize production, without which the present population could not exist.

The rich soil, the plentiful water of the Nile, and the hot sun make maize the nearly perfect crop for Egypt. No other grain crop produces such yields in this environment, and the labor costs of cultivating maize in Egypt are lower than those of any other grain. Today a greater area is devoted to maize than to any other food crop, and "maize forms the principal article of diet of the people."[54]

An examination of the role of crops raised for human consumption in the Far East is more worthwhile than for any other area because the pressure of population on the food supply has been so great for so long that East Asians probably depend less on animals as a source of nourishment than any other large group of people in the world. They cannot afford the extravagant practice of grazing cattle on arable land and then eating the cattle. They know that it is much more efficient, in terms of filling human stomachs, to raise food crops on the land, and let the livestock scavenge for their nourishment. For example, about 98 percent of the caloric content of the Chinese diet is of vegetable origin. In the phrase of Pierre Gourou, the Orient has a "vegetable civilization."[55]

As to the importance of changes and additions to the Orient's vegetable regimen, we can do no better than to quote Warren S. Thompson: "There can be no reasonable doubt that the amount of subsistence is still the chief factor in determining the level of the death rate in such countries as China and India. In the long view, Malthus was fundamentally correct when he said that man's growth in numbers was largely dependent on the supply of subsistence." The staple of the Far East is, of course, rice, but, considering the above quotation, of what significance is the fact that the production of maize and manioc, and probably other American crops, has increased faster in that enormous area in the first half of the twentieth century than that of rice?[56]

The population explosion in the subcontinent of India, as far as we can judge, does not extend farther back than the last decades of the eighteenth century. In 1600 Indians numbered between 100 million of and 125 million. By 1800 the number had changed little; our best estimate is 120 million. Then the awesome rise began: 130 million by 1845; 175 million by 1855; 194 million by 1867; 255 million by 1871.[57] Despite famine, plague, and war, the trend has continued. According to United Nations estimates of 1964, the population of the subcontinent, India and Pakistan combined, is over half a billion.

The beginnings of the population explosion dovetail neatly with the extension of British rule over all of India, bringing political stability, improvement in the transportation system, and at least some of the benefits of modern science. The population expansion also coincides with the widespread adoption of American foods in India. The relationship between the two trends is difficult to trace, for population grew rapidly in some areas where American crops were not raised, but that does not necessarily undermine the contention that they did affect population increase in areas where they *were* cultivated.

Such American fruits as pineapple and guava reached India and were cultivated in appreciable quantities as long ago as the sixteenth century, but they probably had little effect on population growth. These have never been staple foods for any large number of people. The great population builders among the American foods were first cultivated in quantity in the eighteenth century, and did not become major elements in the Indian diet until the nineteenth and twentieth centuries.[58] This seems to have been the case in most of the Eastern hemisphere: Europe, much of Africa and now India.

There is little indication that maize cultivation was widespread in India at the beginning of the nineteenth century, although we do find scattered documentary evidence of its local importance, such as in Kangra, where "the poor people live much on maize." Whatever the extent of its cultivation in 1800, we can be sure that it spread rapidly thereafter, largely displacing millets, as it was doing in the same period in Europe and Africa. By the last decades of the century maize was grown, at least in some quantity, throughout the length and breadth of India. The hill peoples were largely dependent on it, and in the north—in Punjab, the Northwest provinces and Oudh—maize was a staple article of food. George Watt, a British botanist, ventured to "speak of maize as of equal value to the people of India collectively with wheat." He further emphasized its importance (and, incidentally, pointed out one of the chief pitfalls of trying to write food history) by remarking, "So completely has India now appropriated the Makkal [maize] that few of the village fathers would be found willing to admit that it had not always been with them as it is now, a staple article of diet. They may even cite its supposed ancient names and quote wise sayings regarding it, oblivious all the while that a very few years ago these were universally accepted as denoting an altogether different plant." Little has changed since Watt's time, except that now even more maize is raised, and India has edged into the circle of top producers of maize of the entire world.[59]

The sweet potato plant never attained the importance of maize in India, but as Indians learned that it would grow in soil too poor for other crops, its cultivation spread through the hot lowlands, and its root became an item in the diets of all classes in India long before the twentieth century arrived. The Irish potato has usually been raised only as a mountain or winter crop, but it, too, has spread to all suitable parts of India, and its consumption is common, especially on fast days when Hindus are forbidden to eat grain.[60]

Manioc seems to have been a latecomer to India. Not until about 1850 did it become a common crop, but since then no competent writer on Indian alimentation has been able to ignore it. It soon became a staple in Assam, where a Major Jenkins wrote of it in the last century, "There is no barren waste or hill land about us in which this plant does not thrive." Its marvelous adaptability drew the Major's notice: "I have never seen it cultivated in fields or plots, but it appears to be just stuck in the hedges (for which, whilst it grows, it forms a useful post), and when wanted or at maturity, it is dug out."[61]

Manioc has attained greatest importance in southern India in the states of Travancore and Cochin, where it may actually be the principle staple. The reason for its wholesale adoption in these areas of dense population is obvious. Manioc yields the Indians 11.6 million calories per hectare, as compared with 5.5 million and 5 million for paddy rice and maize respectively.

India has become the world's leading grower of peanuts, producing almost 5.3 million metric tons of peanuts in 1963, and they have become common in the diet, especially in southern India. The lima bean is to be found throughout India, as are the pumpkin and the squash. The pumpkin is often to be seen not only in the vegetable gardens of the lower classes, but even spreading over the roofs of their homes.[62]

Although an important source of vitamins, the chile pepper is not usually thought of as a really important item in the diet. It comes close to being just that in India. The American chile pepper was almost completely unknown in seventeenth-century India, began to spread in the eighteenth century, and is now the nearly indispensable ingredient in every Indian meal. The ubiquitous chutney and curry are unimaginable without American chile. George Watt wrote at the end of the nineteenth century that the chile pepper, "ground into a paste, between two stones, with a little mustard oil, ginger and salt . . . , form the only seasoning which the millions of poor can obtain to eat with their rice."[63]

The largest nation of southeast Asia in terms of population and land is Indonesia, the population of which has been growing rapidly for the last century and more, especially on the larger islands. In 1815 the population of Java and Madura was in the vicinity of 4.6 million. In 1890 it was almost 24 million. In 1960 the figure was approximately 62.5 million.[64] In the same century and a half there has been increasingly widespread cultivation of American food plants in Indonesia. A connection between the two phenomena is as certain here as anywhere in the world.

As is so often true of the Orientals, the staple of most Indonesians is rice, but for generations these people have been faced with the simple fact that most of the land suitable to rice and most of the obvious ways to increase rice production were utilized a long time ago. The Indonesian rice farmers and their counterparts in other areas of the Far East are, considering the climate, soils, and tools they have to work with, very good farmers. The amount of rice they can coax out of a hectare of paddy is immense, yet the increase in rice production over the last century or so is insufficient to have alone encouraged the population growth that has characterized the same period.

Amercian Indian food plants arrived in the East Indies practically as soon as the Europeans did. It is probable that the sweet potato arrived before the Europeans. American beans were grown there at least as early as the seventeenth century. As early as 1699, according to the explorer William Dampier, maize was a staple for the people of the coastal plains of Timor. In 1789 Captain William Bligh, late of H.M.S. *Bounty,* reeled ashore at the same island at the end of his epochal 3,600-mile voyage in an open boat, and the natives "brought us a few pieces of dried turtle and some ears of Indian corn." Some time around 1800 the Dutch introduced the Irish potato into the mountains of Java.[65]

In the last century secondary crops, most of them American—maize, manioc, sweet potatoes, peanuts, and chile peppers—have increased in importance relative to rice. This is particularly true in the uplands of Indonesia, generally unfit for rice, where the population growth has equaled that of the coastal lowlands. Of these secondary crops, the most important, as in India, have been maize, manioc and sweet potatoes.[66]

Maize had little significance in the East Indies in the seventeenth century, but by 1800 it may well have become the most important secondary crop, at least in Java. John Crawfurd, in his *History of the Indian Archipelago,* published in 1820, stated that maize cultivation, pushed by population increase, was rapidly spreading, as land suitable for rice grew scarce. Since then, as population expansion has accelerated, so has maize production. In the mid-twentieth century maize ranks second in importance only to rice among the cereals in Indonesia as a whole, and is the staple food in parts of the Celebes, Timor, Lombok, East Java, and Madura.[67]

Manioc made its appearance in the East Indies at least as early as the seventeenth century but, as elsewhere in the world, was adopted rather slowly by local agriculturalists. But the increasing number of mouths calling for food and manioc's incredible productivity combined eventually to make its appeal irresistible. Considering that a portion of the rice crop must be preserved for the next year's seed, then manioc, no part of which need be preserved for planting but the inedible stalk, yields nearly twice as many calories per unit of land in Java as rice. It prospers in areas where only a fool would plant paddy rice and where even maize languishes, such as on the relatively arid limestone plateau of the Gunung Sewu of Java, where it is the chief crop. The United Nations statistics are very sketchy on manioc, but it is worth noting that they place Indonesia second only to Brazil, the homeland of the plant, as a producer of the root.[68]

Indonesia, also, ranks as one of the world's leading sweet potato producers, harvesting an impressive 2.6 million metric tons in 1962. The sweet potato is especially important as an "in-between" crop, like others among the American foods. When the rice of the last harvest is gone and that of the next has not yet arrived, the sweet potato becomes an indispensable source of nourishment for many Indonesians.[69]

Rice production has not been able to keep pace with population expansion on Java, especially in this century. The widening gap between the two has been filled by cultivating other foodstuffs in rotation with rice and back in the areas where the irrigation networks do not reach. In 1900 the people of Java had available to them, per capita, per year 110 kilogram (Kg.) of rice, 30 kg. of tubers and three kg. of pulses. By 1940 the propositions had changed: 85 kg. of rice, 40 kg. of maize, 180 kg. of tubers and about 10 kg. of pulses.[70] The difference between the two diets consists mostly of increased quantities of American foods in the year 1940.

There are many examples elsewhere in Asia of the importance of American foods to growing populations. Japan, for instance, lies too far north for manioc to thrive, and its people have never acquired a liking for maize, but American potatoes, sweet and white, have been an important part of their alimentation for many generations. The sweet potato spread to Japan from China, via the Ryukyu Islands, in the last part of the seventeenth century—so one story goes. The tomb of the Japanese farmer who brought it home is known as the Temple of the Sweet Potato, and there every spring his grateful posterity make him offerings. The sweet potato has proved to be nearly unfailing famine insurance: in four years—1832, 1844, 1872, and 1896—large numbers of the Japanese found themselves depending on sweet potatoes for existence.[71]

The Irish potato has never been a successful rival to the sweet in most parts of Japan, but it does grow well in the colder areas. It arrived no later than 19 June 1615, when an agent of the English East India Company in Japan wrote, "I tooke a garden this day, and planted it with pottatos." Like so many others, the Japanese did not like the taste of the potato at first, but during the floods and famines of the 1680s discovered that potatoes made good cattle feed and would prosper in colder climates and higher altitudes than the sweet potato. Russian introduction of the plant into Hokkaido in the latter part of the century gave further impetus to its cultivation, and when Japan opened her gates to the world in the mid-nineteenth century, visitors found the potato a common item, especially in the north.[72]

The relationship in Japan between growth in population and in production of American foods is not as clear as it is in some other areas of the world, but it is worth taking into consideration. In 1950 Japan raised far more rice than any other food—over 8.5 million metric tons of rice on family farms alone—but these same farms also produced over 4.6 million metric tons of sweet potatoes and over 2.2 million metric tons of Irish potatoes.[73] She is the world's second largest producer of sweet potatoes, which are the staff of life on Okinawa. It is unlikely that any other food plants available to the Japanese could produce the yields that the sweet and Irish potatoes do in the soils in which the Japanese plant them.

The largest producer of sweet potatoes in the world is China. More is known of the impact of American foods in China than in any other area we have examined because of Ping-ti Ho's splendid book, *Studies on the Population of China, 1368–1953;* it is from this work that most of the following remarks have been drawn. Population statistics for China are notoriously vague, and the definition of precisely what is and what is not China has changed so often and is so controversial that perhaps it is an act of self-deception to pay too much attention to exact figures. For as long as man has tried to keep exact records, China's population has been huge, and its growth over the last few centuries has been colossal. In 1661 she had something like 100 million people; in 1900 something like 400 million; and today the Communist regime claims over 687 million subjects.[74]

The Chinese existed in enormous numbers in the seventeenth century chiefly because of their successful exploitation of the rice plant, particularly of the fast maturing varieties first introduced in the eleventh century, which allowed double-cropping. The majority of the Chinese were people of the plains, pinned to the wet lowlands by their dependence on rice. In fact, there is evidence that even as late as 1700 the Chinese farmer had left largely untouched the dry hills and mountains of the northern two-thirds of China. But although the Chinese concentration on growing rice brought vast returns—rice production doubled between the years 1000 and 1850—the problem of diminishing returns became more and more apparent. China's mothers seemed to have a capacity to produce an infinitude of babies, but her land did not have the capacity to produce an infinitude of rice.

Rice and the traditional dry land crops—wheat, millets, and such—could not by themselves have encouraged or enabled China to launch into the upward sweep of population growth that has created as many Chinese today as there were human beings in the entire world two and a half centuries ago. The stable government of the Manchu dynasty undoubtedly was a factor in the seventeenth and eighteenth century, but chaos has been the rule for China's last and most awesome century of population growth; and the life-saving techniques of modern science, the most commonly credited cause of population expansion, are only now beginning to be applied in the rural areas.[75]

No large group of the human race in the Old World was quicker to adopt American food plants than the Chinese. While men who stormed Tenochtitlán with Cortés still lived, peanuts were swelling in the sandy loams near Shanghai; maize was turning fields green in south China and the sweet potato was on its way to becoming the poor man's staple in Fukien.[76]

By the late eighteenth and early nineteenth century maize had become the primary food crop in large areas of the uplands of southwest China. As the valleys of the Yangtse River and its tributaries filled up with people in the eighteenth century, the excess population, forced up into the hills and mountains, found that maize was the key to extract subsistence from the previously barren highlands. The northern Chinese farmer was slower than his southern brothers to take up maize, not cultivating it in quantity until the nineteenth century, but today something like one-seventh of all the food energy in north China is provided by maize. China, which harvested 16,849 million metric tons of maize in 1952–1953, stood second only to the United States as a producer of that food in that year. And, as is the case in Egypt, India and Indonesia, and decidedly not the case in the United States, nearly all China's maize feeds humans, not animals.[77]

However important maize is to China, the sweet potato is an even greater boon. It arrived at least as early as the 1560s and was adopted rapidly because it did not compete with rice and other traditional crops, but prospered in previously unutilized soils, such as the rocky Shantung coast, the rice-deficient southeast provinces and the drought-ridden highlands. By the eighteenth century the sweet potato, its cultivation urged by official edicts, was spreading into nearly every climatically hospitable corner of China. Its admirers have increased ever since, and, next to rice and wheat, the sweet potato is China's most important crop. It is the traditional food of the poorest classes: in fact, to be called a sweet potato eater was an insult in pre-communist China. China is far and away the world's greatest producer of sweet potatoes, averaging at least 18.5 million metric tons a year between 1931 and 1937.[78]

China's agricultural output is so great that she ranks high as a producer of crops which are clearly of secondary importance to her. For example, in the years 1948 through 1952 she produced over 12 million tons of potatoes annually, about as much as the United States. The potato was grown in Fukien before 1800, but since has become most important in the high mountain areas, where it is a staple, and on the high plains of Kansu, Inner Mongolia and Manchuria.[79]

China harvested 2.4 million metric tons of peanuts in 1962–1963, and bows only to India as a producer of this food. Peanuts play a much more important role in China than we who only nibble them at ballgames realize. The plant enables the Chinese peasant to make greater use of the sandy coastal and riverline soils than was ever possible before the sixteenth century, and the peanut even plays an important role in the crop rotation in some rice districts. The peasant, although he has never heard of nitrogen-fixing nodules, does realize that growing peanuts helps to preserve the fertility of the soil. Today peanuts are known throughout China and are a common food in the north.[80]

The impact of American crops on China has, according to Ping-ti Ho, been simply enormous. Rice accounted for perhaps seventy percent of China's total national food output in the early seventeenth century. By 1937 the percentage had dropped to about thirty-six percent. In the last three centuries the dry land crops, such as wheat, millet, maize and sweet potatoes, in contrast to rice, "have increased to about sixty-four percent, and American food plants alone to approximately twenty percent, of the total national food production." "During the last two centuries," Ho continues, "when rice culture was gradually approaching its limit, and encountering the law of diminishing returns, the various dry land food crops introduced from America have contributed most to the increase in national food production and have made possible a continual growth of population."[81]

According to United Nations statistics for world agricultural production in 1963, the crops most heavily produced are as shown in Table 3. (The political situation is such that these figures omit the production of Albania, mainland China, Mongolia, North Korea, and North Vietnam.)

If China's agricultural output were included in these statistics, their order might well be different, but the importance of the plants first cultivated by the American Indian would still be obvious. The statistics would seem to suggest that something like one third of the plant food raised to feed

TABLE 3
LARGEST WORLD CROPS IN 1963
(in million metric tons)[82]

Potatoes	277.6
Rice	257.4
Wheat	250.3
Maize	231.8
Barley[a]	102.9

[a] Below barley the amount produced of each crop drops off sharply.

man and his animals in the world today comes from plants of American origin.

Perhaps the world food production would be sufficient to support the present world population if potatoes, maize, etc., had never existed and the fields they occupy were planted in Old World crops, but I think the reader will agree that that is a very large "perhaps." It seems more likely that the number of human beings on this planet today would be a good deal smaller but for the horticultural skills of the neolithic American.

NOTES

1. Dennis, H. Wrong, *Population and Society*, 13.

2. William H. McNeill, *The Rise of the West*, 627–628, suggests the Columbian exchange as one of the chief causes of the population explosion. The exchange of diseases between and within the Old and New Worlds at first limited population growth; then, as resistance to those maladies built up all over the globe, the population began to expand: "age-old epidemic checks upon population faded into merely endemic attrition."

3. Dorothy S. Thomas, *Social and Economic Aspects of Swedish Population Movements, 1750–1933*, 83–84.

4. George Carter, "Plant Evidence for Early Contacts with America," 162–182; George Carter, "Plants Across the Pacific," 62–71; George Carter, "Maize to Africa," 3–8; Carl O. Sauer,, "Maize into Europe," 777–778; Thor Heyerdahl, "Merrill's Reappraisal of Ethnobotanical Evidence for Prehistoric Contact Between South America and Polynesia," 789–796.

5. Nikolai Ivanovich Vavilov, *The Origin, Variation, Immunity and Breeding of Cultivated Plants*, 44. See also C. D. Darlington, *Chromosome Botany and the Origins of Cultivated Plants*, 132–180.

6. Vavilov, *Cultivated Plants*, 39–43.

7. Uncultivated plants, such as cacti, made the journey from the New to the Old World, also, but their impact seems less than that of their Old World counterparts on the New. As always, "weeds" take hold when the ecology of a given area has been disturbed. Henry N. Ridley found Singapore Island to be entirely covered

with dense forest in 1822. Man had stripped the jungle off by his return in 1888, and he found a number of alien invaders among the new growth: "thirty-nine came from South America and the West Indies, nineteen from other parts of tropical Asia, three from China, seven from Africa, four from Europe, and fourteen were typical weeds now so widely distributed that their homes of origin is uncertain." Henry N. Ridley, *The Dispersal of Plants Throughout the World*, 639.

8. Vance Bourjaily, "The Corn of Coxcatlán," 55; Richard S. MacNeish, "Ancient Mesoamerican Civilization," 531–537; Paul C. Mangelsdorf, Richard S. MacNeish, Walton C. Galinat, "Domestication of Corn," 538–545.

9. Food and Agricultural Organization of the United Nations, *Production Yearbook, 1963*, 17:37–38, 46–48; David Mitrany, *The Land and the Peasant in Rumania*, 304.

10. Désiré Bois, *Les Plantes Alimentaires Chez Tous les Peuples et à Travers les Ages*, 1:331; William L. Langer, "Europe's Initial Population Explosion," 11; Cecil Woodham-Smith, *The Great Hunger: Ireland 1845–1849*, 30; Berthold Laufer, *The American Plant Migration*, part I: *The Potato*, 11.

11. FAO *Production Yearbook, 1963*, 52, 79; Ping-ti Ho, *Studies on the Population of China, 1368–1953*, 186; A. Hyatt Verrill, *Foods America Gave the World*, 46, 48; Ruth McVey, ed., *Indonesia*, 131.

12. Herbert J. Spinden, "Thank the American Indian," 331; Wilbur H. Youngman, "America—Home of the Bean," 228; Carl O. Sauer, *Agricultural Origins and Dispersals*, 65; W. R. Arkroyd, *Legumes in Human Nutrition*, vi, 38, 109; Artemas Ward, *Encyclopedia of Food*, 29; Bois, *Plantes Alimentaires*, 1:142.

13. Sauer, *Agricultural Origins*, 66.

14. William O. Jones, *Manioc in Africa*, 4.

15. Ibid., 5.

16. Roger Barlow, *A Brief Summe of Geographie*, 154–155.

17. Jones, *Manioc*, 4, 6, 256; Donald D. Brand, "Tapioca from a Brazilian Root," 93.

18. Brand, "Tapioca," 93–94; Jones, *Manioc*, 15.

19. These figures are obtained by multiplying the yield statistics in kilograms in the FAO *Production Yearbook, 1963*, passim, by the caloric value statistics in the FAO *Food Composition Tables for International Use*, passim.

20. Arthur Young, *Travels During the Years 1787, 1788 and 1789*, 2:41.

204 | THE COLUMBIAN EXCHANGE

21. Bois, *Plantes Alimentaires,* 1:142; Rafael Altamira, *A History of Spain,* 470; John Locke, *Locke's Travels in France, 1675–1679,* 207.

22. Jean Lamarck, ed., *Encyclopédie Méthodique, Botanique,* 3:71.

23. Paul Weatherwax, *Indian Corn in Old America,* 45–47; C. E. P. Brooks, *Climate Through the Ages,* 310.

24. Márton Pécsi and Béla Sárfalvi, *The Geography of Hungary,* 251; Lamarck, *Encyclopédie Méthodique,* 3:682; Food and Agricultural Organization, *Maize and Maize Diets, A Nutritional Survey,* 62.

25. Locke, *Travels,* 236; Jorge Nadal, *La Población Española (Siglos XVI a XX),* 20; J. W. Goethe, *Italian Journey, 1786–1788,* trans. W. H. Auden and Elizabeth Mayer, 20; Young, *Travels,* 1:643, 645, 647, 650, 2:353; *Annual Register* (1810), 52:672; Sauer, "Maize into Europe," 777–778; Marion I. Newbegin, *Southern Europe, a Regional and Economic Geography,* 181; J. H. G. Lebon, *An Introduction to Human Geography,* 123–124; Edmond Soreau, *L'Agriculture du XVIIe Siècle à la Fin du XVIIIe,* 103, 179; D. V. Glass and D. E. C. Eversley, eds., *Population in History,* 455, 472, 573; Marcel R. Reinhard and André Armengaud, *Histoire Générale de la Population,* 144.

26. *The Statesman's Yearbook, Statistical and Historical Annual of the States of the World for the Year 1964–1965,* xix.

27. Elisee Reclus, *Universal Geography,* 3:145; Henry Marczali, *Hungary in the Eighteenth Century,* 46, 50, 55; Reinhard and Armengaud, *Histoire Générdle,* 179.

28. J. E. Worcester, *A Geographical Dictionary or Universal Gazetteer,* 2:101, 788; L. C. Vialla de Sommières, *Voyage Historique et Politique au Montenegro,* 2:75; Mitrany, *Rumania,* 304; L. S. Stavrianos, *The Balkans Since 1453,* 420; Doreen Warriner, ed., *Contrasts in Emerging Societies: Readings in the Social and Economic History of South-Eastern Europe in the Ninetheenth Century,* 298, 300, 308, 322, 326, 354, 368.

29. Mitrany, *Rumania,* 305; Bernard Newman, *Balkan Background,* 95; Eugène Pittard, *La Romanie,* 147–149; Reclus, *Universal Geography,* 1:147.

30. Charles Eliot, *Turkey in Europe,* 328.

31. Joel Martin Halpern, *A Serbian Village,* 57–58.

32. Langer, "Population Explosion," 1–17.

33. As quoted in Redcliffe N. Salaman, *The History and Social Influence of the Potato,* 424, 425, 428.

34. As quoted in Laufer, *Potato,* 62–63.

35. Salaman, *The Potato,* 135, 189, 190, 251; Woodham-Smith, *The Great Hunger,* 30; Langer, "Population Explosion," 12.

36. Langer, "Population Explosion," 14; B. H. Slicher Van Bath, *The Agrarian History of Western Europe,* A.D. *500–1850,* 267.

37. *Annual Register* (1803), 45:850–853.

38. Slicher Van Bath, *Agrarian History,* 268; Langer, "Population Explosion," 14; Marczali, *Hungary,* 55–56; Alexander von Humbolt, *Voyage de Humbolt et Bonpland, Première Partie Physique Générale, et Relation Historique du Voyage,* 1:29; Warriner, *Contrasts,* 66.

39. Worcester, *Geographical Dictionary,* 2:466; Langer, "Population Explosion," 15–16; Peter I. Layshchenko, *History of the National Economy of Russia,* 453; FAO *Production Yearbook, 1963,* 76.

40. FAO *Production Yearbook, 1963,* 76; Quoted from Salaman, *The Potato,* 102.

41. Vavilov, *Cultivated Plants,* 44; L. Dudley Stamp, *Africa: A Study in Tropical Development,* 142; Sauer, *Agricultural Origins,* 34; Roland Oliver and J. D. Fage, *A Short History of Africa,* 28.

42. George Peter Murdock, *Africa, Its People and Their Culture History,* 223, 233–234 and passim; George Petter Murdock, "Staple Subsistence Crops of Africa," 522–540; Roland Portères, "L'Introduction du Maïs en Afrique," 221; William A. Hance, *The Geography of Modern Africa,* 9.

43. Some even claim that maize was present in Africa prior to Columbus's voyages. Few, as yet, accept this view, which, of course, does not mean that it is incorrect. For those interested in further reading on this theory, George Carter's "Maize to Africa" is a good place to start.

44. Marvin P. Miracle, "The Introduction and Spread of Maize in Africa," 39, 41, 44, 45.

45. Ibid., 52; S. M. Molena, *The Bantu, Past and Present,* 118; William J. Burchell, *Travels in the Interior of Southern Africa,* 1:225; Hance, *Geography of Modern Africa,* 547; Marvin P. Miracle, "Murdock's Classification of Tropical African Food Economies," 219–244.

46. Jones, *Manioc,* 3, 16.

47. Ibid., 38; W. B. Harrison, Review of *Manioc in Africa,* by William O. Jones, 159; R. J. Harrison Church, *West Africa, A Study of the Environment and Man's Use of It,* 489; Miracle, "Murdock's Classification," 219, 224.

48. There are those who think that maize was grown in the

Middle East before the sixteenth century and that Arab sailors were in contact with America as early as the ninth century. See M. D. W. Jeffreys, "Pre-Columbian Maize into Africa," 965–966.

49. Portères, "Maïs en Afrique," 99; *Déscription de l'Egypte ou Recueil des Observations et des Recherches qui ont été faites en Egypte Pendant l'Expédition de l'Armée Française*, 19:55.

50. John Ray, ed., *Collection of Curious Travels and Voyages Containing Dr. Leonhart Rauwolf's Journey into the Eastern Countries*, 2:50, 72, 124, 130, 133–134, 187, 189, 215; Karl H. Dannenfeldt, *Leon Rauwolf*, 97, 254.

51. Ömer Lufti Barkan, "Essai sur les Données Statistiques des Registres de Recensement dans l'Empire Ottoman aux XVe et XVIe Siècles," 27; Spinden, "Thank the American Indian," 331; John Payne, *Universal Geography*, 1:335, 415; Henry Blunt, *A Voyage into the Levent*, passim; Chevalier Chardin, *Voyages de Chevalier Chardin en Perse et Autres Lieux de l'Orient*, passim.

52. Reader Bullard, ed., *The Middle East, a Political and Economic Survey*, 55; Vivi and Gunnar Täckholm, *Flora of Egypt*, 1:546; J. D. Tothill, *Agriculture in the Sudan*, 319; Charles Issawi, *Egypt at Mid-Century, An Economic Survey*, 20; Payne, *Universal Geography*, 1:453; Helen Anne B. Rivlin, *The Agricultural Policy of Muhammad 'Ali in Egypt*, 158.

53. Marcel R. Reinhard, *Histoire de la Population Mondiale de 1700 à 1948*, 446–447.

54. Issawi, *Egypt*, 111; W. B. Fisher, *The Middle East*, 468.

55. Pierre Gourou et al., *The Development of Upland Areas in the Far East*, 1:8.

56. Warren S. Thompson, "Population," 11; V. D. Wickizer and M. K. Bennett, *The Rice Economy of Monsoon Asia*, 208ff.

57. Kingsley Davis, *The Population of India and Pakistan*, 24, 25.

58. Irfan Habib, *The Agrarian System of Mughal India, 1556–1707*, 38, 47–48, 56.

59. George Watt, *A Dictionary of the Economic Products of India*, 6:334–335; *Statesman's Yearbook, 1964–1965*, xix.

60. Watt, *Products of India*, 4:479–482, 6:266; Laufer, *Potato*, 91.

61. Watt, *Products of India*, 5:159; Jones, *Manioc*, 25, 33.

62. Statistical Office of the United Nations, *Statistical Yearbook, 1964*, 138; Watt, *Products of India*, 1:286, 2:639.

63. Watt, *Products of India*, 2:137.

64. Nitisastro Widjojo, *Migration, Population Growth, and Eco-*

*nomic Development in Indonesia: A Study of the Economic Conse-
quences of Alternative Patterns of Inter-Island Migration*, 6, 254.

65. I. H. Burkhill, *A Dictionary of the Ecónomic Products of
the Malay Peninsula*, 2:1709, 2047–2048; Charles Robequain, *Malaya,
Indonesia, Borneo and the Philippines*, 95; William Bligh, *The Mutiny
of H.M.S. Bounty*, 193; Laufer, *Potato*, 95.

66. McVey, *Indonesia*, 125; Gourou et al., *Upland Areas*, 2:53.

67. Gourou et al., *Upland Areas*, 1:74–75; McVey, *Indonesia*,
120; Burkill, *Products of the Malay Peninsula*, 2:2280.

68. Burkill, *Products of the Malay Peninsula*, 2:1413; Jones,
Manioc, 25; McVey, *Indonesia*, 17; FAO *Production Yearbook, 1963*,
81–82; Clifford Geertz, *Agricultural Involution: The Process of
Ecological Change in Indonesia*, n. 92.

69. MvVey, *Indonesia*, 131; Gourou et al., *Upland Areas*,
2:84–85.

70. Geertz, *Agricultural Involution*, 96.

71. J. S. Cooley, "Origin of the Sweet Potato and Primitive
Storage Practices," 328–329; Berthold Laufer, "The American Plant
Migration," 244–245.

72. Peter Pratt, *History of Japan Compiled from the Records
of the English East India Company, at the Instance of the Court
of Directors*, 2:60; Laufer, *Potato*, 81–82; Rutherford Alcock, *The
Capital of the Tycoon, A Narrative of Three Years Residence in
Japan*, 245, 263; Henry Dyer, *Dai Nippon*, 242.

73. FAO *Report on the 1950 World Census of Agriculture* [no
pagination].

74. L. Carrington Goodrich, *A Short History of China*, n. 202;
Kenneth S. Latourette, *A Short History of the Far East*, 714.

75. William Peterson, *Population*, 372–373.

76. Ho, *Population of China*, 183–184.

77. Ibid., 187–189; John King Fairbank, *The United States and
China*, 127; FAO *Production Yearbook, 1963*, 47; FAO, *Maize and
Maize Diets*, 62–63.

78. Ho, *Population of China*, 186–187; Iago Galdston, ed., *Human
Nutrition, Historic and Scientific*, 68.

79. *Statesman's Yearbook, 1964–1965*, xxi; Ho, *Population of
China*, 189.

80. Ho, *Population of China*, 184–186.

81. Ibid., 184, 191–192.

82. United Nations, *Statistical Yearbook, 1964*, 21.

The
Columbian
Exchange
Continues

6

The Columbian exchange continues and will continue. The men of the Old World continue to enjoy the benefits of biological warfare as American Indians continue to die of Old World diseases. Between 1871 and 1947, the total number of natives of Tierra del Fuego dropped from between 7,000 and 9,000 to 150, many of them victims of a malady which is even now one of the chief killers of the aborigines of the Chaco: measles.[1]

Most of the really devastating killers among the diseases crossed the oceans to the New World in the first post-Columbian century, but the migration of sicknesses has, of course, never stopped. The arrivals of cholera epidemics, with their high mortality rates, were among the most awesome events of the nineteenth century in America. The African anopheles mosquitos, which arrived in Brazil about 1929, did not initiate the spread of malaria in America—it had existed in the New World for several centuries, at least—but they could breed in conditions under which American mosquitos could not. Hundreds of thousands of humans fell sick and about 20,000 died before these immigrant insects were eliminated.[2]

Most of the diseases native to the New World have proved to be inexportable. *Verruga Peruana,* which sickened the comrades of Pizarro and still takes its toll, is a disease whose most notable symptom is great warts or ulcers. This malady "of granulomatous erruption" is, fortunately for the rest of the world, still confined to Peru, Colombia, and Ecuador. *Oroya* fever strikes down the healthy in Peru, Ecuador, Bolivia, Colombia, Chile, and probably Guatemala, but has never established a beachhead in the Old World. Rocky Mountain spotted fever stays on its own side of the Atlantic. Pinta, probably the cause of the strange complexions of Moctezuma's servants whom Cortes called "tiger men," never has crossed oceans—never has, that is, unless we consider it as just another form of treponematosis.[3]

The one disease—if we can call it that—which experts agree is American in origin and which has laid thousands low in the Old World is that ailment caused by the sandflea or chigger of the tropics. Oviedo's description of its depredations is as accurate for America or Africa (where the insect appeared about 1872) today as it was for Española four hundred years ago. He recorded that the chigger

> penetrates the skin of the feet and forms a pocket as large as a chickpea between the skin and the flesh. It swells with nits, which are the eggs which the insect deposits. If it is not taken out in time the *niguas* (for that is the name of this small animal) grow and increase so that the men are so severely affected that they are crippled and remain lame forever.[4]

The chief danger from this insect is that the site in which its eggs are deposited will become an avenue for really dangerous infection. The nigua has often served as a pathfinder for tetanus.[5]

But the chigger is no maker of history like the tsetse fly or the anopheles mosquito. The most important pathological organism that America ever exported is probably the

Treponema pallidum. It has spread everywhere since the fifteenth century, and the wounds it inflicts upon society suppurate beneath the cosmetic of hypocrisy. Among its victims have been men whose physical health or lack of it has shaped our history and culture. Saint-Simon's *Mémoires* inform us that Louis XIV's celebrated general, the Duc de Vendôme, had syphilis. Guy de Maupassant and Friederich Nietzsche, both of whom died insane, were probably syphilitics.[6]

Finally, in the mid-twentieth century a way to cure syphilis quickly and thus limit its spread was discovered: penicillin. It was hoped that the widespread use of penicillin would soon wipe out the disease completely, but, instead, the effectiveness of the medication has led to overconfidence. A drop in the number of syphilitics in the 1950s has been followed by a resurgence of the disease. In 1964 in England and Wales, for instance, syphilis was second only to tuberculosis as a cause of death among the infectious diseases.[7]

The other set of biological exchanges initiated by the Columbian voyages consisted of life forms visible to the naked eye, ranging from pumpkins to water buffalo. The results of this exchange—from the human viewpoint—have been mixed. Pumpkins, for instance, are eaten with pleasure by millions of the Old World's people, and the *Vrat Kaumudi* of India recommends the worship of this fruit. The water buffalo, introduced into the lower Amazon region in the hope that it would prove as valuable a beast of burden as in Asia, has rather become a dangerous wild animal.[8]

The exchange of plants and animals between the hemispheres goes on continually. The transfer of organisms which conduct themselves in a manner contrary to the interests of man is naturally better recorded than the stories of helpful migrants. According to tradition, that enemy of American wheat, the Hessian Fly, arrived with the Hessians during the American Revolution. The starling and English sparrow have dispossessed millions of American birds and swept across North America. The carp, first succesfully introduced into America in 1877, has spread explosively, driving native American fish and water fowl out of many ponds, lakes, and rivers. Importations, intentional and unintentional, have made it possible for the twentieth-century American to be trampled by Barbary sheep in New Mexico and gored by Russian hogs in North Carolina. If he sits at home, he can watch his flowers succumb to Japanese beetles and his trees to the Dutch elm disease and the chestnut tree fungus mentioned in Chapter 4. All of these, excepting only the Hessian fly, have arrived in the New World well within the last century.[9]

The results of biological transfers from the eastern to western hemispheres are, then, mixed at best. The ecology of vast areas of the Americas has been changed by the arrival and propagation of Old World life forms. Native animals, such as the bighorn sheep, which once roamed over huge areas, have been destroyed or driven back into the mountains, where they gaze down on the enormous herds of horses and cattle, which have usurped their ancient homes. In thousands and thousands of square miles of the Americas, the indigenous plants have been eliminated completely or restricted to uncultivated strips along the side of roads; and sugar, coffee, bananas, wheat, barley, and rye occupy the greater part of the land. The positive result has been an enormous increase in food production and, thereby, in human population. The negative results have been the destruction of ecological stability over enormous areas and an increase of erosion that is so great that it amounts to a crime against posterity. The Spaniards initiated the process, and it is perhaps significant that many Spanish-American words adopted into the Anglo-American vocabulary have to do with domesticated animals or erosion: bronco, lariat, chaps, bukaroo, arroyo, and barranca, to name a few.

The New World has few valuable animals to offer the Old. The turkey, guinea pig, and Muscovy duck crossed the Atlantic very early. The muskrat was purposely introduced into Europe in 1905 in hopes of profits to be gained from its pelts and spread so quickly that by 1917 Europeans were trying to bring it under control. Most Europeans agree that its importation was a mistake.[10]

Of valueless animals the New World has supplied the Old with plenty. For instance, North American gray squirrels have nearly driven Britain's red squirrels right off the island in the last seventy years. In the 1860s, an American vine aphid nearly destroyed the French wine industry, which was saved only by grafting European vines onto American rootstock resistant to that aphid. The Colorado potato beetle followed the white potato across the Atlantic about 1920 and by 1955 had advanced as far east as Russia.[11]

It is in plants that America has made its really positive contribution to the Old World. There were American plants, which the European wished he had never seen, such as the Canadian water weed that choked British waterways in the middle of the last century, but the food plants developed by the American Indian proved to be an enormously valuable acquisition for the Old World farmer. The dependence of Old World peoples on American crops in some instances may even be increasing today. For instance, the dependence on the sweet potato has undoubtedly increased in China since World War II. During the "Great Leap Forward" of the late 1950s, the intention of China's leaders was—and still may be—to have this root satisfy 20 to 30 percent of China's dietary needs.[12]

The most obvious element in the Columbian exchange—at least from the human viewpoint—is the last to be dealt with in this book: people. Few, very few, aborigines of the New World have crossed the Atlantic to colonize in the Old World, but aborigines of Europe and Africa have crossed by the tens of millions to found nations in the regions of America where their pioneers had done the heroic work of bringing diseases to destroy or reduce the resistance of the native Americans. Indeed, the Euro- and Afro-Americans now often consider themselves to be the natives of those nations, and the Indians to be the aliens.

The source of the earliest mass migration of Old World peoples to the New World was not Europe, despite the impression that history textbooks give. The mass of African immigrants arrived in America before the mass of Europeans. With perhaps millions of Native Americans succumbing to cold steel, the musketball, whiskey, and disease in the sixteenth, seventeenth, and eighteenth centuries, especially in the coastal regions, European exploitation of America was slowed by the shortage of servants and slaves. Europeans could not or would not offer themselves in sufficient numbers to make up this shortage, and so the white conquistadors and plantation masters and merchant princes turned to Africa. The shortage of labor was most pressing in the islands and littoral of tropical America, where the swords and maladies of the Old World had made the cleanest sweep of the aborigines and where the profits to be made from the mass production of tobacco, rice, indigo, coffee, and especially sugar were potentially the greatest. Almost 90 percent of the Africans who were torn from their homes to serve as slaves in America were brought to the tropics of the New World, 38 percent to Brazil and 42 percent to the Antilles alone. The total number brought to America probably falls between 8 million and 10.5 million, and almost all of these had arrived by 1850. In 1950 their descendants, both of pure and part African ancestry, numbered at least 47 million, as compared with the entire African population, Caucasians and Asians included, of 198 million.[13]

The migration of masses of aborigines from Europe to America is an event of no more than the last century and a half. The port officials of Seville recorded only 150,000 people embarking for the New World from 1509 to 1740, and, while this is a serious underestimation of the numbers of Spaniards who made that choice, it does suggest that relatively few did. In the seventeenth century only a quarter million left the British Isles for America, and, in the eighteenth century, only a million and a half. Germany sent only 200,000 before 1800, and other European countries even fewer.[14] Despite interbreeding with the Indians and Afro-Americans and despite what were sometimes fantastically high birth rates, these few people would have never filled up the regions vacated by the Indians if they had not been aided by the multitudes that have followed them since.

In the nineteenth century, news that the American settlements were now more than beachheads and that American land was good and cheap spread throughout Europe. The spacious and dependable steamship replaced the cramped and undependable sailing ship. Population pressure in rural Europe made it more and more difficult to obtain even a small plot of ground, and the early industrial revolution made wages low and unemployment frequent in her cities. The greatest transoceanic migration in all human history began, at first a freshet in the 1830s and then a torrent of Englishmen, Scots, Irishmen, Germans, Swedes, Poles, Spaniards, Portuguese, Czechs, Italians, and Russians, Protestants, Catholics, and Jews crossing the Atlantic to fill in the lands left vacant by the Indians or defined as vacant by the ethnocentric immigrants. From 1851 to 1960, over 61 million Europeans migrated to continents other than that of their birth.[15] The great bulk of these men and women, 45 million by 1924, migrated to the Americas. Of these 45 million, the majority, about 34 million, chose the United States of America as their new home. Those who went to Latin America went chiefly to Argentina and Brazil, the total to Argentina between 1850 and 1940 approaching 7 million and the total to Brazil from 1821 to 1945 about 4.5 million. Non-American recipients of European immigrants, like Australia and South Africa, lagged far behind.[16]

In 1930 about 20 million people born in Europe were living in other continents: nearly 14 million in North America—12 million in the United States and most of the remainder in Canada—and about 5 million in Latin America, chiefly Argentina and Brazil. And the migration to the New World continues. Between 1946 and 1957 Europe lost 5.4 million emigrants and the Americas gained 4.4 million immigrants.[18]

As of the 1950s the population of the United States was over 85 percent of European ancestry, and the corresponding percentage for Brazil was 42, for Chile 46, for Uruguay 96, and for Argentina 99.[19] There are two Europes, as there are two Africas: one on either side of the Atlantic. The European and African in America are the most blatant products of the Columbian exchange.

The effects of the transatlantic crossing of Old World emigrants, along with their agricultures and industries, has been, of course, enormous, and whole legions of historians have devoted their careers to tracing those influences. We will only briefly note a few of those influences.

All the populations of all the continents have increased in the last two hundred years, but Europe's has increased fastest, from 19 or 20 percent of the world's population in 1750 to 23 percent in 1850. In 1960 the proportion was still 21 percent.[20] This relative increase over the last two centuries must have played a role in enabling the expansion of the area of the world settled by Europeans from no more than 22 percent in 1750 to a peak figure of 36 percent in 1950.[21]

Why did Europeans gain in number relative to Asians and Americans? Because they made fuller use of American crops? Probably not. Because of more efficient government, better sanitation, and other advantages? Probably so. Cer-

TABLE 4
INTERCONTINENTAL MIGRATION, SELECTED
COUNTRIES AND PERIODS[17]

Country of Emigration	Emigration Period	Number of Emigrants
Austria and Hungary	1846–1932	5,196,000
Belgium	1846–1932	193,000
British Isles	1846–1932	18,020,000
Denmark	1846–1932	387,000
Finland	1871–1932	371,000
France	1846–1932	519,000
Germany	1846–1932	4,889,000
Holland	1846–1932	224,000
Italy	1846–1932	10,092,000
Norway	1846–1932	854,000
Poland	1920–1932	642,000
Portugal	1846–1932	1,805,000
Russia	1846–1924	2,253,000
Spain	1846–1932	4,653,000
Sweden	1846–1932	1,203,000
Switzerland	1846–1932	332,000

Country of Immigration	Immigration Period	Number of Immigrants
Argentina	1856–1932	6,405,000
Australia	1861–1932	2,913,000
Brazil	1821–1932	4,431,000
British West Indies	1836–1932	1,587,000
Canada	1821–1932	5,206,000
Cuba	1901–1932	857,000
Mexico	1911–1931	226,000
New Zealand	1851–1932	594,000
South Africa	1881–1932	852,000
United States	1821–1932	34,244,000
Uruguay	1836–1932	713,000

tainly the removal of more than 50 millions across the Atlantic must have done a great deal to lessen population pressure on the resources of the continent of their birth and, thus, to encourage population growth there. And certainly the export of Europeans and Africans to America helped to bring a manifold return on European investments in the New World, and by thus lessening the burden of poverty, to encourage an increase in marriages and births.

An admittedly extreme example of what Europeans and Africans working in America to enrich Europe could mean in terms of wealth streaming back to Europe is the following: between 1714 and 1773, Britain imported £101,264,818 worth of goods, mostly sugar, from her West Indian colonies—20.5 percent of her total imports for that period—much of which was re-exported, at profit, to the continent. A contemporary estimated that every Englishman driving slaves in the cane fields brought twenty times greater clear profit to England than a similar person in the home country.[22]

The emigration of masses of Europeans to America created giant markets for European manufacturers and, thus, a return of enormous profits to Europe. Even if we select only those American nations whose citizens are most nearly completely European in ancestry, and exclude such nations as Brazil, which has millions of European ancestry, we discover that Euro-Americans make up an immense market for European exports. To illustrate, the United States, Canada, and Argentina received 17 percent of Great Britain's exports in 1860 and 21 percent in 1960. Britain, of course, provides extreme examples of the sort we are looking for, because she has been so long one of the greatest manufacturing and trading nations in the world. But even France, which has lagged behind her rival across the Channel in these categories, sent 11 percent of her exports to the United States in 1860 and 6 percent in 1960.[23]

There are, of course, a thousand other ways in which America has been a device for making capital for Europe, but that is a subject for another book. We have indicated the truth of the claim that the Columbian exchange has created markets for Europe without which she would have been and would be now a very different and a much poorer region of the earth, and poverty a palpably heavier burden on the connubial propensities of young adults.

This book must end on a note of pessimism for we have tried to take the long view and, at least to some extent, the view of the historian of life rather than that of human institutions. The long-range biological effects of the Columbian exchange are not encouraging.

If one values all forms of life and not just the life of one's own species, then one must be concerned with the genetic pool, the total potential of all living things to produce descendants of various shapes, sizes, colors, internal structures, defenses against both multicellular and unicellular enemies, maximum fertility, and, to speak generally, maximum ability to produce offspring with maximum adaptive possibilities. The genetic pool is usually expanded when continents join. As plants and creatures move into virgin territory, the adaptations to new environments of those who survive the increased competition produce new types and even many new species. Paleontologists and comparative zoologists call the event "explosive evolution," meaning that it often only takes a few million years.[24] This is what normally would have happened and would be happening after the joining of the Old and New Worlds in 1492—but for man.

Not for half a billion years, at least, and probably for long before that, has an extreme or permanent physical change affected the whole earth. The single exception to this generality may be European man and his technologies, agricultural and industrial. He has spread all over the globe, and non-

European peoples have adopted his techniques in all but the smallest islets. His effect is comparable to an increase in the influx of cosmic rays or the raising of whole new chains of Andes and Himalayas.

The Columbian exchange has included man, and he has changed the Old and New Worlds sometimes inadvertently, sometimes intentionally, often brutally. It is possible that he and the plants and animals he brings with him have caused the extinction of more species of life forms in the last four hundred years than the usual processes of evolution might kill off in a million. Man kills faster than the pace of evolution: there has been no million years since Columbus for evolution to devise a replacement for the passenger pigeon. No one can remember what the pre-Columbian flora of the Antilles was like, and the trumpeter swan and the buffalo and a hundred other species have been reduced to such small numbers that a mere twitch of a change in ecology or man's wishes can eliminate them. The flora and fauna of the Old and especially of the New World have been reduced and specialized by man. Specialization almost always narrows the possibilities for future changes: for the sake of present convenience, we loot the future.[25]

The Columbian exchange has left us with not a richer but a more impoverished genetic pool. We, all of the life on this planet, are the less for Columbus, and the impoverishment will increase.

NOTES

1. Jehan Vellard, "Causas Biologicas de la Desaparición de los Indios Americanos," 83 and passim.

2. Charles S. Elton, *The Ecology of Invasions by Animals and Plants,* 20.

3. William H. Prescott, *History of the Conquest of Mexico*

and the History of the Conquest of Peru, 894; Philip H. Manson-Bahr, *Manson's Tropical Diseases,* 181, 184; Alfonso Elizondo Langagne, "Program for the Eradication of Pinta (Spotted Sickness) in Mexico," 172.

4. Gonzalo Fernández Oviedo y Valdés, *Natural History of the West Indies,* trans. Sterling A. Stoudemire, 23. See also Fray Bartolomé de Las Casas, *Historia de las Indias,* 5:349; Luis L. Dominguez, ed., *The Conquest of the River Plate, 1535–1555,* 74; François Pyrard, *The Voyage of François Pyrard of Laval to the East Indies, the Maldives, the Moluccas and Brazil,* trans. Albert Gray, 319; Hans Staden, *Hans Staden: The True History of His Captivity,* trans. Malcolm Letts, 166.

5. Manson-Bahr, *Tropical Diseases,* 622–623.

6. J. D. Rolleston, "Syphilis in Saint-Simon's *Mémoires,*" 183; Guy de Maupassant, *The Portable Maupassant,* ed. Lewis Galantière, 21; H. A. Reyburn, H. E. Hinderks, and J. G. Taylor, *Nietzsche, The Story of a Human Philosopher,* 497–498. A good place to begin a search for other great men with syphilis is in Judson B. Gilbert and Gordon E. Mestler, *Disease and Destiny,* a bibliographical guide to medical references to famous figures of history.

7. R. S. Morton, *Venereal Diseases,* 38–44.

8. Julian H. Steward, ed., *Handbook of South American Indians,* 6:424; George A. Watt, *A Dictionary of Economic Products of India,* 1:286, 2:639.

9. George Laycock, *The Alien Animals,* 10, 13, 28–45, 47, 51, 61–62, 75, 83, 110–117, 162–170.

10. Ibid., 95–100.

11. Ibid., 91, 93; Elton, *Ecology of Invasions,* 59; Carl Lindroth, *The Faunal Connections Between Europe and North America,* 136.

12. Iago Galdston, ed., *Human Nutrition, Historic and Scientific,* 74.

13. Philip D. Curtin, *The African Slave Trade, A Census,* 87–91, 265–266.

14. Brinley Thomas, "Migration, Economic Aspects," 293.

15. I realize that an appreciable number of the 61 million eventually returned to Europe, but those who did had usually spent at least several years outside of Europe, and I feel that it is no more necessary to subtract them than I feel it necessary to subtract those who emigrated and then died within five or ten years.

16. B. Thomas, "Migration," 296; William Woodruff, *Impact of Western Man, A Study of Europe's Role in the World Economy, 1750–1960,* 106; Population Division, Department of Social Affairs,

United Nations, *The Determinants and Consequences of Population Trends*, 101–103.

17. B. Thomas, "Migration," 294.

18. Ibid., 295; United Nations, *Determinants and Consequences of Population Trends*, 101.

19. Woodruff, *Impact of Western Man*, 112; United States, Bureau of the Census, Department of Commerce, *Pocket Data Book, 1969*, 36–49.

20. These percentages include Asian Russians, a relatively insignificant number.

21. Woodruff, *Impact of Western Man*, 103.

22. Eric Williams, *Capitalism and Slavery*, 52–53, 225.

23. Woodruff, *Impact of Western Man*, Tables VII/14 and VII/16.

24. George Gaylord Simpson, *The Geography of Evolution*, 7.

25. George Gaylord Simpson, *The Meaning of Evolution, A Study of the History of Life and of its Significance for Man*, 194–195, 249.

Bibliography

Biologists are rarely historians and historians are rarely biologists, so bio-historians are forced to process a great deal of ore in order to obtain a very few nuggets of what is to them gold. Therefore, the bibliography of this brief book is rather long and probably will prove to be a source of frustration rather than of help to the student who wishes to probe more deeply into the subject of the Columbian exchange. Perhaps a short essay on the sources which were most helpful to me will provide a guide.

The writings of the early European explorers and settlers are, of course, extremely helpful in pointing out the contrasts between the Old and New Worlds and the impact of Old World microlife, flora and fauna, on the Americas. Particularly useful are *The Journals and Other Documents of the Life of Christopher Columbus,* trans. Samuel Eliot Morison (New York: Heritage Press, 1963) and Ferdinand Columbus, *The Life of Admiral Christopher Columbus by His Son Ferdinand,* trans. Benjamin Keen (New Brunswick: Rutgers University Press, 1959). For discriptions of the interiors of the continents of the New World, the equivalents are

Hernando Cortés, *Five Letters,* trans. J. Bayard Morris (New York: W. W. Norton and Co., 1962), *The Bernal Díaz Chronicles,* trans. Albert Idell (Garden City: Double- day and Co., 1956), Francisco López de Gómara, *Cortés, The Life of the Conqueror by His Secretary,* trans. Lesley Byrd Simpson (Berkeley and Los Angeles: University of California Press, 1964), and Pedro Pizarro, *Relation of the Discovery and Conquest of the Kingdoms of Peru,* 2 vols., trans. Philip A. Means (New York: Cortes Society, 1921).

The great contemporary histories of Gonzalo Fernández Oviedo y Valdés and Bartolomé de Las Casas are gold mines, though the percentage of dross to metal runs quite high throughout most of their pages. The great exception is Oviedo's *Natural History of the West Indies,* which is a boon to the bio-historian and readily available to the English reader in Sterling A. Stoudemire's translation (Chapel Hill: University of North Carolina Press, 1959). Oviedo's full comments on the New World are found in his *Historia General y Natural de las Indias,* 4 vols. (Madrid: Ediciones Atlas, 1959). The best edition of Las Casas's *Historia de las Indias* is that of Agustín Millares Carlo and Lewis Hanke (3 vols., Mexico: Fondo de Cultura Económica, 1951), which I unfortunately did not have available to me.

The generations of colonists who followed the above men included, especially among the priests and monks, writers who were more actively conscious of the significance of the Columbian Exchange than anyone since. Joseph de Acosta's *The Natural and Moral History of the Indies,* trans. Edward Grimston 2 vols. (New York: Burt Franklin, n.d.), and Bernabé Cobo's *Obras,* 2 vols. (Madrid: Atlas Ediciones, 1964), run close to one hundred percent gold, according to my assay. Other early writers whose works are of special value to the bio-historian, full reference to which can be found below, are Bernandino de Sahagún, Juan López de Velasco, Antonio Vasquez de Espinosa, Diego de Durán,

Toribio Motolinía, Alonso de Zorita, Pedro de Cieza de León, Pero de Magalhães, Pedro Sarmiento de~Gamboa, and these wanderers whose accounts were collected by Richard Hakluyt and Samuel Purchas. Also helpful is the *Colección de Documentos Inéditos Relativos al Descubrimiento, Conquista y Colonización de las Posesiones Espãnoles en América y Oceanía* (Madrid: Imprenta de Quiros, 1864–1884), 42 vols., which, unfortunately, has not been indexed with the bio-historians' interests in mind.

The twentieth-century work which proved most valuable to me was P. M. Ashburn's *The Ranks of Death, A Medical History of the Conquest of America* (New York: Coward-McCann, 1947). The books and articles of Sherburne F. Cook, Woodrow Borah, Henry F. Dobyns, Alexander Marchant, Mervyn Ratekin, Arthur P. Whitaker, Carl Otwin Sauer, John J. Johnson, Madaline W. Nichols, François Chevalier, Charles J. Bishko, Donald D. Brand, Rollie E. Poppino, Alfred J. Tapson and Clark Wissler (full references below) provided me, quite frankly, with my most beneficial material. Without Julian H. Steward, ed., *Handbook of South American Indians* (Washington D. C., United States Government Printing Office, 1946–1959), 7 vols., the problem of researching the impact of the Columbian exchange on the Indians of the southern half of the Americas would be impossibly unwieldy.

Those particularly interested in the smallpox pandemic of the 1520s and those that followed should read with care C. W. Dixon's medical text, *Smallpox* (London: J. and A. Churchill, 1962), and E. Wagner Stearn's and Allen E. Stearn's provocative *The Effect of Smallpox on the Destiny of the Amerindian* (Boston: Bruce Humphries, 1945).

It is more difficult to research the impact of America's diseases, animals, and plants on the Old World than that of the Old World on the New. Except for the matter of syphilis, few took much notice of the effects of the Columbian exchange on Europe, Africa, and Asia until the twentieth century. The American food whose influence has attracted the most attention is the potato, and for this I highly recommend Berthold Laufer, *The American Plant Migration,* Part I, *The Potato,* Anthropological Series, Vol. 28 (Chicago: Field Museum of Natural History, 1938), and Redcliffe N. Salaman, *The History and Social Influence of the Potato* (Cambridge: Cambridge University Press, 1949). William L. Langer's article, "Europe's Initial Population Explosion," *The American Historical Review* 69 (October 1963), 1–17 is especially valuable for the impact of the potato on European demography. William O. Jones, *Manioc in Africa* (Stanford: Stanford University Press, 1959) should be read by anyone interested in that food source, no matter in what continent. George P. Murdock, *Africa, Its People and Their Culture History* is probably the most helpful book to refer to for the general impact of the Columbian exchange on Africa.

The problem of finding material on the influence of the Columbian Exchange on the Far East is a very discouraging one. The one nugget of pure gold is Ping-ti Ho's *Studies on the Population of China, 1368–1953* (Cambridge: Harvard University Press, 1959), a book which should be inspiring dozens of scholars to follow up his theory of the impact of American crops on Chinese demography. For India, Irfan Habib, *The Agrarian System of Mughal India, 1556–1707* (New York: Asia Publishing House, 1963), is of some assistance. I. H. Burkill, *A Dictionary of the Economic Products of the Malay Peninsula* (London: Published on behalf of the Governments of the Straits Settlements and Federated Malay States by the Crown Agents for the Colonies, 1935), 2 vols., and George Watt, *A Dictionary of the Economic Products of India* (Calcutta: Superintendant of the Government Printing, India, 1889–1899), 7 vols., are another lode for the diligent searcher. For those who are interested in food plant migrations, it is, of course, necessary to know where the plants originated. For that, despite all the research of the last decades, one must turn to Nikolai Ivanovich Vavilov, *The Origin, Variation, Immunity and Breeding of Cultivated Plants* (New York: Ronald Press Co., 1951).

In contrast to all the other aspects of the Columbian exchange, the early history of syphilis has been exhaustively researched. A very good place to start, both to learn something about the disease per se and about its history is R. S. Morton, little book, *Venereal Diseases* (Baltimore: Penguin Books, 1966). The primary sources on the subject include Ruy Díaz de Isla, *Tractado llamado fructo de todos Sanctos: contra el mal Serpentino* (Seville: 1542), Ulrich von Hutten, *Of the Wood Called Guaiacum,* trans. Thomas Paynel (London: Thomas Bertheletregii, 1540), Girolamo Fracastoro, *Fracastor, Syphilis or the French Disease, a Poem in Latin Hexameters,* trans. Heneage Wynne-Finch (London: William Heinemann 1935), and the works of Las Casas, Oviedo, and Ferdinand Columbus mentioned above. One can then attempt to scale that massif of secondary works crowned by Iwan Bloch's *Der Ursprung der Syphilis* (Jena: Verlag von Gustav Fischer, 1901), which argues the Columbian view of the origin of the disease. (It is especially helpful in that it contains the pertinent pages of Díaz de Isla's book, which are difficult to obtain). Samuel Eliot Morison his *Admiral of the Ocean Sea, A Life of Christopher Columbus* (Boston: Little, Brown and Co., 1942), 2 vols., speaks most persuasively for the American origin. The view that venereal syphilis, as a separate and distinct disease, was present in the pre-Columbian Old World is put forth in some detail by Richmond C. Holcomb, "Ruiz Díaz de Isla and the Haitian Myth of European Syphilis," *Medical Life* 43 (July, August, September, November 1936): 270–316, 318–364, 415–470, 487–514. The classic version of this view is that of Karl Sudhoff, which can be found in his *Essays in the History of Medicine,* various translators (New York: Medical File Press, 1926). There have been many publications by those who follow the Unitarian view; a good introduction to them is the articles of E. H. Hudson (full references below). Although over two hundred years old, Jean Astruc's *A Treatise on Venereal Diseases* (London: W. Innys and J. Richardson, C. Davis, J. Clarke, R. Manby and H. S. Cox, 1754) is still very valuable.

The study of demographic history is at present in a stage of rapid expansion, and many of the more common truisms of today are apt to be disproved tomorrow. Until a synthesis of the very latest work is made, however, I will continue to recommend *Histoire Générale de la Population* by Marcel R. Reinhard and André Armengaud (Paris: Editions Montchrestien, 1961) to those who wish to examine the record of population expansion since the Columbian exchange began. Statistics on black migration to the New World are to be found in Philip D. Curtin's *The African Slave Trade, A Census* (Madison: University of Wisconsin Press, 1969) and for European migration in Brinley Thomas's "Migration" in the *International Encyclopedia of the Social Sciences* (New York: Macmillan Co. and the Free Press, 1968), vol. 10. Statistics on the production of American foods today are to be found in the Food and Agricultural Organization of the United Nations's publications listed below.

CHAPTER 1

Acosta, Joseph de. *The Natural and Moral History of the Indies.* 2 vols. Translated by Edward Grimston. New York: Burt Franklin [n.d.].

Bendyshe, T. "The History of Anthropology." *Memoirs of the Anthropological Society of London* 1 (1863–1864): 335–458.

Brooks, Charles W. *Japanese Wrecks Stranded and Picked*

Up Adrift in the North Pacific Ocean. Fairfield, Washington: Ye Galleon Press, 1964.

Castañeda, Pedro. *The Journey of Coronado.* Translated by George Parker Winship. Ann Arbor: Microfilms, 1966.

Champlain, Samuel. *Narrative of a Voyage to the West Indies and Mexico in the Years 1599–1602.* Translated by Alice Wilmere. London: The Hakluyt Society, 1859.

Cobo, Bernabé. *Obras.* 2 vols. Madrid: Atlas Ediciones, 1964.

Colbert, Edwin H. *Evolution of the Vertebrates.* New York: John Wiley and Sons, 1955.

Columbus, Christopher, *Journals and Other Documents on the Life of Christopher Columbus.* Translated by Samuel Eliot Morison. New York: Heritage Press, 1963.

Commager, Henry Steele, ed. *Documents of American History.* New York: Appleton-Century-Crofts, Inc., 1949.

———, and Giordanetti, Elmo, eds. *Was America a Mistake? An Eighteenth Century Controversy.* Columbia: University of South Carolina Press, 1968.

Darlington, C. D. *Chromosome Botany and the Origins of Cultivated Plants.* New York: Hafner Publishing Co., 1963.

Darlington, Philip J. *Zoogeography: The Geographical Distribution of Animals.* New York: John Wiley and Sons, 1966.

Edwards, William E. "The Late-Pleistocene Extinction and Diminution in Size of Mammalian Species." In *Pleistocene Extinctions, The Search for a Cause,* edited by P. S. Martin and H. E. Wright, Jr. New Haven: Yale University Press, 1967.

Gleason, Henry A., and Cronquist, Arthur. *The Natural Geography of Plants.* New York: Columbia University Press, 1964.

Good, Ronald. *The Geography of the Flowering Plants.* New York: John Wiley and Sons, 1964.

Hale, Matthew. *The Primitive Origination of Mankind, Considered and Examined According to the Light of Nature.* London: Printed by W. Godbid for W. Shrowsbery, 1677.

Hanke, Lewis. *The Spanish Struggle for Justice in the Conquest of America.* Boston: Little, Brown and Co., 1965.
————. *History of Latin American Civilization, Sources and Interpretations.* 2 vols. Boston: Little, Brown and Co., 1967.

Hazard, Paul. *The European Mind, 1680–1715.* London: Hollis and Carter, 1953.

Hodge, Frederick W., and Lewis, Theodore H., eds. *Spanish Explorers in the Southern United States, 1528–1543.* New York: Charles Scribner's Sons, 1907.

Hodgen, Margaret T. *Early Anthropology in the Sixteenth and Seventeenth Centuries.* Philadelphia: University of Pennsylvania Press, 1964.

Hopkins, David M. "The Cenozoic History of Beringia—A Synthesis." In *The Bering Land Bridge.* Edited by David M. Hopkins. Stanford: Stanford University Press, 1967.

Huddleston, Lee Eldridge, *Origins of the American Indians. European Concepts, 1492–1729.* Austin: University of Texas Press, 1967.

Hulse, Frederick S. *The Human Species, An Introduction to Physical Anthropology.* New York: Random House, 1963.

Laughlin, W. S. "Human Migration and Permanent Occupation in the Bering Sea Area." In *The Bering Land Bridge,* edited by David M. Hopkins. Stanford: Stanford University Press, 1967.

Léry, Jean de. *Journal de Bord de Jean de Léry en la Terre de Brésil*. Edited by M. R. Mayeux. Paris: Editions de Paris, 1957.

Li, Hui-Lin. "Floristic Relationships Between Eastern Asia and Eastern North America." *Transactions of the American Philosophical Society* 42 N.S. (1952):371–430.

Lindroth, Carl H. *The Faunal Connections Between Europe and North America*. New York: John Wiley and Sons, 1957.

Lorant, Stefan, ed. *The New World*. New York: Duell, Sloan and Pearce, 1965.

Mannix, D. P., and Cowley, Malcolm, *Black Cargoes*. New York: Viking Press, 1965.

Martin, P. S. "Prehistoric Overkill." In *Pleistocene Extinction, The Search for a Cause,* edited by P. S. Martin and H. E. Wright, Jr. New Haven: Yale University Press, 1967.

McKee, David Rice. "Isaac de la Peyrère, A Precursor of Eighteenth-Century Critical Deists." *Publications of the Modern Language Association of America* 59 (June 1944):456–485.

Montaigne, Michel Eyquem de. *Montaigne, Selected Essays*. Edited by Blanchard Bates. New York: Modern Library, 1949.

Moore, Raymond C., *Introduction to Historical Geology* (New York, Toronto and London: McGraw-Hill Book Co., 1958).

Mourant, A. E.; Kopéc, Ada; and Domaniewska-Sobczak, Kasimiera. *The ABO Groups, Comprehensive Tables and Maps of World Distribution*. Springfield, Illinois: Charles C. Thomas, 1958.

Müller-Beck, Hansjurgen. "On Migration Across the Bering Land Bridge in the Upper Pleistocene." In *The Bering Land Bridge,* edited by David M. Hopkins. Stanford: Stanford University Press, 1967.

Neel, J. V., and Salzano, F. M. "A Prospectus for Genetic Studies on the American Indians." In *The Biology of Human Adaptability,* edited by Paul T. Baker and J. S. Weiner. Oxford: Clarendon Press, 1966.

Peyrère, Isaac de La. *Prae-Adamita.* n.p.: 1655.

Quinn, David B., ed. *The Voyages and Colonising Enterprises of Sir Humphrey Gilbert.* 2 vols. London: The Hakluyt Society, 1940.

Rowse, A. L. *The Elizabethans and America.* New York: Harper and Row, 1959.

Sclater, Philip L. "On the General Geographical Distribution of the Members of the Class Aves." *Journal of the Proceedings of the Linnean Society (Zoological)* 2 (1858):130–145.

Simpson, George Gaylord. *The Geography of Evolution.* New York: Capricorn Books, 1965.

Stewart, T. D. "A Physical Anthropologist's View of the Peopling of the New World." *Southwestern Journal of Anthropology* 16 (Autumn 1960):259–279.

Strachey, William. *The Historie of Travell into Virginia Britania.* London: The Hakluyt Society, 1953.

Thevet, André. *The New Found Worlde, or Antarctike.* Translated by Thomas Hacket. London: Henrie Bynneman, 1568.

Wallace, Alfred Russel. *The Geographical Distribution of Animals.* 2 vols. New York: Hafner Publishing Co., 1962.

Waldseemüller, Martin. *Cosmographiae Introductio by Martin Waldseemuller . . . To Which Are Added the Four Voyages of Amerigo Vespucci.* Edited and translated by Joseph Fischer and Franz von Wiesser. Ann Arbor: University Microfilms, 1966.

Winchell, Alexander. *Preadamites, or a Demonstration of the Existence of Men Before Adam.* Chicago: Scott, Foresman and Co., 1901.

Zeuner, Frederick E. *A History of Domesticated Animals.* London: Hutchinson and Co., 1963.

CHAPTER 2

Adams, Charles Francis. *Three Episodes of Massachusetts History.* 2 vols. New York: Russell and Russell, 1965.

Alba C., M. M. *Etnología y Población Historica.* Panama: Imprento Nacional, 1928.

Alvarez Rubiano, Pablo. *Pedrarias Dávila.* Madrid: Consejo Superior de Investigaciones Cientificas, Instituto Gonzalo Fernández de Oviedo, 1944.

Anales de Tlatelolco, Unos Anales Historicos de la Nación Mexicana y Códice de Tlatelolco. Edited by Heinrich Berlin. Mexico: Antigua Rebredo de José Porrua e Hijos, 1948.

Andagoya, Pascual de. *Narrative of the Proceedings of Pedrarias Dávila.* Translated by Clements R. Markham. London: The Hakluyt Society, 1865.

The Annals of the Cakchiquels and Title of the Lords of Totonicapán. Translated by Adrian Recinos, Dioniscio José Chonay, and Delia Goetz. Norman: University of Oklahoma Press, 1953.

Ashburn, P. M. *The Ranks of Death: A Medical History of the Conquest of America.* New York: Coward-McCann, Inc., 1947.

Ayala, Felipe Gaumán Poma. *Neuva Corónica y Buen Govierno.* Lima: Arqueologia e Historia del Ministerio de Educacion Publica de Peru, 1956.

Bailey, Alfred G. *The Conflict of European and Eastern Algonkian Cultures, 1504–1700: A Study in Canadian Civilization.* St. John: New Brunswick Museum, 1937.

Bancroft, Hubert Howe. *History of Alaska, 1730–1885.* San Francisco: A. L. Bancroft and Co., 1886.

Bedson, S. P., et al. *Virus and Rickettsial Diseases*. Baltimore: Williams and Wilkins Co., 1950.

Blair, Emma H., and Robertson, James A., eds. *Philippine Islands*. 55 vols. Cleveland: Arthur H. Clark Co., 1903–1909.

Borah, Woodrow. "America as Model: The Demographic Impact of European Expansion upon the Non-European World." *Actas y Memorias del XXXV Congresso Internacional de Americanistas* 3 (Mexico: 1964): 379–387.

The Book of Chilam Balam of Chumayel. Edited and translated by Ralph L. Roy. Washington, D.C.: Carnegie Institution of Washington, 1933.

Cieza de León, Pedro de. *The Incas of Pedro de Cieza de León*. Edited by Victor W. von Hagen. Translated by Harriet de Onis. Norman: University of Oklahoma Press, 1959.

Colección de Documentos Inéditos Relativos al Descubrimiento, Conquista y Colonización de las Posesiones Españolas en América y Oceanía. 42 vols. Madrid: Imprenta de Quiros, 1864–1884.

Colección de Documentos para la Historia de Costa Rica. 10 vols. Paris: Imprenta Pablo Dupont, 1886.

Colección de Varios Documentos para la Historia de la Florida y Tierras Adyacentes. London: La Casa de Trübner and Co., 1857.

Cook, Sherburne F. "The Incidence and Significance of Disease Among the Aztecs and Related Tribes." *Hispanic American Historical Review* 26 (August 1946):320–325.

Cook, Sherburne F., and Borah, Woodrow. *The Indian Population of Central Mexico 1531–1610*. Berkeley: University of California Press, 1960.

———. *The Aboriginal Population of Central Mexico on the Eve of the Spanish Conquest*. Berkeley: University of California Press, 1963.

Cooper, Donald B. *Epidemic Disease in Mexico City, 1761–1813*. Austin: University of Texas Press, 1965.

Cortés, Hernando. *Five Letters*. Translated by J. Bayard Morris. New York: W. W. Norton and Co., 1962.

Díaz del Castillo, Bernal. *The Bernal Díaz Chronicles: The True Story of the Conquest of Mexico*. Translated by Albert Idell. Garden City: Doubleday and Co., 1956.

Dixon, C. W. *Smallpox*. London: J. and A. Churchill, 1962.

Dobyns, Henry F. "An Outline of Andean Epidemic History to 1720." *Bulletin of the History of Medicine* 37 (November–December 1963):493–515.

Duffy, John. *Epidemics in Colonial America*. Baton Rouge: Louisiana State University Press, 1953.

Durán, Diego. *The Aztecs: The History of the Indies of New Spain*. Translated by Doris Heyden and Fernando Horcasitas. New York: Orion Press, 1964.

Figueroa Marroquin, Horacio. *Enfermedades de los Conquistadores*. San Salvador: Ministerio de Clutura, 1955.

Fuentes, Patricia de, ed. and trans. *The Conquistadores. First Person Accounts of the Conquest of Mexico*. New York: Orioh Press, 1963.

Garcilaso de la Vega. *First Part of the Royal Commentaries of the Yncas*. Translated by Clements R. Markham. London: The Hakluyt Society, 1871.

Gibson, Charles. *The Aztecs Under Spanish Rule*. Stanford: Stanford University Press, 1964.

———. *Spain in America*. New York: Harper and Row, 1966.

D'Harcourt, Raoul and Marie. *La Médecine dans l'Ancien Pérou*. Paris: Librairie Maloine, 1939.

Herrera y Tordesillas, Antonio de. *Historia General de los Hechos de los Castellanos en las Islas y Tierra Firme del Mar Océano*. 17 vols. Madrid: Real Academia de Historia, 1934–57.

Jarcho, Saul. "Some Observations on Diseases in Prehistoric

America." *Bulletin of the History of Medicine* 38 (January–February 1964):1–19.

Landa, Diego de. *Landa's Relación de las Cosas de Yucatán.* Translated by Alfred M. Tozzer. Cambridge, Massachusetts: Peabody Museum, 1941.

Las Casas, Fray Bartolomé de. *Obras Escogidas de Fray Bartolomé de Las Casas.* 5 vols. Madrid: Ediciones Atlas, 1957–1958.

León-Portilla, Miguel, ed. *The Broken Spears. The Aztec Account of the Conquest of Mexico.* Boston: Beacon Press, 1962.

Lévi-Strauss, Claude. *A World on the Wane.* London: Hutchinson and Co., 1961.

Lizárrago, Reginaldo de. *Descripción Colonial por Fr. Reginalao de Lizárrago.* Buenos Aires: J. Roldán, 1928.

López de Gómara, Francisco. *Cortés, the Life of the Conqueror by His Secretary.* Translated by Lesley Byrd Simpson. Berkeley: University of California Press, 1964.

López de Velasco, Juan. *Geografía y Descripción Universidad de las Indias.* Madrid: Establecimiento Tipográfico de Fortanet, 1894.

Marchant, Alexander. *From Barter to Slavery: The Economic Relations of the Portuguese and Indians in the Settlement of Brazil, 1500–1580.* Baltimore: The Johns Hopkins Press, 1942.

Markham, Clements R., ed. and trans. *Narratives of the Rites and Laws of the Incas.* London: The Hakluyt Society, 1873.

May, Jacques M., ed. *Studies in Disease Ecology.* New York: Hafner Publishing Co., 1961.

McBryde, F. Webster. "Influenza in America During the Sixteenth Century (Guatemala: 1523, 1559–1562, 1576)." *Bulletin of the History of Medicine* 8 (February 1940):296–302.

Montesinos, Fernando. *Memorias Antiguas Historiales del Perú.* Translated by Philip A. Means. London: The Hakluyt Society, 1920.

Morison, Samuel Eliot. *Admiral of the Ocean Sea, A Life of Christopher Columbus.* Boston: Little, Brown and Co., 1942, 2 vols.

Motolinía, Toribio. *Motolinía's History of the Indians of New Spain.* Translated by Elizabeth A. Foster. Berkeley: The Cortés Society, 1950.

Murúa, Martín de. *Historia General del Perú, Origen y Descendencia de los Incas.* 2 vols. Madrid: Instituto Gonzalo Fernández de Oviedo, 1962.

Oviedo y Valdés, Gonzalo Fernández. *Historia General y Natural de las Indias.* 4 vols. Madrid: Ediciones Atlas, 1959.

Phelan, John L. *The Hispanization of the Philippines.* Madison: University of Wisconsin Press, 1959.

Pizarro, Pedro. *Relation of the Discovery and Conquest of the Kingdoms of Perus.* 2 vols. Translated by Philip A. Means. New York: Cortés Society, 1921.

Porras Barrenechea, Raúl, ed. *Cartas del Perú, 1524–1543.* Lima: Sociedad de Bibliófilos Peruanos, 1959.

Prescott, William H. *History of the Conquest of Mexico and the History of the Conquest of Peru.* New York: Modern Library, [n.d.].

Quinn, David B., ed. *The Roanoke Voyages.* London: The Hakluyt Society, 1955.

Relaciones Históricas y Geograficas de América Central. Madrid: Libreria General de Victoriano Suarez, 1908.

Rhodes, A. J., and van Rooyen, C. E. *Textbook of Virology for Students and Practitioners of Medicine.* Baltimore: The Williams and Wilkins Co., 1962 and 1968.

Sahagún, Bernardino de. *Florentine Codex: General History of the Things of New Spain.* 12 vols. Translated by Arthur J. O. Anderson and Charles E. Dibble. Santa

Fe: School of American Research and the University of Utah, 1950–1959.

Sarmiento de Gamboa, Pedro. *History of the Incas*. Translated by Clements R. Markham. Cambridge: The Hakluyt Society, 1907.

Schultz, Myron G. "A History of Bartonellosis (Carrion's Disease)." *The American Journal of Tropical Medicine and Hygiene* 17 (1968):503–515.

Scott, Henry H. *A History of Tropical Medicine*. 2 vols. London: Edward Arnold and Co., 1939.

Staden, Hans. *The True History of His Captivity*. Translated by Malcolm Letts. New York: Robert M. McBride and Co., 1929.

Stearn, E. Wagner, and Stearn, Allen E. *The Effect of Smallpox on the Destiny of the Amerindian*. Boston: Bruce Humphries, 1945.

Sudhoff, Karl. *Essays in the History of Medicine*. Various translators. New York: Medical File Press, 1926.

Top, Franklin H., et al. *Communicable and Infectious Diseases*. St. Louis: C. V. Mosby Co., 1964.

Valboa, Miguel Cabello. *Miscelánea Antártica, una Historia del Perú Antiguo*. Lima: Universidad Nacional Major de San Marcos, Facultad de Letras, Instituto de Etnología, 1951.

Vasquez de Espinosa, Antonio. *Compedium and Description of the West Indies*. Translated by Charles Upson Clark. Washington D.C.: Smithsonian Institute, 1948.

Vellard, Jehan. "Causas Biologicas de la Desaparición de los Indios Americanos." *Boletín del insituto Riva-Agüero* (Pontifica Universidad Catolica del Perú), no. 2 (1956):77–93.

von Hagen, Victor W. *Realm of the Incas*. New York: Mentor, 1957.

Zinsser, Hans. *Rats, Lice and History*. New York: Bantam Books, 1960.

CHAPTER 3

Acosta, Joseph de. *The Natural and Moral History of the Indies.* 2 vols. Translated by Edward Grimston. New York: Burt Franklin, n.d.
Anderson, Edgar. *Plants, Man and Life.* Berkeley: University of California Press, 1967.
Arcila Farias, Eduardo. *Económica Colonial de Venezuela.* Mexico: Fondo de Cultura Económica, 1946.
Aschmann, Homer. "The Head of the Colorado Delta." In *Geography as Human Ecology, Methodology by Example,* edited by S. R. Eyre and G. R. Jones. New York: St. Martins Press, 1966.
Benzoni, Girolamo. *History of the New World.* Translated by W. H. Smyth. New York: Burt Franklin, [n.d.].
Bidwell, Percy W., and Falconer, John I. *History of Agriculture in the Northern United States, 1620–1860.* Washington, D.C.: Carnegie Institute of Washington, 1925.
Bishko, Charles J. "The Peninsular Background of Latin-American Cattle Ranching." *Hispanic American Historical Review* 32 (November 1952):491–515.
Brand, Donald D., "The Early History of the Range Cattle Industry in Northern Mexico." *Agricultural History* 35 (July 1961):132–139.
Burns, Alan. *History of the British West Indies.* Great Britain: George Allen and Unwin, 1954.
Cervantes Saavedra, Miguel de. *Don Quixote.* Translated by Samuel Putnam. New York: Viking Press, 1949.
Champlain, Samuel. *Narrative of a Voyage to the West Indies and Mexico in the Years 1599–1602.* Translated by Alice Wilmere. London: The Hakluyt Society, 1859.
Chevalier, François. *Land and Society in Colonial Mexico.* Translated by Alvin Eustis. Berkeley: University of California Press, 1963.
Cieza de León, Pedro de. *The Incas of Pedro de Cieza de*

León. Translated by Harried de Onis. Edited by Victor W. von Hagen. Norman: University of Oklahoma Press, 1959.

Cobo, Bernabé. *Obras*. 2 vols. Madrid: Atlas Ediciones, 1964.

Columbus, Christopher. *Journals and Other Documents on the Life of Christopher Columbus*. Translated by Samuel Eliot Morison. New York: Heritage Press, 1963.

Columbus, Ferdinand. *The Life of the Admiral Christopher Columbus by His Son Ferdinand*. Translated by Benjamin Keen. New Brunswick: Rutgers University Press, 1959.

Commager, Henry Steele, and Geordanetti, Elmo, eds. *Was America a Mistake: An Eighteenth Century Controversy*. Columbia: University of South Carolina, 1968.

Coni, Emilio A. "La Agricultura, Ganadería e Industrias Hasta el Virrcinato." *Historia de la Nación Argentina*, vol. 4. Buenos Aires: Imprenta de la Universidad, 1938, 357–371.

Cook, Sherburne F. *The Historical Demography and Ecology of Teotlalpán*. Berkeley: University of California Press, 1949.

———. *Soil Erosion and Population in Central Mexico*. Berkeley: University of California Press, 1949.

Darwin, Charles. *The Voyage of the Beagle*. Garden City: Doubleday and Co., 1962.

Deerr, Noel. *The History of Sugar*. 2 vols. London: Chapman and Hall, 1949 and 1950.

Denhardt, Robert M. "The Role of the Horse in the Social History of Early California." *Agricultural History* 14 (January 1940):13–22.

Dobie, J. Frank. "The First Cattle in Texas and the Southwest Progenitors of the Longhorns." *Southwestern Historical Quarterly* 42 (January 1939):171–197.

———. *The Mustangs*. New York: Bramhall House, 1952.

Dominguez, Luis L., ed. *The Conquest of the River Plate,* 1535–1555. New York: Burt Franklin [n.d.].

Driver, Harold E., ed. *The Americas on the Eve of Discovery.* Englewood Cliffs: Prentice-Hall, 1964.

Dusenberry, William H. "Woolen Manufacture in Sixteenth-Century New Spain." *The Americas* 4 (October 1947): 223–234.

Edwards, Bryan. *The History, Civil and Commercial, of the British West Indies.* New York: AMS Press, 1966.

Encyclopaedia Britannica. 1959 ed., s.v. "rats."

Ewers, John C. *The Horse in Blackfoot Indian Culture with Comparative Material from Other Western Tribes.* Washington, D.C.: Smithsonian Institute, 1955.

Forbes, Jack D. *Apache, Navaho and Spaniard.* Norman: University of Oklahoma Press, 1960.

Gage, Thomas. *A New Survey of the West Indies, 1648.* New York: Robert M. McBride and Co., 1929.

Gibson, Charles. *The Aztecs Under Spanish Rule.* Stanford: Stanford University Press, 1964.

González, Julio V. *Historia Argentina.* Vol. 1: *La Era Colonial.* Mexico and Buenos Aires: Fondo de Cultura Económica, 1957.

Graham, R. B. Cunningham. *The Conquest of the River Plate.* Garden City: Doubleday, Page and Co., 1924.

———. *The Horses of the Conquest.* Norman: University of Oklahoma Press, 1949.

Haenke, Tadeo. *Viáje Por el Virreinato del Río de la Plata.* Buenos Aires: Emece Editores, 1943.

Hakluyt, Richard, ed. *The Principal Navigations, Voyages, Traffiques and Discoveries of the English Nation.* 12 vols. New York: AMS Press, 1965.

Haring, Clarence H. *Trade and Navigation Between Spain and the Indies in the Time of the Hapsburgs.* Cambridge: Harvard University Press, 1918.

———. *The Buccaneers in the West Indies in the XVIII Century.* Hamden, Connecticut: Archon Books, 1966.

Harrell, Taylor M. "The Development of the Venezuelan Llanos in the Sixteenth Century." Master's Thesis, University of California, 1957.

Hendry, Gorge W. "The Source Literature of Early Plant Introduction into Spanish America." *Agricultural History* 8 (April 1934):64–71.

Herrera y Tordesillas, Antonio de. *Historia General de los Hechos de los Castellanos en las Islas y Tierra Tirme del Mar Océane.* 17 vols. Madrid: Real Academia de Historia, 1934–1957.

Jiménez de la Espada, Marcos, ed. *Relaciones Geograficas de Indias–Perú.* 2 vols. Madrid: Ediciones Atlas, 1965.

Johannessen, Carl L. *Savannas of Interior Honduras.* Berkeley: University of California Press, 1963.

Johnson, John J. "The Introduction of the Horse into the Western Hemisphere." *Hispanic American Historical Review* 23 (November 1942):587–610.

———. "The Spanish Horse in Peru Before 1550." In *Greater America, Essays in Honor of Herbert Eugene Bolton.* Berkeley: University of California Press, 1945.

Juan [y Santacilla], Jorge, and de Ulloa, Antonio. *A Voyage to South America.* Translated by John Adams. New York: Alfred A. Knopf, 1964.

Kalm, Peter. "Peter Kalm's Description of Maize, How It is Planted and Cultivated in North America, Together with Many Uses of This Crop Plant." Translated by Esther L. Larsen. *Agricultural History* 9 (April 1935):97–117.

Lammons, Frank B. "Operation Camel: An Experiment in Animal Transportation in Texas, 1857–1860." *Southwestern Historical Quarterly* 41 (July 1957):20–50.

Laycock, George. *The Alien Animals.* New York: Natural History Press, 1966.

Levene, Ricardo. *A History of Argentina.* Translated by William S. Robertson. Chapel Hill: University of North Carolina Press, 1937.

López de Velasco, Juan. *Geografía y Descripción Universidad de las Indias*. Madrid: Establecimiento Tipográfico de Fortanet, 1894.

Mendez Nadal, Dolores, and Alberts, Hugo W. "The Early History of Livestock and Pastures in Puerto Rico." *Agricultural History* 21 (January 1947):61–64.

Morrisey, Richard J. "Colonial Agriculture in New Spain." *Agricultural History* 31 (July 1957):24–29.

Morse, Richard M., ed. *The Bandeirantes*. New York: Alfred A. Knopf, 1965.

Nichols, Madaline W. "The Spanish Horse of the Pampas." *American Anthropologist* 41 N.S. (January–March 1939):119–129.

Oviedo y Valdés, Gonzalo Fernández. *Natural History of the West Indies*. Translated by Sterling A. Stoudemire. Chapel Hill: University of North Carolina Press, 1959.

Paez, Ramon. *Wild Scenes in South America or, Life in the Llanos of Venezuela*. New York: Charles Scribner, 1862.

Parry, J. H., and Sherlock, P. M. *A Short History of the West Indies*. London: Macmillan and Co., 1963.

Pereyra, Carlos. *La Obra de España en América*. Madrid: Biblioteca Neuva [n.d.].

Poppino, Rollie E. "Cattle Industry in Colonial Brazil." *Mid-America* 31 (October 1949):219–238.

Prado, Caio, Jr. *The Colonial Background of Modern Brazil*. Translated by Suzette Macedo. Berkeley: University of California Press, 1967.

Purchas, Samuel, ed. *Hakluytus Posthumus or Purchas His Pilgrimes*. 12 vols. Glasgow: James MacLehose and Sons, 1906.

Ratekin, Mervyn. "The Early Sugar Industry in Española." *Hispanic American Historical Review* 34 (February 1954):1–19.

Ridley, Henry N. *The Dispersal of Plants Throughout the World*. Ashford, Kent, U.K.: L. Reeve and Co., 1930.

Romero, Emilio. *Historia Económica del Perú*. Buenos Aires: Editorial Sudamerica, 1949.

Sauer, Carl O. *The Early Spanish Main*. Berkeley: University of California Press, 1966.

Simpson, Lesley Byrd. *Exploitation of Land in Central Mexico in the Sixteenth Century*. Berkeley: University of California Press, 1952.

Spicer, Edward H. *Cycles of Conquest*. Tucson: University of Arizona Press, 1962.

Steward, Julian H., ed. *Handbook of South American Indians*. 7 vols. Washington, D.C.: United States Government Printing Office, 1946–1959.

Tapson, Alfred J. "Indian Warfare on the Pampa during the Colonial Period." *Hispanic American Historical Review* 42 (February 1962):1–28.

Thomas, William L., Jr., ed. *Man's Role in Changing the Face of the Earth*. Chicago: University of Chicago Press, 1956.

Unanue, Hipólito. *Observaciones Sobre El Clima de Lima*. Lima: Comision Nacional de Cooperación Intelectual, 1940.

Underhill, Ruth M. *Red Man's America*. Chicago: University of Chicago Press, 1953.

Vazquez de Espinosa, Antonio. *Compendium and Description of the West Indies*. Translated by Charles Upson Clark. Washington, D.C.: Smithsonian Institute, 1948.

Walker, Alexander. *Columbia: Being a Geographical, Statistical, Agricultural, Commercial, and Political Account of that Country*. 2 vols. London: Baldwin, Cradock and Joy, 1822.

Warren, Harris. *Paraguay, An Informal History*. Norman: University of Oklahoma Press, 1949.

Webb, Walter P. *The Great Plains*. New York: Grosset and Dunlap, 1931.

Wentworth, Edward N. *America's Sheep Trails*. Ames: Iowa State College Press, 1948.

Whitaker, Arthur P. "The Spanish Contribution to American Agriculture." *Agricultural History* 3 (January 1929): 1–14.

White, C. Langdon. "Cattle Raising: A Way of Life in the Venezuelan Llanos." *The Scientific Monthly* 83 (September 1956):122–129.

Wissler, Clark. "The Influence of the Horse in the Development of Plains Culture." *American Anthropologist* 16 (January–March 1914):1–25.

Zeuner, Frederick E. *A History of Domesticated Animals.* London: Hutchinson and Co., 1963.

Zorita, Alonso de. *Life and Labor in Ancient Mexico.* Translated by Benjamin Keen. New Brunswick: Rutgers University Press, 1963.

CHAPTER 4

Abraham, J. Johnston. "The Early History of Syphilis." *The British Journal of Surgery* 32 (October 1944):225–237.

Anderson, James E. "Human Skeletons of Tehuacan." *Science* 148 (23 April 1965):496–497.

Astruc, Jean. *A Treatise of Venereal Diseases.* London: W. Innys and J. Richardson, C. Davis, J. Clarke, R. Manby and H. S. Cox, 1754.

Barrack, Bruce. "Syphilis and Yaws." *Archives of Dermatology* 73 (May 1956):510–515.

Billings, W. D. *Plants and the Ecosystem.* London: Macmillan and Co., 1964.

Bloch, Ivan. *Der Ursprung des Syphilis.* Jena: Verlag von Gustav Fischer, 1901.

Burckhardt, Jacob. *The Civilization of the Renaissance in Italy.* U.S.A.: Albert and Charles Boni, 1935.

The Cambridge Modern History. Vol. 1: *The Renaissance.*

Edited by A. W. Ward; G. W. Prothero; and Stanley Leathes. New York: The Macmillan Co., 1902.

The New Cambridge Modern History. Vol. 1: *The Renaissance.* Edited by G. R. Potter. Cambridge: Cambridge University Press, 1957.

Castiglione, A. *History of Medicine.* Translated by E. B. Krumbhaar. New York: Alfred A. Knopf, 1947.

Cellini, Benvenuto. *The Memoirs of Benvenuto Cellini.* Translated by Anne MacDonell. New York: E. P. Dutton and Co., 1907.

Clowes, William. *The Selected Writings of William Clowes.* Edited by F. N. L. Poynter. London: Harvey and Blythe, 1948.

Cockburn, Thomas A. "The Origin of the Treponematoses." *Bulletin of the World Health Organization* 24 (1961):221–228.

Columbus, Ferdinand. *The Life of the Admiral Christopher Columbus by His Son Ferdinand.* Translated by Benjamin Keen. New Brunswick: Rutgers University Press, 1959.

Cervantes Saavedra, Miguel de. *Don Quixote.* Translated by Samuel Putman. New York: Viking Press, 1949.

Díaz de Isla, Ruy. *Tractado llamado fructo de todos Sanctos: contra el mal Serpentino.* Selville: 1542.

Dennie, Charles C. *A History of Syphilis.* Springfield, Illinois: Charles C. Thomas, 1962.

Durant, Will. *The Renaissance, A History of Civilization in Italy from 1304–1576* A.D. New York: Simon and Schuster, 1953.

Elgood, Cyril. *A Medical History of Persia and the Eastern Caliphate.* Cambridge: Cambridge University Press, 1951.

Elizondo Langagne, Alfonso. "Program for the Eradication of Pinta (Spotted Sickness) in Mexico." *Proceedings of the World Forum on Syphilis and Other Treponema-*

toses. Washington, D.C.: United States Department of Health, Education and Welfare, 1964.

Erasmus, Desiderius. *The Colloquies of Erasmus.* Translated by Craig R. Thompson. Chicago: University of Chicago Press, 1965.

Finch, B. E., and Green, Hugh. *Contraception through the Ages.* Springfield, Illinois: Charles C. Thomas, 1963.

Fisher, John. *The English Works of John Fisher.* The Early English Text Society, Extra Series, no. 27. Edited by J. E. B. Mayor. London: N. Trübner and Co., 1876.

Fracastoro, Girolamo. *Fracastor, Syphilis or the French Disease, A Poem in Latin Hexameters.* Translated by Heneage Wynne-Finch. London: William Heinemann Medical Books, 1935.

Gilbert, Judson B., and Mestler, Gordon E. *Disease and Destiny.* London: Dawsons of Pall Mall, 1962.

Goff, C. W. "Syphilis." In *Diseases in Antiquity: A Survey of the Diseases, Injuries and Surgery of Early Populations.* Edited by Don Brothwell and A. T. Sandison. Springfield, Illinois: Charles C. Thomas, 1967.

Guthe, Thorstein. "The Treponematoses as a World Problem." *British Journal of Venereal Diseases* 36 (June 1960):67–77.

Hackett, C. J. "On the Origin of Human Treponematoses." *Bulletin of the World Health Organization* 29 (1963):7–41.

Hendrickson, G. L. "The 'Syphilis' of Girolamo Frascatoro with Some Observations on the Origin and History of the Word 'Syphilis.' " *Bulletin of the History of Medicine* 2 (November 1934):515–546.

Henschen, Folke. *The History and Geography of Diseases.* Translated by Joan Tate. New York: Delacorte Press, 1966.

Hermans, Eduard H. "Interrelationship of Syphilis Incidence

and Maritime Activity." *Proceedings of the World Forum on Syphilis and Other Treponematoses.* Washington, D.C.: United States Department of Health, Education and Welfare, 1964, 131–133.

Holcomb, Richmond C. "Ruiz Díaz de Isla and the Haitian Myth of European Syphilis." *Medical Life* 43 (July, August, September, November 1936):270–316, 318–364, 415–470, 487–514.

————. Letter to the Editor, 14 March 1944. *American Journal of Syphilis, Gonorrhoea and Venereal Disease* 28 (July 1944):515.

Huard, P. "La Syphilis Vue Par Les Médecins Arabo-Persans, Indiens et Sino-Japonais du XVe et XVIe Siècles." *Histoire de la Médicine* 6 (July 1956):9–13.

Hudson, E. H. "Treponematosis and African Slavery." *British Journal of Venereal Diseases* 40 (March 1964): 43–52.

————. "Treponematosis and Man's Social Evolution." *American Anthropologist* 67 (August 1965):885–901.

————. "Treponematosis in Perspective." *Bulletin of the World Health Organization* 32 (1965):735–748.

Isenberg, Max. "Syphilis in the Eighteenth and Early Nineteenth Centuries." *Medical Record* 152 (18 December 1940):456–460.

Jeanselme, Edouard. *Traité de la Syphilis.* Paris: G. Doin et Cie., 1931.

Jos, Emiliano. "Centenario de Fernando Colón (Enfermedad de Martín Alonso) e Impugnaciones a la Historia del Almirante." *Revista de Indias* 3 (1942):85–110.

Kemble, James. *Idols and Invalids.* New York: Doubleday, Doran and Co., 1936.

Lane, John E. "A Few Early Notes on Syphilis in the English Colonies in North America." *Archives of Dermatology and Syphilis* 7 (August 1920):215–219.

Las Casas, Fray Bartolomé de. *Historia de las Indias*. 5 vols. Madrid: Imprenta de Miguel Ginestra, 1876.

Léry, Jean de. *Journal de Bord de Jean de Léry*. Edited by M. R. Mayeux. Paris: Editions de Paris, 1957.

Luther, Martin. *Luther's Letters of Spiritual Counsel*. Edited and translated by Theodore Tappert. Library of Christian Classics, vol. 17. Philadelphia: Westminster Press, 1955.

Manson-Bahr, Philip H. *Manson's Tropical Diseases*. Baltimore: The Williams and Wilkens Co., 1966.

Monardes, Nicolás. *Ioyfull Newes Out of the Newe Founde Worlde*. Translated by John Frampton. London: Willyam Norton, 1577.

Morison, Samuel Eliot. *Admiral of the Ocean Sea, A Life of Christopher Columbus*. 2 vols. Boston: Little, Brown and Co., 1942.

Morton, R. S. *Venereal Diseases*. Baltimore: Penguin Books, 1966.

———. "St. Denis Patron Saint of Syphilitics." *British Journal of Venereal Diseases* 37 (December 1961):285–288.

———. "Some Aspects of the Early History of Syphilis in Scotland." *British Journal of Venereal Diseases* 38 (December 1962):175–180.

Munger, Robert S. "Guaiacum, the Holy Wood from the New World." *Journal of the History of Medicine and Allied Sciences* 4 (Spring 1949):196–229.

Parran, Thomas. *Shadow on the Land, Syphilis*. New York: Reynal and Hitchcock, 1937.

Pusey, William A. *The History and Epidemiology of Syphilis*. Springfield, Illinois: Charles C. Thomas, 1933.

Oviedo y Valdés, Gonzalo Fernández. *Historia General y Natural de las Indias*. 4 vols. Madrid: Imprenta de la Real Academia de la Historia, 1851–55.

Rabelais, François. *The Five Books of Gargantua and*

Pantagruel. Translated by Jacques Le Clercq. New York: Modern Library,· [n.d.].

Rhodes and C. E. van Rooyen, *Textbook of Virology for Students and Practitioners of Medicine.* Baltimore: The Williams and Wilkens Co., 1962.

Shrewsbury, J. F. D. "Henry VIII, A Medical Study." *Journal of the History of Medicine and Allied Sciences* 7 (Spring 1952):141–185.

Sigerist, Henry E. *Civilization and Disease.* Chicago: University of Chicago Press, 1962.

———. *A History of Medicine.* Vol. 1: *Primitive and Archaic Medicine.* New York: Oxford University Press, 1951.

Smith, Preserved. *The Age of the Reformation.* New York: Henry Holt and Co., 1920.

Stewart, T. D., and Spoehr, Alexander. "Evidence of Paleopathology of Yaws." *Bulletin of the History of Medicine* 26 (November–December 1952):538–553.

Thevet, André. *The New Found Worlde, or Antarctike.* Translated by Thomas Hacket. London: Henrie Bynneman, 1568.

Voltaire [François Marie Arouet]. *Voltaire: Candide and Other Stories.* Translated by Joan Spencer. London, New York, Toronto: Oxford University Press, 1966.

von Hutten, Ulrich. *Of the Wood Called Guaiacum.* Translated by Thomas Paynel. London: Thomas Bertheletregii, 1540.

Weisman, Abner I. "Syphilis: Was It Endemic in Pre-Columbian America or Was It Brought Here from Europe?" *New York Academy Medical Bulletin* 42 (April 1966):284–300.

Wong, K. Chimin, and Wu, Lien-teh. *History of Chinese Medicine.* Shanghai: National Quarantine Service, 1936.

Zimmermann, E. L. "An Early English Manuscript on Syphilis: A Fragmentary Translation from the Second Edition of Gaspar Torrella's *Tractatus cum Consiliis contra Pudendagram seu Mordum Gallicum." Bulletin of the History of Medicine* 5 (May 1937):461–482.

———. "Extragenital Syphilis as Described in the Early Literature (1497–1624) with Special Reference to Focal Epidemics." *American Journal of Syphilis, Gonorrhoea and Veneral Disease* 22 (November 1938):757–780.

CHAPTER 5

Alcock, Rutherford. *The Capital of the Tycoon, A Narrative of Three Years Residence in Japan.* New York: Harper and Brothers, 1868.

Altamira, Rafael. *A History of Spain.* New York: Van Nostrand Co., 1949.

Annual Register, n.p.: 1803 and 1810.

Arkroyd, W. R. *Legumes in Human Nutrition.* Food and Agriculture Organization of the United Nations Study No. 19, 1964.

Barkan, Ömer Lufti. "Essai sur les Données Statistiques des Registres de Recensement dans l'Empire Ottoman aux XVe et XVIe Siècles." *Journal of the Economic and Social History of the Orient* 1 (1958):9–36.

Barlow, Roger. *A Brief Summe of Geographie.* London: The Hakluyt Society, 1932.

Bligh, William. *The Mutiny of H.M.S. Bounty.* New York: New American Library of World Literature, 1962.

Blount, Henry. *A Voyage into the Levant.* London: Printed by I. L. for Andrew Crooke, 1638.

Bois, Désiré. *Les Plantes Alimentaires Chez Tous les Peuples et à Travers les Ages.* Paris: Paul Lechevalier, 1927.

Bolinder, Gustaf. *Indians on Horseback*. London: Dennis Dobson, 1957.

Bourjaily, Vance. "The Corn of Coxcatlan." *Horizon* 7 (Spring 1966):50–55.

Brand, Donald D. "Tapioca from a Brazilian Root." *Agriculture in the Americas* 3 (May 1943):93–96.

Brooks, C. E. P. *Climate Through the Ages*. New York: McGraw-Hill Book Co., 1949.

Bullard, Reader, ed. *The Middle East, a Political and Economic Survey*. London: Oxford University Press, 1961.

Burchell, William J. *Travels in the Interior of Southern Africa*. London: Batchworth Press, 1953.

Burkill, I. H. *A Dictionary of the Economic Products of the Malay Peninsula*. 2 vols. London: Published on behalf of the Governments of the Straits Settlements and Federated Malay States by the Crown Agents for the Colonies, 1935.

Carter, George F. "Plant Evidence for Early Contacts with America." *Southwestern Journal of Anthropology* 6 (Summer 1950):161–182.

————. "Plants Across the Pacific." *Memoirs of the Society for American Archaeology*, no. 9. Supplement to *American Antiquity* 18, no. 3, part 2 (January 1953): 62–71.

————. "Maize to Africa." *Anthropological Journal of Canada* 1, no. 2 (1963):3–8.

Chardin, Chevalier. *Voyages de Chevalier Chardin en Perse et Autres Lieux de l'Orient*. Paris: Le Normant, 1811.

Church, R. J. Harrison. *West Africa, A Study of the Environment and of Man's Use of It*. London: Longmans, Green and Co., 1960.

Cooley, J. S. "Origin of the Sweet Potato and Primitive Storage Practices." *The Scientific Monthly* 72 (May 1951): 325–331.

Dannenfeldt, Karl H. *Leonhard Rauwolf.* Cambridge: Harvard University Press, 1968.

Davis, Kingsley. *The Population of India and Pakistan.* Princeton: Princeton University Press, 1951.

Déscription de l'Egypte ou Recueil des Observations et des Recherches qui ont été faites en Egypte Pendant l'Expédition de l'Armée Française. 24 vols. Paris: C. L. F. Panckoncke, 1824.

Dyer, Henry. *Dai Nippon.* New York: Charles Scribner's Sons, 1904.

Eliot, Charles. *Turkey in Europe.* New York: Barnes and Noble, 1965.

Fairbank, John King. *The United States and China.* New York: Viking Press, 1962.

Fisher, W. B. *The Middle East.* London: Methuen and Co., 1950.

Food and Agricultural Organization of the United Nations. *Food Composition Tables for International Use* (FAO Nutritional Studies, no. 3). Rome: 1949.

————. *Maize and Maize Diets, a Nutritional Survey.* (FAO Nutritional Studies, no. 9). Rome: 1963.

————. *Production Yearbook, 1963.* Rome: 1964. XVII.

————. *Report on the 1950 World Census of Agriculture.* Vol. I: *Census Results by Countries.* Rome, 1955.

Galdston, Iago, ed. *Human Nutrition, Historic and Scientific,* Monograph III. New York: International Universities Press, 1960.

Geertz, Clifford. *Agricultural Involution: The Process of Ecological Change in Indonesia.* Berkeley: University of California Press, 1963.

Glass, D. V., and Eversley, D. E. C., eds. *Population in History.* Chicago: Andine Publishing Co., 1965.

Goethe, J. W. *Italian Journey, 1786–1788.* Translated by W. H. Auden and Elizabeth Mayer. New York: Pantheon Press, 1962.

Goodrich, L. Carrington. *A Short History of China.* New York: Harper and Brothers, 1943.

Gourou, Pierre, et al. *The Development of Upland Areas in the Far East.* 2 vols. New York: International Secretariat, Institute of Pacific Relations, 1949, 1951.

Habib, Irfan. *The Agrarian System of Mughal India, 1556–1707.* New York: Asia Publishing House, 1963.

Halpern, Joel Martin. *A Serbian Village.* New York: Columbia University Press, 1958.

Hance, William A. *The Geography of Modern Africa.* New York: Columbia University Press: 1964.

Heyerdahl, Thor. "Merrill's Reappraisal of Ethnobotanical Evidence for Prehistoric Contact between South America and Polynesia." *Akten des 34. Internationalen Amerikanisten Kongresses.* Vienna: Verlag Ferdinand Berger, Horn, 1962.

Ho, Ping-ti. *Studies on the Population of China, 1368–1953.* Cambridge: Harvard University Press, 1959.

Issawi, Charles. *Egypt at Mid-Century, An Economic Survey.* London: Oxford University Press, 1954.

Jeffreys, M. D. W. "Pre-Columbian Maize into Africa." *Nature* 172 (21 November 1953):965–966.

Jones, William O. *Manioc in Africa.* Stanford: Stanford University Press, 1959.

Lamarck, Jean, ed. *Encyclopédie Méthodique, Botanique.* 8 vols. Paris: Chez Panckoncke and Chez H. Agasse, 1783–1808.

Langer, William L. "Europe's Initial Population Explosion." *American Historical Review* 69 (October 1963):1–17.

Latourette, Kenneth S. *A Short History of the Far East.* New York: The Macmillan Co., 1964.

Laufer, Berthold. "The American Plant Migration." *Scientific Monthly* 28 (March 1929):239–251.

————. *The American Plant Migration.* Part I: *The Potato.*

Anthropological Series, vol. 28. Chicago: Field Museum of Natural History, 1938.

Lebon, J. H. G. *An Introduction to Human Geography.* New York: Capricorn Books, 1966.

Locke, John. *Locke's Travels in France, 1675–1679.* Cambridge: Cambridge University Press, 1953.

Lyashchenko, Peter I. *History of the National Economy of Russia.* New York: The Macmillan Co., 1949.

McNeill, William H. *The Rise of the West.* New York: Mentor, 1965.

MacNeish, Richard S. "Ancient Mesoamerican Civilization." *Science* 143 (7 February 1964):531–537.

McVey, Ruth, ed. *Indonesia.* New Haven: Southeast Asia Studies, Yale University, 1963).

Mangelsdorf, Paul C.; MacNeish, Richard S.; and Galinat, Walton C. "Domestication of Corn." *Science* 143 (7 February, 1964):538–545.

Marczali, Henry, *Hungary in the Eighteenth Century.* Cambridge: Cambridge University Press, 1910.

Miracle, Marvin P. "The Introduction and Spread of Maize in Africa." *Journal of African History* 6 (1965):39–55.

———. "Murdock's Classification of Tropical African Food Economies." In *Reconstructing African Culture History,* edited by Creighton Gabel and Norman R. Bennett. Boston: Boston University Press, 1967.

Mitrany, David. *The Land and the Peasant in Rumania.* London: Oxford University Press, 1930.

Molena, S. M. *The Bantu, Past and Present.* Cape Town: C. Struik, 1963.

Morgan, W. B. Review of *Manioc in Africa,* by W. O. Jones. *Journal of African History* 3 (1962):159–160.

Murdock, George Peter. *Africa, Its Peoples and Their Culture History.* New York: McGraw-Hill Book Co., 1959.

———. "Staple Subsistence Crops of Africa." *Geographical Review* 50 (October 1960):522–540.

Nadal, Jorge. *La Población Española (Siglos XVI a XX)*. Barcelona: Ediciones Ariel, 1966.

Newbigin, Marion I. *Southern Europe, A Regional and Economic Geography of the Mediterranean Lands*. New York: E. P. Dutton and Co., [n.d.].

Newman, Bernard. *Balkan Background*. New York: The Macmillan Co., 1945.

Oliver, Roland, and Fage, J. D. *A Short History of Africa*. Baltimore: Penguin Books, 1962.

Payne, John. *Universal Geography Formed into a New and Entire System Describing Asia, Africa, Europe and America*. 2 vols. Dublin: Zachariah Jackson, 1794.

Pécsi, Márton, and Sárfalvi, Béla. *The Geography of Hungary*. London: Collet's, 1964.

Pelzer, Karl J. "The Agricultural Foundation." In *Indonesia*, edited by Ruth T. McVey. New Haven: Southeast Asia Studies, Yale University, 1963.

Petersen, William. *Population*. New York: The Macmillan Company, 1961.

Pittard, Eugène. *La Romanie*. Paris: Editions Bossard, 1917.

Population Division, Department of Social Affairs, United Nations. *The Determinants and Consequences of Population Trends*. New York: 1953.

Portères, Roland. "L'Introduction du Maïs en Afrique." *Journal d'Agriculture Tropicale et de Botanique Appliquée* 2 (May–June 1955):221–231.

Pratt, Peter. *History of Japan Compiled from the Records of the English East India Co., at the Instance of the Court of Directors*. Kobe: J. L. Thompson and Co., 1931.

Ray, John, ed. *Collection of Curious Travels and Voyages Containing Dr. Leonhart Rauwolf's Journey into the Eastern Countries*, vol. 2. London: n.p., 1738.

Reclus, Elisee. *Universal Geography*. London: J. S. Virtue and Co. [n.d.].

Reinhard, Marcel R. *Histoire de la Population Mondiale de 1700 à 1948.* Paris: Editions Domat-Montchrestien, [n.d.].

Reinhard, Marcel R., and Armengaud, André. *Histoire Générale de la Population.* Paris: Editions Montchrestien, 1961.

Ridley, Henry N. *The Dispersal of Plants Throughout the World.* Ashford, Kent, U. K.: L. Reeve and Co., 1930.

Rivlin, Helen Anne B. *The Agricultural Policy of Muhammad Ali in Egypt.* Cambridge: Harvard University Press, 1961.

Robequain, Charles. *Malaya, Indonesia, Borneo and the Philippines.* London: Longmans, Green and Co., 1954.

Salaman, Redcliffe N. *The History and Social Influence of the Potato.* Cambridge: Cambridge University Press, 1949.

Sauer, Carl O. *Agricultural Origins and Dispersals.* New York: The American Geographical Society, 1952.

————. "Maize into Europe." *Akten des 34. Internationalen Amerikanisten Kongresses.* Vienna: Verlag Ferdinand Berger, Horn, 1962.

Slicher Van Bath, B. H. *The Agrarian History of Western Europe,* A.D. *500–1850.* New York: St. Martin's Press, 1963.

Soreau, Edmond. *L'Agriculture du XVIIe Siècle à la Fin du XVIIIe.* Paris: E. de Boccard, 1952.

Spinden, Herbert, J. "Thank the American Indian." *Scientific American* 138 (April 1928):330–332.

Stamp, L. Dudley. *Africa: A Study in Tropical Development.* New York: John Wiley and Sons, 1964.

Statistical Office of the United Nations, Department of Economic and Social Affairs. *Statistical Yearbook, 1964.* New York: 1965.

The Statesman's Yearbook, Statistical and Historical Annual of the States of the World for the Year 1964–1965.

Edited by S. H. Steinberg. London: Macmillan and Co., 1964.

Stavrianos, L. S. *The Balkans Since 1453*. New York, Holt, Rinehart and Winston, 1958.

Täckholm, Vivi and Gunnar. *Flora of Egypt*. 2 vols. Cairo: Fouad I University Press, 1941.

Thomas, Dorothy Swaine. *Social and Economic Aspects of Swedish Population Movements, 1750–1933*. New York: The Macmillan Co., 1941.

Thompson, Warren S. "Population." *Scientific American* 182 (February 1950):11–15.

Tothill, J. D. *Agriculture in the Sudan*. London: Oxford University Press, 1948.

Vavilov, Nikolai Ivanovich. *The Origin, Variation, Immunity and Breeding of Cultivated Plants*. New York: Ronald Press Co., 1951.

Verrill, A. Hyatt. *Foods America Gave the World*. Boston: L. C. Page and Co., 1937.

Vialla de Sommières, L. C. *Voyage Historique et Politique au Montenegro*. Paris: Alexis Eymery, 1820.

von Humbolt, Alexander. *Voyage de Humbolt et Bonpland, Première Partie Physique Générale, et Relation Historique du Voyage*. Paris: Chez Fr. Schoell, Libraire and A. Tübingue, Chez J. G. Cotta, Libraire, 1807.

Ward, Artemas. *Encyclopedia of Food*. New York: Peter Smith, 1941.

Warriner, Doreen, ed. *Contrasts in Emerging Societies: Readings in the Social and Economic History of South-Eastern Europe in the Nineteenth Century*. Bloomington: Indiana University Press, 1965.

Watt, George. *A Dictionary of the Economic Products of India*. 7 vols. Calcutta: Superintendant of Government Printing, India, 1889–1899.

Weatherwax, Paul. *Indian Corn in Old America*. New York: The Macmillan Co., 1954.

Wickizer, V. D., and Bennett, M. K. *The Rice Economy of Monsoon Asia*. Stanford: Stanford University Food Research Institute, 1941.

Widjojo, Nitisastro. "Migration, Population Growth, and Economic Development in Indonesia: A Study of the Economic Consequences of Alternative Patterns of Inter-Island Migration." Ph.D. dissertation, University of California, Berkeley, 1961.

Willett, Frank. "The Introduction of Maize into West Africa: An Assessment of Recent Evidence." *Africa: Journal of the International African Institute* 32 (January 1962):1–13.

Woodham-Smith, Cecil. *The Great Hunger: Ireland 1845–1849*. New York: The New American Library of World Literature, 1964.

Worcester, J. E. *A Geographical Dictionary or Universal Gazetteer*. 2 vols. Boston: Cummings and Hilliard, 1823.

Wrong, Dennis H. *Population and Society*. New York: Random House, 1965.

Young, Arthur. *Travels During the Years 1787, 1788 and 1789*. 2 vols. Dublin: n.p., 1793.

Youngman, Wilbur H. "America—Home of the Bean." *Agriculture in the Americas* 3 (December 1943):228–232.

CHAPTER 6

Curtin, Philip D. *The African Slave Trade, A Census*. Madison: University of Wisconsin Press, 1969.

Dominguez, Luis L., ed. *The Conquest of the River Plate, 1535–1555*. New York: Burt Franklin, n.d.

Elizondo Langagne, Alfonso. "Program for the Eradication

of Pinta (Spotted Sickness) in Mexico," *Proceedings of the World Forum on Syphilis and Other Treponematoses*. Washington, D.C.: U.S. Dept. of Health, Education and Welfare, 1964, 171–177.

Elton, Charles S. *The Ecology of Invasions by Animals and Plants*. London: Methuen and Co., 1958. New York: John Wiley and Sons, 1958.

Galdston, Iago, ed. *Human Nutrition, Historic and Scientific, Monograph III*. New York: International Universities Press, 1960.

Gilbert, Judson B., and Mestler, Gordon E. *Disease and Destiny*. London: Dawsons of Pall Mall, 1962.

Las Casas, Bartolomé de. *Historia de las Indias*. 5 vols. Madrid: Imprenta de Miguel Ginesta, 1876.

Laycock, George. *The Alien Animals*. New York: Natural History Press, 1966.

Lindroth, Carl H. *The Faunal Connections Between Europe and North America*. New York: John Wiley and Sons, 1957.

Maupassant, Guy de. *The Portable Maupassant*. Edited by Lewis Galantière. New York: Viking Press, 1947.

Morton, R. S. *Venereal Diseases*. Baltimore: Penguin Books, 1966.

Manson-Bahr, Philip H. *Manson's Tropical Diseases*. Baltimore: The Williams and Wilkins Co., 1966.

Oviedo y Valdés, Gonzalo Fernández. *Natural History of the West Indies*. Translated by Sterling A. Stoudemire. Chapel Hill: University of North Carolina Press, 1959.

Prescott, William H. *History of the Conquest of Mexico and the History of the Conquest of Peru*. New York: Modern Library [n.d.].

Pyrard, François. *The Voyage of François Pyrard of Laval to the East Indies, the Maldives, the Moluccas and Brazil*. Translated by Albert Gray. New York: Burt Franklin [n.d.].

Reyburn, H. A.; Hinderks, H. E.; and Taylor, J. G. *Nietzsche, The Story of a Human Philosopher.* London: Macmillan and Co., 1948.

Rolleston, J. D. "Syphilis in Saint-Simon's *Mémoires.*" *British Journal of Dermatology* 53 (June 1941):183–186.

Simpson, George Gaylord. *The Geography of Evolution.* New York: Capricorn Books, 1965.

————. *The Meaning of Evolution, A Study of the History of Life and of Its Significance for Man.* New Haven: Yale University Press, 1967.

Steward, Julian H. Ed. *Handbook of South American Indians.* Washington, D.C.: United States Government Printing Office, 1946–1959, 7 vols.

Thomas, Brinley. "Migration, Economic Aspects." *International Encyclopedia of the Social Sciences,* vol. 10. New York: The Macmillan Co. and the Free Press, 1968.

United Nations. Department of Social Affairs. Population Division. *The Determinants and Consequences of Population Trends.* New York: 1953.

U.S. Bureau of the Census. Department of Commerce. *Pocket Data Book, 1969.* Washington, D.C.: Government Printing Office, 1969.

Vellard, Jehan, "Causas Biologicas de la Desaparición de los Indios Americanos." *Boletín del instituto Riva-Agüero* (*Pontifica Universidad Catolica del Perú*), no. 2 (1956):77–93.

Watt, George. *A Dictionary of the Economic Products of India.* 7 vols. Calcutta: Superintendent of Government Printing, 1889–1899.

Williams, Eric. *Capitalism and Slavery.* New York: Capricorn Books, 1966.

Woodruff, William. *Impact of Western Man, A Study of Europe's Role in the World's Economy, 1750–1960.* New York: St. Martin's Press, 1967.

Bibliography
to the 2003 Edition

Compiled by Frederic Vallvé,
Georgetown University

CHAPTER 1: THE CONTRASTS

Axtell, James. *Beyond 1492: Encounters in Colonial North America.* New York: Oxford University Press, 1992.

Black, Francis L. "Infectious Diseases in Primitive Societies." *Science* 187 (14 February 1975):515–518.

Bonavía, Duccio. "Apuntes sobre los orígenes de la civilización andina." *Revista del Museo de Arqueología e Historia* 6 (1966):7–30.

Brokensha, David; Warren, D.M.; and Werner, Oswald. *Indigenous Knowledge Systems and Development.* Lanham, MD: University Press of America, 1980.

Butzer, Karl W. "No Eden in the New World (Evidence of environmental degradation during prehispanic agricultural practices in Mexico." *Nature* 362, no. 6415 (1993):15–18.

Clutton-Brock, Juliet. *Domesticated Animals from Early Times.* Austin: University of Texas Press, 1981.

Crawford, Michael H. *The Origins of Native Americans: Evidence from Anthropological Genetics.* Cambridge: University of Cambridge Press, 1998.

Deagan, Kathleen A. *Columbus' Outpost among the Taínos: Spain and America at La Isabela, 1493–1498.* New Haven: Yale University Press, 2002.

Denevan, William M. "The Pristine Myth: The Landscape of the Americas in 1492." *Annals of the Association of American Geographers* 82 (1992):369–385.

Earls, John. "Ecología y agronomía en los Andes." In *Alternativas étnicas al desarrollo*, edited by Javier Medina and David Tuschneider. La Paz: Hisbol, 1991.

Flannery, Kent V. "The Origins of Agriculture." *Annual Review of Anthropology* 2 (1973):271–310.

Gade, Daniel W. "The Andes as a Dairyless Civilization: Llamas and Alpacas as Unmilked Animals." In *Nature and Culture in the Andes*, edited by Daniel W. Gade. Madison: University of Wisconsin Press, 1999.

Gade, Daniel W. *Nature and Culture in the Andes.* Madison: University of Wisconsin Press, 1999.

Garavaglia, Juan Carlos. "Human Beings and the Environment in America: on 'determinism' and 'possibilism.' " *International Social Science Journal/UNESCO* 134 (November 1992):569–577.

Garza, Mercedes de la. *Sueño y alucinación en el mundo nahuatl y maya.* México, DF: Instituto de Investigaciones Filológicas, Centro de Estudios Mayas, UNAM, 1990.

Grigg, D.B. *The Agricultural Systems of the World: An Evolutionary Approach.* Cambridge: Cambridge University Press, 1974.

Harlan, Jack R. "The Plants and Animals that Nourish Man." *Scientific American* 253 (September 1976):94–95.

Kidwell, Clara Sue. "Science and Ethnoscience: Native American World Views as a Factor in the Development of Native Technologies." In *Environmental History: Critical Issues in Comparative Perspective*, edited by Kendall E. Bailes. Lanham: University Press of America, 1985, pp. 277–285.

Knapp, Gregory; Denevan, William M.; and Mathewson, K., eds.

Pre-Hispanic Agricultural Fields in the Andean Region. Oxford: BAR International Series, 1987.

León-Portilla, Miguel, ed. *Broken Spears: The Aztec Account of the Conquest of Mexico.* Boston: Beacon Press, 1992.

LeVine, Terry Y., ed. *Inka Storage Systems.* Norman: University of Oklahoma Press, 1992.

Lockhart, James. *We People Here: Nahuatl Accounts of the Conquest of Mexico.* Berkeley: University of California Press, 1993.

López Austin, Alfredo. *The Human Body and Ideology: Concepts of the Ancient Nahuas.* 2 vols. Salt Lake City: University of Utah Press, 1988.

Martin, Calvin. *The Keepers of the Game: Indian-Animal Relationships and the Fur Trade.* Berkeley: University of California Press, 1978.

Mourant, A.E.; Kopéc, Ada C.; and Domaniewska-Sobczak, Kazimiera. *The Distribution of the Human Blood Groups and Other Polymorphisms.* Oxford: Oxford University Press, 1976.

Piperno, Dolores R., and Pearsall, Deborah M. *The Origins of Agriculture in the Lowland Neotropics.* San Diego: Academic Press, 1998.

Ramos Pérez, Demetrio. *El descubrimiento 'humano' de América: las suposiciones colombinas sobre los Caribes y su importancia como guía conductora.* Granada: Excelentísima Diputación Provincial, 1982.

Renfrew, Jane M. *Palaeoethnobotany, The Prehistoric Food Plants of the the Near East and Europe.* New York: Columbia University Press, 1973.

Sanders, William T., and Nichols, Deborah L. "Ecological Theory and Cultural Evolution in the Valley of Oaxaca." *Current Anthropology* 29, no. 1 (February 1998):33–80.

Simoons, Frederick J. "The Geographical Hypothesis and Lactose Malabsorption, A Weighing of the Evidence." *American Journal of Digestive Diseases* 23 (November 1978):964.

Spalding, Karen. *Huarochirí: An Andean Society Under Inca and Spanish Rule.* Stanford: Stanford University Press, 1984.
Todorov, Tzvetan. *La Conquête de l'Amérique: la question de l'autre.* Paris: Seuil, 1982.
Wright, Ronald. *Stolen Continents: The Americas Through Indian Eyes Since 1492.* New York: Houghton Mifflin, 1992.

CHAPTER 2: CONQUISTADOR Y PESTILENCIA

Alchon, Suzanne Austin. *Native Society and Disease in Colonial Ecuador.* Cambridge: University of Cambridge Press, 1991.
Alden, Dauril, and Miller, Joseph C. "Unwanted Cargoes: The Origin and Dissemination of Smallpox via the Slave Trade, c. 1560–1830." In *The African Exchange: Toward a Biological History of Black People*, edited by Kenneth F. Kiple. Durham: Duke University Press, 1998, pp. 35–109.
Ashburn, P.M. *The Ranks of Death: A Medical History of the Conquest of America.* New York: Porcupine Press, 1980.
Berte, J.P. "Les epidemies au Mexique au XVIe siècle." *Asclepio* 35 (1083):357–363.
Bono, Juan Angel del. *Peripecias y enfermedades en la conquista de América.* Buenos Aires: Editorial Plus Ultra, 1993.
Borah, Woodrow. "Introduction." In *The Secret Judgements of God: Native Peoples and Old World Disease in Colonial Spanish America,* edited by Noble David Cook and W. George Lovell. Norman: University of Oklahoma Press, 1992.
Brooks, Francis J. "Revising the Conquest of Mexico: Smallpox, Sources and Populations." *Journal of Interdisciplinary History* 24 (1993):1–29.
Butzer, Karl W., ed. "The Americas Before and After 1492: Current Geographical Research." *Annals of the Association of American Geographers* 82, no. 3 (September 1992).
Cook, Noble David. *Born to Die, Disease and New World Conquest, 1492–1650.* Cambridge: Cambridge University Press, 1998.

Florescano, Enrique, and Malvido, Elsa, eds. *Ensayos sobre la historia de las epidemias en México.* 2 vols. México: Instituto Mexicano del Seguro Social, 1980.

Flórez Miguel, Marcelino. *Ambición y muerte en la conquista de América.* Valladolid: Ambito, 1992.

Gade, Daniel W. "Inca and Colonial Settlements, Coca Cultivation and Endemic Disease in the Tropical Forest." *Journal of Historical Geography* 5 (1979):263–279.

Grohs, Waltraud. "Los indios del Alto Amazonas del siglo XVI al siglo XVIII." *Bonner Amerikanistische Studien*, 2. Bonn, FRG: Univ. Bonn, Seminar für Völkerkunde, 1974.

Guerra, Francisco. "The Influence of Disease on Race, Logistics, and Colonization in the Antilles." *Journal of Tropical Medicine* 49 (1966):23–35.

Guerra, Francisco. "El efecto demográfico de las epidemias tras el descubrimiento de América." *Revista de Indias* 46 (1986): 41–58.

Gutiérrez Estévez, Manuel, ed. *Sustentos, aflicciones y postrimerías de los indios de América.* Madrid: Casa de América, 2000.

Henige, David. "When Did Smallpox Reach the New World (and Why Does It Matter?)." In *Africans in Bondage: Studies in Slavery and the Slave Trade,* edited by Paul E. Lovejoy. Madison: University of Wisconsin Press, 1986, pp. 11–26.

Henige, David P. *Numbers from Nowhere: The American Indian Population Debate.* Norman: University of Oklahoma Press, 1998.

Jackson, Robert H. *Indian Population Decline: The Missions of Northwestern New Spain, 1687–1840.* Albuquerque: University of New Mexico Press, 1994.

Jennings, Francis. *The Invasion of America: Indians, Colonialism, and the Cant of Conquest.* Chapel Hill: University of North Carolina Press, 1975.

Joralemon, Donald. "New World Depopulation and the Case of Disease." *Journal of Anthropological Research* 38 (1982): 108–127.

Kiple, Kenneth F., ed. *The African Exchange: Toward a Biological History of Black People.* Durham: Duke University Press, 1987.

Kiple, Kenneth F., et al., eds. *The Cambridge World History of Human Disease.* Cambridge: Cambridge University Press, 1993.

Krech, Shepart. "Disease, Starvation and North Athapaskan Social Organization." *American Ethnologist* 5 (1978):710–732.

Larsen, Clark Spencer. *Native American Demography in the Spanish Borderlands.* New York: Garland Publishers, 1991.

Lenihan, John, and Fletcher, William W., eds. *Health and the Environment.* New York: Academic Press, 1976.

López Austin, Alfredo. *Textos de medicina nahuatl.* México, DF: UNAM, 1975.

López Pinero, José María. "Las 'nuevas medicinas' americanas en la obra (1565–1574) de Nicolás Monardes." *Asclepio* 42 (1990):3–68.

Lovell, W. George. "Disease and Depopulation in Early Colonial Guatemala." In *The Secret Judgements of God: Native Peoples and Old World Disease in Colonial Spanish America,* edited by Noble David Cook and George W. Lovell. Norman: University of Oklahoma Press, 1992, pp. 51–85.

Lovell, W. George. "Enfermedades del Viejo Mundo y mortandad amerindia: la viruela y el tabardillo en la sierra de los Cuchumatanes de Guatemala (1780–1810)." *Mesoamérica* 169 (1988):239–285.

Lovell, W. George. " 'Heavy Shadows and Dark Night': Disease and Depopulation in Colonial Spanish America." *Annals of the Association of American Geographers* 82 (1992):426–443.

Lovell, W. George, and Lutz, Christopher H. "The Historical Demography of Colonial Central America." *Yearbook/CLAG* 17/18 (1990):127–138.

Malvido, Elsa, and Viesca, Carlos. "La epidemia de cocoliztli de 1576." *Historias* (México) 11 (1985):27–33.

McCaa, Robert. "Spanish and Nahuatl Views on Smallpox and Demographic Catastrophe in Mexico." *Journal of Interdisciplinary History* 25 (1995):397–431.

McNeill, William H. *Plagues and Peoples*. Garden City, NY: Doubleday Anchor, 1976.

Mellardo Campos, Virginia, et al. "La medicina tradicional de los pueblos indígenas de México." In *Biblioteca de la medicina mexicana*. Colaboración de Soledad Mata Pinzón et al. Dirección de Carlos Zolla. Coordinación de Virginia Mellado Campos. Revisión de María del Carmen Carrillo Farga. 3 vols. México: Instituto Nacional Indigenista, 1994.

Melvido, Elsa. "Factores de despoblación y reposición de Cholula (1641–1810)." *Historia Mexicana* 89 (1973):52–110.

Merbs, Charles F. "Patterns of Health and Sickness in the Precontact Southwest." In *Precolumbian Consequences I: Archaeological and Historical Perspectives on the Spanish Borderlands West,* edited by David Hurst Thomas. Washington, DC: Smithsonian Institute Press, 1989, pp. 41–56.

Milner, G.R. "Epidemic Disease in the Postcontact Southeast: A Reappraisal." *Midcontinental Journal of Archaeology* 5 (1980):39–56.

Molina del Villar, América. *La Nueva España y el matlazahuatl*. México, DF: CIESAS/Colegio de Michoacán, 2001.

Myers, Thomas P. "El efecto de las pestes sobre las poblaciones de la Amazonía alta." *Amazonía Perú* 8, no. 15 (Agosto 1988):61–82.

Narvaja, Benito R., and Pinotti, Luisa V. *Violencia, población e identidad en la colonización de América hispánica: las secuelas demográficas de la conquista*. Buenos Aires: Universidad de Buenos Aires, Oficina de publicaciones del CBC, 1996.

Newman, Linda A. *Indian Survival in Colonial Nicaragua*. Norman: University of Oklahoma Press, 1987.

Newman, Linda A. *The Cost of Conquest: Indian Decline in Honduras Under Spanish Rule*. Boulder: Westview Press, 1986.

Newman, Linda A. *Life and Death in Early Colonial Ecuador.* Norman: University of Oklahoma Press, 1995.

Newman, M.T. "Aboriginal New World Epidemiology and Medical Care, and the Impact of Old World Disease Imports." *American Journal of Physical Anthropology* 45 (1976):667–672.

Orellana, Sandra L. *Indian Medicine in Highland Guatemala.* Albuquerque: University of New Mexico Press, 1987.

Platt, Anne, and Patterson, Jane A., ed. *Infecting Ourselves: How Environmental and Social Disruptions Trigger Disease.* Washington, DC: Worldwatch Institute, 1996.

Platt, Stephen D., et al., eds. *Locating Health: Sociological and Historical Explorations.* Aldershot, Hants.; Brookfield, VT: Avebury, 1993.

Powell, Mary Lucas. "Health and Disease in the Late Prehistoric Southeast." In *Disease and Demography in the Americas*, edited by John W. Verano and Douglas H. Ubelaker. Washington, DC: Smithsonian Institution Press, 1992, pp. 41–53.

Prem, Hanns J. "Disease Outbreaks in Central Mexico during the Sixteenth Century." In *The Secret Judgements of God: Native Peoples and Old World Disease in Colonial Spanish America*, edited by Noble David Cook and W. George Lovell. Norman: University of Oklahoma Press, 1992, pp. 22–50.

Ramenofsky, Ann F. *Vectors of Death: The Archaeology of European Contact.* Albuquerque: University of New Mexico Press, 1987.

Raudzens, George, ed. *Technology, Disease, and Colonial Conquests, Sixteenth to Eighteenth Centuries: Essays Reappraising the Guns and Germs Theories.* Boston: Brill, 2001.

Reff, Daniel T. *Disease, Depopulation and Culture Change in Northwestern New Spain, 1518–1764.* Salt Lake City: University of Utah Press, 1991.

Rosenblat, Angel. "The Population of Hispaniola at the Time of Columbus." In *The Native Population of the Americas in 1492,* second edition, edited by William M. Denevan. Madison: University of Wisconsin Press, 1992, pp. 43–66.

Rouse, Irving. *The Taínos: Rise and Decline of the People Who Greeted Columbus.* New Haven: Yale University Press, 1992.

Royal, Robert. *1492 and All That: Political Manipulations of History.* Washington, DC: Ethics and Public Policy Center, 1992.

Sánchez-Albornoz, Nicolás. *La población de América latina: desde los tiempos precolombinos al año 2025.* Madrid: Alianza Editorial, 1985.

Sánchez-Albornoz, Nicolás. *The Population of Latin America: A History.* Translated by W.A.R. Richardson. Berkeley: University of California Press, 1974.

Settipane, Guy A. *Columbus and the New World: Medical Implications.* Providence: OceanSide Publications, 1995.

Smith, Marvin T. *Archaeology of Aboriginal Culture Change in the Interior Southeast: Depopulation during the Early Historic Period.* Gainesville: University of Florida Press, 1987.

Stannard, David E. *American Holocaust: Columbus and the Conquest of the New World.* New York: Oxford University Press, 1992.

Stodder, Ann L. W., and Martin, Debra L. "Health and Disease in the Southwest Before and After Spanish Contact." In *Disease and Demography in the Americas,* edited by John W. Verano and Douglas H. Ubelaker. Washington, DC: Smithsonian Institution Press, 1992.

Storey, Rebecca. *Life and Death in the Ancient City of Teotihuacán: A Modern, Paleodemographic Synthesis.* Tuscaloosa: University of Alabama Press, 1992.

Sweet D.G., *'A Rich Realm of Nature' Destroyed: The Middle Amazon Valley, 1640–1750.* Madison: University of Wisconsin Press, 1974.

Thornton, Russell. *American Indian Holocaust and Survival: A History Since 1492*. Norman: University of Oklahoma Press, 1987.

Verano, John W. "Prehistoric Disease and Demography in the Andes." In *Disease and Demography in the Americas*, edited by John W. Verano and Douglas H. Ubelaker. Washington, DC: Smithsonian Institution Press, 1992, pp. 15–24.

Verano, John W., and Ubelaker, Douglas H., eds. *Disease and Demography in the Americas*. Washington, DC: Smithsonian Institution Press, 1992.

Verlinden, Charles. "La population de l'Amérique précolumbienne: Une question de méthode." In *Méthodologie de l'histoire et des sciences humanes: mélanges en honneur de Fernand Braudel*. Paris: N.p., 1972, pp. 453–462.

Way, A.B. "Diseases of Latin America." In *Biocultural Aspects of Disease,* edited by H. Rothschild. New York: Academic Press, 1981, pp. 253–291.

Weisman, Abner I. *Medicine Before Columbus: As Told in Pre-Columbian Medical Art*. New York: Pre-Cortesian Publications, 1979.

Whitmore, Thomas M. *Disease and Death in Early Colonial Mexico: Simulating Amerindian Depopulation*. Boulder: Westview Press, 1992.

Williams, Barbara J. "Contact Period Rural Overpopulation in the Basin of Mexico Carrying Capacity Models Tested with Documentary Data." *American Antiquity* 54, no. 4 (October 1998):715–732.

Wood, Peter H. "The Impact of Smallpox on the Native Population of the Eighteenth Century South." *New York State Journal of Medicine* 87 (1987):30.

Zambardino, Rudolph A. "Critique of David Heninge's 'On the Contact Population of Hispaniola: History of Higher Mathematics.' " *Hispanic American Historical Review* 58 (1978): 700–708.

Zambardino, Rudolph A. "Mexico's Population in the Sixteenth

Century: Demographic Anomaly or Mathematical Illusion?"
Journal of Interdisciplinary History 11 (1980):1–27.

CHAPTER 3: OLD WORLD PLANTS AND ANIMALS IN THE NEW WORLD

Angulo, Rafael. *Historia de la alimentación del nuevo mundo.* Mérida, Venezuela: Editorial Futuro, 1991.

Antúnez de Mayolo, Santiago. "La nutrición en el antiguo Perú." A paper delivered at the III Congreso Peruano, *El hombre y la cultura andina,* Lima, 1977.

Archetti, Eduardo P. *Guinea-pigs, Food, Symbol and Conflict of Knowledge in Ecuador.* Translated by Valentina Napolitano and Peter Worsley. New York: Berg, 1997.

Bergman, Roland. "Subsistence Agriculture in Latin America." In *Food, Politics and Society in Latin America,* edited by John C. Super and Thomas C. Wright. Lincoln and London: University of Nebraska Press, 1985.

Clausen, Curtis P., Bartlett, Blair Ralph, et al. *Introduced Parasites and Predators of Arthropod Pests and Weeds: A World Review.* Washington, DC: Agricultural Research Service, U.S. Dept. of Agriculture, 1978.

Cronk, Quentin C.B., and Fuller, Janice L. *Plant Invaders: The Threat to Natural Ecosystems.* London: Chapman and Hall, 1995.

Cronon, William. *Changes in the Land: Indians, Colonists and the Ecology of New England.* New York: Hill and Wang, 1983.

Elton, Charles S. *The Ecology of Invasions by Animals and Plants.* Chicago: University of Chicago Press, 2000.

Groves, R.H., and Burdon, J.J., eds. *Ecology of Biological Invasions.* Cambridge: Cambridge University Press, 1986.

Horkheimer, Hans. "Alimentación y obtención de alimentos en los Andes prehispánicos." Translated by Ernesto More. In *Alternativas étnicas al desarrollo,* edited by David Tuchshneider and Javier Medina. La Paz: Hisbol, 1990.

Johannessen, Sissel, and Hastorf, Christine A., eds. *Corn and Culture in the Prehistoric New World.* Boulder: Westview Press, 1994.

Koopowitz, Harold, and Kaye, Hilary. *Plant Extinction: A Global Crisis.* Washington, DC: Stone Wall Press; Harrisburg, PA: Distributed by Stackpole Books, 1983.

Levin, Donald A. *The Origin, Expansion, and Demise of Plant Species.* New York: Oxford University Press, 2000.

Long, John L. *Introduced Birds of the World: The Worldwide History, Distribution and Influence of Birds Introduced to New Environments.* New York: Universe Books, 1981.

Melville, Elinor G.K. *A Plague of Sheep: Environmental Consequences of the Conquest of Mexico.* Cambridge: Cambridge University Press, 1994.

Milne, Lorus Johnson, and Milne, Margery. *Ecology Out of Joint: New Environments and Why They Happen.* New York: Scribner, 1977.

Parodi, Lorenzo R., and Mazocca, Angel. *Agricultura prehispánica y colonial: Edición conmemorativa del V centenario del descubrimiento de América.* Buenos Aires: Academia Nacional de Agronomía y Veterinaria, 1992.

Peloso, Vincent C. "Succulence and Sustenance: Region, Class, and Diet in Nineteenth-Century Peru." In *Food, Politics and Society in Latin America,* edited by John C. Super and Thomas C. Wright. Lincoln and London: University of Nebraska Press, 1985.

Plasencia, Pedro. *Episodios gastronómicos de la conquista de Indias.* Madrid: Mileto Ediciones, 2001.

Roosevelt, Anna Curtenius. *Parmana: Prehistoric Maize and Manioc Subsistence along the Orinoco and the Amazon.* New York: Academic Press, 1980.

Slatta, Richard W. *Comparing Cowboys and Frontiers.* Norman: University of Oklahoma Press, 1997.

Super, John C. *Food, Conquest and Colonization in Sixteenth-Century Spanish America.* Albuquerque: University of New Mexico Press, 1988.

Super, John C. "The Formation of Nutritional Regimes in Colonial Latin America." In *Food, Politics, and Society in Latin America*, edited by John C. Super and Thomas C. Wright. Lincoln and London: University of Nebraska Press, 1985.

Todd, Kim. *Tinkering with Eden: A Natural History of Exotics in America*. New York: W.W. Norton, 2001.

Tortolero, Alejandro, coord. *Tierra, agua y bosques: historia y medio ambiente en el México central*. México, DF: Centre Français d'Études Mexicaines et Centroaméricaines, 1996.

Tortolero, Alejandro. *El agua y su historia: México y sus desafíos hacia el siglo XXI*. México, DF: Siglo XXI Eds., 2000.

Weismantel, Mary J. *Food, Gender, and Poverty in the Ecuadorian Andes*. Philadelphia: University of Pennsylvania Press, 1988.

Williams, David F., ed. *Exotic Ants: Biology, Impact and Control of Introduced Species*. Boulder: Westview Press, 1994.

Wilson, Charles L., and Graham, Charles L. *Exotic Plant Pests and North American Agriculture*. New York: Academic Press, 1983.

Wright, Thomas C., and Super, John C., eds. *Food, Politics, and Society in Latin America*. Lincoln and London: University of Nebraska Press, 1985.

CHAPTER 4: THE EARLY HISTORY OF SYPHILIS: A REAPPRAISAL

Allison, Marvis J., et al. "La sífilis ¿una enfermedad americana?" *Chungará/Arica* 9 (Agosto 1982):275–283.

Arrizabalaga, Jon. *The Great Pox: The French Disease in Renaissance Europe*. New Haven: Yale University Press, 1997.

Baker, Brenda J., and Amelagos, George J. "The Origin and Antiquity of Syphilis: Paleopathological Diagnosis and Interpretation." *Current Anthropology* 29 (1988):703–737.

Costa, Enzo Fernando. *Historia de la sífilis y de los hombres que lucharon contra ella.* Buenos Aires: Editorial Universitaria de Buenos Aires, 1977.

Crissey, John T. *The Dermatology and Syphilology of the Nineteenth Century.* New York: Praeger, 1981.

French, Roger, et al. *Medicine from the Black Death to the French Disease.* Aldershot, Hants.; Brookfield, VT: Ashgate Pub., 1998.

Guerra, Francisco. "The Dispute over Syphilis: Europe versus America." *Clio Medica* (Netherlands) 13 (1978):39–62.

Guerra, Francisco. "The Problem of Syphilis." In *First Images of America: The Impact of the New World on the Old,* edited by Fredi Chiappelli. 2 vols. Berkeley: University of California Press, 1972, pp. 845–851.

Luna Calderón, Fernando. *Primeras evidencias de sífilis en las Antillas Precolombinas.* Santo Domingo, DR: Universidad Autónoma de Santo Domingo, 1977.

Quéntel, Claude. *History of Syphilis.* Translated by Judith Braddock and Brian Pike. Baltimore: Johns Hopkins University Press, 1990.

Quéntel, Claude. *Le mal de Naples: Histoire de la syphilis.* Paris: Seghers, 1986.

Tosti, Antonio. *Storie all'ombra del malfrancese.* Palermo: Sellerio editore, 1992.

CHAPTER 5: NEW WORLD FOODS AND OLD WORLD DEMOGRAPHY

Coats, Alice M. *The Plant Hunters: Being a History of the Horticultural Pioneers, Their Quests and Their Discoveries from the Renaissance to the Twentieth Century.* New York: McGraw-Hill, 1970.

Coe, Sophie D. *America's First Cuisines.* Austin: University of Texas Press, 1994.

Masson Meiss, Luis, et al. *De papa a patata: la difusión española del tubérculo andino.* Editor científico e iconográfico Javier López Linage. Barcelona: Lunwerg Editores, 1991.

National Research Council. *Lost Crops of the Incas: Little-Known Plants of the Andes with Promise for Worldwide Cultivation.* Washington, DC: National Academy Press, 1989.

Remesal, Agustín. *Un banquete para los dioses: comidas, ritos y hambres en el Nuevo Mundo.* Madrid: Alianza Editorial, 1993.

CHAPTER 6: THE COLUMBIAN EXCHANGE CONTINUES

Abernethy, David B. *The Dynamics of Global Dominance: European Overseas Empires, 1415–1980.* New Haven: Yale University Press, 2000.

Crosby, Alfred W. *Ecological Imperialism: The Biological Expansion of Europe, 900–1900.* Cambridge: Cambridge University Press, 1986.

Curtin, Phillip D. *Death by Migration: Europe's Encounter With the Tropical World in the Nineteenth Century.* Cambridge: Cambridge University Press, 1989.

Curtin, Phillip D. *Migration and Mortality in Africa and the Atlantic World, 1700–1900.* Aldershot, Hants.; Burlington, VT: Ashgate/Variorum, 2001.

Dean, Warren. *Brazil and the Struggle for Rubber: A Study in Environmental History.* Cambridge: Cambridge University Press, 1987.

Dean, Warren. "Ecological and Economic Relationships in Frontier History: São Paulo." In *Essays on Frontiers and World History,* by Philip Wayne Powell, et al.; edited by George Wolfskill and Stanley Palmer. College Station: Texas A & M University Press, 1983.

Dean, Warren. "Indigenous Populations of the São Paulo-Rio de Janeiro Coast: Trade, Aldeamento, Slavery, and Extinction." *Revista Histórica* (São Paulo) 117 (1984):3–26.

Dean, Warren. *With Broadax and Firebrand: The Destruction of*

276 | BIBLIOGRAPHY TO THE 2003 EDITION

the Brazilian Atlantic Forest. Berkerley: University of California Press, 1995.

Dobyns, Henry F. *Their Numbers Became Thinned: Native American Population Dynamics in Eastern North America.* Knoxville: University of Tennessee Press, 1983.

Karlen, Arno. *Man and Microbes: Disease and Plagues in History and Modern Times.* New York: G.P. Putnam's Sons, 1995.

Kiple, Kenneth F., and Beck, Stephen V. *Biological Consequences of the European Expansion, 1450–1800.* Aldershot, Hants.; Brookfield VT: Ashgate/Variorum, 1997.

Pohl, Hans, ed. *The European Discovery of the World and Its Economic Effects on Pre-Industrial Society, 1500–1800.* Stuttgart: Franz Steiner, 1990.

Rosset, Peter, and Benjamins, Medea, eds. *The Greening of the Revolution: Cuba's Experiment with Organic Agriculture.* Melbourne, Vic., Australia: Ocean Press, 1994.

Trexler, Richard C. *Sex and Conquest: Gendered Violence, Political Order and the European Conquest of the Americas.* Ithaca: Cornell University Press, 1995.

Tucker, Richard P. *Insatiable Appetite: The United States and the Ecological Degradation of the Tropical World.* Berkeley: University of California Press, 2000.

Tyrrell, Ian R. *True Gardens of the Gods: Californian-Australian Environmental Reform, 1960–1930.* Berkeley: University of California Press, 1999.

Zarrilli, Adrián Gustavo. "Capitalism, Ecology and Agrarian Expansion in the Pampean Region, 1890–1950." *Environmental History* 6, no. 4 (October 2001).

Index

277

horses in, 81, 82–83
livestock in, 82, 85, 87–88, 93, 99,
    112, 113
maize in, 171
olive trees in, 72
pigs in, 79
smallpox in, 48–50, 52–53, 54, 56–
    57, 77
Spanish conquest of, 48
sugar in, 69
wheat in, 70
wine in, 71
Middle East, importance of American
    foods and plants in the, 188–
    190
Migration of people, 212–218
Millet, 186, 192, 199, 201
Mining, 68
Moles, 8
Monkeys, 6, 8
Monogeneticism, 11
Montaigne, 10
Montejo y Robledo, 140
Montezuma, 54
Moose, 30
Morbo Gallico, De (Falloppio), 160
Morfi, Fray, 83
Mosquitos, 208, 209
Motolinía, Toribio, 52–53, 57
Mules, 96, 101
Murúa, Martín de, 53
Muskrats, 212
Mutton, 92

Narváez, 48
Nature, balance of, 113
New Granada, 94
New Zealand, 20
    sweet potatoes in, 169
Nietzsche, Friedrich, 210
Niguas, 209

Oats, 175
Olive oil, 70, 72–73
Olive trees, 67, 72–73
On the Origin of Species (Darwin),
    14
Oranges, 66–67, 68
Oroya fever, 209
Overgrazing, 112
Oviedo y Valdés, Gonzalo Fernández

de, 45, 50, 68, 87, 138, 139,
    209
on origin of syphilis, 138, 139
Oxen, 108, 110

Palm trees, 9
Panama
    disease in, 50–51
    sheep in, 93
Pandemic, 39, 43, 52, 54
Papaya, 170
paprika, 66, 177
Paracelsus, Philippus, 12, 140, 155
Paraguay
    cattle in, 91
    horses in, 84, 105
    sheep in, 100
Passenger pigeons, 219
Patagonia, 91, 95
Peanuts, 170, 185, 186, 193, 195,
    199, 200
Peccary, 77
Penicillin, 210
Peoples, migration of, 212–218
Pereyra, Carlos, 77
Peru, 11, 18, 38, 39, 66, 98
    camels in, 96
    cattle in, 91
    dogs in, 95
    horses in, 83, 84
    olive trees in, 72–73
    pigs in, 79
    sheep in, 92, 93–94
    smallpox in, 50, 53, 54–56, 77
    sugar in, 69
    wheat in, 70–71
    wine in, 72
Pestilence, 35–58
Pigeons, passenger, 219
Pigs, 75–76, 77–79, 98, 101
Pineapples, 170, 192
Ping-ti Ho, 198, 201
Pinta, 143, 145, 209
Pinzón, Martin Alonso, 140–141
Pinzón family, 139
Pizarro, Francisco, 36, 50, 55, 79, 83
Pizarro, Gonzalo, 78
Pizarro, Hernando, 81
Pizarro, Pedro, 55, 56
Plants
    contrast between Old World and
        New World, 3–31

ABOUT THE AUTHOR

ALFRED W. CROSBY, JR., is Professor Emeritus of American Studies, History, and Geography at the University of Texas, Austin. He is the author of *Ecological Imperialism: The Biological Expansion of Europe, 900–1900* (1986), *America's Forgotten Pandemic: The Influenza of 1918* (1989), *The Measure of Reality: Quantification and Western Society, 1250–1600* (1997), and most recently *Throwing Fire: Projectile Technology through History* (2002).